Eggs Benedict, **Ch. 5** (see page 61)

Best Basic Burger, **Ch. 6** (see page 95)

Minestrone Soup, **Ch. 7** (see page 108)

Savory Roast Beef, **Ch. 9** (see page 180)

Fried Chicken, **Ch. 10** (see page 219)

Shrimp Scampi, **Ch. 11** (see page 228)

Poached Salmon with Dill Sauce, **Ch. 11** (see page 230)

Country-Style Strawberry Shortcake, **Ch. 16** (see page 351)

ABSOLUTE
BEGINNER'S
GUIDE

TO

Cooking

Deb Roussou

800 East 96th Street,
Indianapolis, Indiana 46240

Absolute Beginner's Guide to Cooking
Copyright © 2005 by Que Publishing

International Standard Book Number: 0-7897-3370-6

Library of Congress Catalog Card Number: 2004118435

Printed in the United States of America

First Printing: June 2005

08   07   4   3   2

Trademarks

All terms mentioned in this book that are known to be trademarks or service marks have been appropriately capitalized. Que Publishing cannot attest to the accuracy of this information. Use of a term in this book should not be regarded as affecting the validity of any trademark or service mark.

Old Bay Seasoning is a registered trademark of McCormick and Company, Inc.

Nestlé and Toll House are registered trademarks of Nestlé, Inc.

Saran Wrap is a registered trademark of SC Johnson & Son, Inc.

Tabasco Sauce is a registered trademark of McIlhenny Company.

A-1 Steak Sauce is a registered trademark of Intercorp Excelle Inc.

Warning and Disclaimer

Every effort has been made to make this book as complete and as accurate as possible, but no warranty or fitness is implied. The information provided is on an "as is" basis. The author and the publisher shall have neither liability nor responsibility to any person or entity with respect to any loss or damages arising from the information contained in this book.

Bulk Sales

Que Publishing offers excellent discounts on this book when ordered in quantity for bulk purchases or special sales. For more information, please contact

U.S. Corporate and Government Sales
1-800-382-3419
corpsales@pearsontechgroup.com

For sales outside of the U.S., please contact

International Sales
international@pearsoned.com

Executive Editor
Candace Hall

Development Editor
Sean Dixon

Managing Editor
Charlotte Clapp

Project Editor
Andrew Beaster

Copy Editor
Laura W. Town

Indexer
Lisa Wilson

Proofreader
Elizabeth Finney

Publishing Coordinator
Cindy Teeters

Interior Designer
Ann Jones

Cover Designer
Dan Armstrong

Page Layout
Susan Geisleman

Contents at a Glance

INTRODUCTION

We live in a time when culinary awareness has become commonplace. An entire television network dedicated to cooking, and mid-priced bistros serving haute cuisine, have introduced good food to the average Joe. With global products available at the local grocery store, there is no reason why you can't create great tasting meals in your own kitchen—this is actually much easier than you think! A desire to eat and a willingness to try new things are the only requirements you need to get started!

Cooking is a simple combination of food, equipment, and techniques that does not need to be complicated, intimidating, or terribly time-consuming. The first part of this book introduces you to these components in a reference format. The recipe chapters are lessons that give you the opportunity to practice the techniques and prepare the food.

This book is recipe-based, and is organized to maximize cooking and minimize reading. The cooking lessons are the recipes themselves, each with detailed steps to teach you the absolute basics of the culinary arts. For example, learning about the process of poaching is necessary; but actually poaching salmon, or artichokes, creates a memory that can be recalled the next time you need to poach a food. At the end of each recipe where you've learned how to poach, steam, or bake, you will have a completed dish to enjoy.

How This Book Is Organized

Absolute Beginner's Guide to Cooking takes you through the fundamentals: tells you what you need to get started, describes all cooking terms and techniques, and provides tips that will help you get meals on the table in the minimum amount of time with maximum efficiency. By the time you finish the first four chapters, you will be ready to use all the great recipes included in this book.

Chapter 1: Cookware and Tool Essentials

Included in this chapter is a suggested short list of essential kitchen cookware and tools that will be adequate to get started. Purchasing cookware can be daunting, so we have provided some basic guidelines to follow while shopping. It is best to start small and add items as you discover that you cannot live without them.

Chapter 2: Food Essentials for Your Pantry

This chapter includes suggestions and recommendations for food pantry items and refrigerated/freezer foods that are frequently used. Having these foods on hand will reduce unnecessary trips to the store for small items such as a box of baking soda.

I've also included a *Basic Cheese Chart* for your information and reference. You can create your own style of seasoning suited to your tastes with the help of the handy *Herb and Spice Chart* and *Spice Blends Chart*. These charts are quick and easy references for flavors, characteristics, and use of your basic food pantry essentials.

Chapter 3: Glossary of Terms and Techniques, Conversions and Equivalents

The glossary includes detailed explanations of cooking terms and techniques used in the recipes. Terms such as *dicing* are explained along with detailed food-specific instructions (dicing an onion, for example). This section also includes a *Weight and Measurement Conversions* list, and a *Food Yield Equivalents Chart*, both valuable reference tools. It is not necessary to read this book start to finish. You may find a recipe you like, so jump right in, and use the glossary for further explanations of any recipe steps you may not understand.

tip

To make the glossary easier to find, we have highlighted the edge of the page with a dark margin.

Chapter 4: Getting a Meal on the Table

Full of helpful tips on how to plan a menu, choose and read a recipe, and shop for food, this chapter will assist you with the organization of cooking. The ultimate goal is to have a complete meal on the table with a minimum amount of time, money, and frustration. This chapter is your guide to actually making that happen!

The Recipe Chapters

Each recipe chapter contains easy-to-follow preparation and cooking instructions. Some chapters also include handy reference charts that are particular to the foods included in the chapter. You can learn how to separate an egg in Chapter 5, "Eggs and Other Breakfast Fare," as well as how to make yummy omelets using those eggs. In Chapter 9, "Meat—Beef, Pork, and Lamb," you will find *Meat Roasting Charts*, as well as instructions on how to use a meat thermometer. There is a *Vegetable Steaming Chart* located in Chapter 13, "Side Dishes—Vegetables and Potatoes."

Whether you have depleted your trust fund or are just sick of fast food, sooner or later you will have to put a pan to the stove and cook something. Remember, learning to cook should be fun, not a chore. The payoff is a fantastic meal you created yourself. So keep it simple and enjoy the process. Bon appétit!

How to Use This Book

You will find several special elements in this book designed to help you better understand the text: notes, tips, and cautions.

note

A note is designed to provide a useful piece of extra information we do not want you to miss. Take an extra moment to read each note; you will be glad you did.

tip

A tip is a piece of advice—a little trick or shortcut—that will help save you time and frustration as you cook. Tips can also help you maneuver around potential problems or limitations.

caution

A caution warns you of potentially dangerous acts or situations. In some cases, cautions alert you to potential mistakes that can ruin the meal you are preparing. In other cases, cautions warn you against actions that could cause you physical harm if attempted. Don't ignore any cautions! Always read them carefully.

cim

1

COOKWARE AND TOOL ESSENTIALS

As a beginning cook, purchasing cookware can be daunting. There are many gauges, finishes, weights, and famous brands from which to choose, and just as many opinions as to what is best. Materials range from light to heavy gauges of aluminum, sometimes coated with a nonstick surface; light to heavy gauges of stainless steel, usually not coated; and cast iron coated with enamel. Nonstick surfaces are great if you prefer to cook with a limited amount of oil, while stainless steel allows lots of little browned bits to collect on the bottom of the pan, perfect for deglazing and creating great sauces. If you use pans with a nonstick surface, it is important to use wooden or plastic utensils because metal utensils will scratch and destroy the nonstick surface.

Cookware Basics and Purchasing Guidelines

To get started, purchase just a few quality pieces that will do a number of jobs. For example, a medium-sized skillet or saucepan will do the same job as a small one. The more you cook, the more familiar you will become with your own needs and preferences, and the particular qualities of cookware that you desire. Any specific cookware requirements will show themselves as you notice that you repeatedly wish you had a wok or a Dutch oven. At this point, shopping for additional cookware items will be an enjoyable experience because you will have a clear idea of your needs. As you shop, be sure to handle the cookware in the store. Handling the cookware is not only acceptable, but it is expected. You want to be able to lift the cookware comfortably without straining your wrist, and the handle should fit nicely in your hand. As you purchase, keep the following guidelines in mind.

Saucepans or Pots

Make sure the bases are flat and solid; a bit of weight is desirable and an indicator of durability. Thin pans tend to warp when heated and can cook unevenly. These pans eventually become unusable. The pan lids should fit well, and the handles should be sturdy, comfortable, and heat resistant.

Skillets or Sauté Pans

As with pots and pans, a fairly heavy, solid, flat bottom will keep the skillet in contact with the heat in an even manner. Size will be determined by your needs. If you make eggs for breakfast every morning, for example, it's suggested that you get a small or medium skillet while *Chicken Cacciatore* (page 213) for the family will require a large skillet with a tight-fitting lid. Heat resistant handles give you the option of stove top browning with the completion of cooking in the oven, a technique you will find, for example, in *Horseradish Encrusted Pork Loin with Mushroom Stuffing* (page 189).

Roasting Pan

If purchasing only one roasting pan, then you might as well get one that is large enough to roast a turkey. You can always fit a small chicken in a large pan, but not a large turkey in a small pan. A solid weight can be added alongside a small chicken to keep a large pan from twisting when it gets hot. Deep sides on the roasting pan will keep food from splattering and allow you to roast vegetables along with your meat.

Dutch Oven

As with a roasting pan, you might as well get a Dutch oven that is large enough to cook a whole chicken. Make sure the lid fits snugly, and the handles are sturdy and large enough for a good grip. Expect the Dutch oven to be heavy, but not so heavy that you need help lifting it. This can be an expensive item, but you can find them at garage sales and secondhand shops for a fraction of the cost for a new Dutch oven.

Knives

Worth the investment and the time to keep it sharp, a good knife is worth its weight in truffles. Trying to cut or dice with a dull knife is frustrating and can be dangerous. When undue pressure is put on a dull knife, you sacrifice control, and can end up with cut fingers or worse. If you know what to look for in a knife, you can get a good one at a reasonable price. Choose a high-carbon stainless steel knife with an extension of the blade, called a *tang*, running the full length of the handle and held in place with three rivets. If you plan on splurging on an expensive knife, be sure to test how it feels in your hand before purchasing. A knife should have good balance and weight, which will become apparent once you test a few. A knife that is too light or too heavy is harder to control. See the following descriptions of specific knives for shopping guidelines. It is wise to learn how to sharpen a knife with a knife steel or, at the least, purchase an electric knife sharpener.

Chef's Knife

The most important tool in your kitchen, the chef's knife comes in a range of sizes. It will be used in almost every recipe to chop, slice, dice, and mince. Choose a size that feels best. If you have small hands, a large 12-inch chef's knife could be too large. Test a knife by firmly grasping the knife handle. It should feel comfortable in your hand with a good balance and weight; substantial, but not too heavy to control. There should be ample space under the handle to allow the knuckles to sit comfortably with- . out hitting a cutting surface.

HOW TO USE A CHEF'S KNIFE

When cutting vegetables, use a chef's knife, because the recessed handle allows space for your hand. Your knuckles won't smack the chopping board while you cut.

Firmly grasp the knife handle with your whole hand: fingers curled around the handle, forefinger tucked up snug against the heel (the large end of the knife blade), and your thumb draped over the top of the handle and just down the other side. For best control, hold the knife comfortably in your hand, neither too loose nor with a death grip.

The hand not holding the knife should hold the food with the fingertips curled safely under and away from the knife, with knuckles extended toward the side of the knife. This protects the fingertips from getting cut because the blade of the knife rests against the extended knuckles.

Place the tip of your blade on the cutting board, and pump your knife up and down, cutting through the food on the down motion.

Slowly move your fingertips backward, exposing the uncut food for slicing.

Paring Knife

This small knife is used for peeling small vegetables and cleaning meat or chicken. Look for one that feels good in your hand with a substantial, high-carbon stainless steel blade. As with the chef's knife, the tang should run the full length of the handle and be held in place with three rivets. A quality paring knife will last a lifetime.

Serrated Knife

If you have ever tried to slice a loaf of French bread with any knife other than a serrated knife, you know that it just doesn't work. This knife works well on all delicate items that are difficult to cut with a regular knife. Choose a serrated knife that has an 8- to 10-inch long, high-carbon stainless steel blade. The blade should have an extension that runs the full length of the handle and be held in place by three rivets.

The Short List of Basic Cookware and Tools

This is a guideline for the basic equipment you will need to get started. It is not necessary to purchase everything on the list—just start with a few items and then add to your arsenal as your interest and skills develop. Remember to keep it simple. If a kitchen item has only one purpose, such as a citrus zester, it is probably not a necessary item in the beginning kitchen. If it seems you are always thinking, "Gosh, I sure could use a citrus zester," while you scrape the outer skin from a lemon with a paring knife, then invest in one. But remember, the more stuff you have, the more likely you'll end up with a drawer full of gadgets that get in the way of finding your vegetable peeler when you need it.

Pots, Pans, and Baking Dishes

The following list details what pots, pans, and baking dishes are essential for every kitchen.

- Small (1-quart) saucepan with lid: good for melting butter, heating milk or stock, or reheating small quantities of food.
- Medium (3-quart) saucepan with lid: good for boiling and simmering vegetables, potatoes, pastas, grains, soups, and sauces or reheating medium quantities of food.

- Large (8- to 10-quart) stock pot: good for boiling and simmering pasta, making large batches of stock or soup, or cooking large vegetables like corn on the cob or boiling whole potatoes.

- Medium 10-inch skillet: good for frying meats, eggs, grilled cheese sandwiches, or sautéing or stir-frying vegetables and/or meats.

- Large roasting pan with rack: heavy-gauge aluminum or stainless steel for roasting meats, poultry, and vegetables. Cooking rack can double as a cooling rack.

- Small (1-quart) baking dish with lid: glass or ceramic for baking casseroles, dips, chicken or fish, reheating foods, or marinating meats.

- Rectangular 13×9×2-inch baking dish: glass or ceramic for baking large casseroles like lasagna, or chicken and fish.

- Square 9×9×2-inch baking pan: glass or ceramic for baking brownies and cakes, or roasting potatoes and vegetables.

- Pie pan, 9-inch: aluminum, glass, or ceramic for baking pies, roasting small quantities of food, or toasting nuts.

- Baking sheet with a rim (18×12×1-inch): nonstick or heavy-duty aluminum for baking savory hors d'oeuvres, cookies, biscuits, or roasting potatoes and vegetables. The rim prevents oven spills. This can also be used as a handy carrying tray.

Kitchenware

The following is a list of the gadgets that every kitchen needs.

- Can opener.

- Chef's knife, 9-inch: for chopping, dicing, or slicing just about everything you cook or prepare in your kitchen, including fruits, vegetables, meats, fish, and prepared foods.

- Colander: for draining pasta or vegetables.

- Corkscrew and bottle opener.

- Cutting board.

- Grater: four-sided, freestanding.

- Measuring cups: Dry ingredients, plastic or metal (preferably stainless steel), set of four (1 cup, 1/2 cup, 1/3 cup, 1/4 cup). Liquid ingredients, plastic or glass (preferably glass), with measurement markings on the side. The 2-cup size is suggested. Sizes available are 1-, 2-, and 4-cup.

- Measuring spoons (preferably stainless steel): Set of five (1 tablespoon, 1 teaspoon, 1/2 teaspoon, 1/3 teaspoon, 1/4 teaspoon).

- Mixing bowls: preferably both glass and stainless steel.
- Oven-safe dial meat thermometer: this is not cheap, but worth it.
- Oven thermometer: saves cookies from burning.
- Paring knife, 3-inch: for peeling, coring, and cutting bad spots from fruits and vegetables.
- Pepper grinder.
- Plastic storage containers: inexpensive and reusable; available at the grocery store.
- Pot holders.
- Potato masher.
- Serrated knife, 9-inch: for cutting breads and slicing other foods that squish easily, such as tomatoes.
- Slotted spoon.
- Soup ladle.
- Flipping spatulas: One metal and one hard plastic for non-stick surfaces.
- Scraping spatulas (flexible rubber): One large and one that is small and narrow for scraping bowls or jars.
- Timer: unless your microwave or stove has a built-in timer.
- Tongs.
- Vegetable peeler.
- Wire-mesh strainer: large.
- Wire whisk: stainless steel.
- Wooden stirring spoons.

Absolute Additions When You Have Some Extra Money

The following is a list of items that make cooking easier. These items should be purchased when you have extra money in your kitchen fund.

- Blender.
- Citrus zester.
- Collapsible vegetable steamer: fits in any pot.
- Dutch oven: Ovenproof, heavy-bottomed pot with lid that can be used on the stove top and in the oven. Used for browning meat on the stovetop, then transferring to the oven to complete the cooking by braising or roasting.
- Electric hand mixer.
- Food processor: to blend, grate, slice, or chop large amounts of foods. If you cook a lot, you will wonder how you got along without it. If you don't cook

much, forget the food processor and look upon vigorous stirring and chopping as your weekly workout.

- Mini-food processor: to chop herbs and blend small amounts of ingredients.
- Long-handled fork.
- Funnel.
- Kitchen shears.
- Loaf pans: Two 9×5×3-inch pans for baking breads, pound cake, or meat loaf.
- Meat pounder: smooth bottomed.
- Muffin tin: for baking muffins or quick breads, mini-cheesecakes, or puff-pastry hors d'oeuvres.
- Pastry brush.
- Rolling pin: heavy.
- Round cake pans: Two 8×2-inch or 9×2-inch pans. Used for baking layer cakes.
- Salad spinner.
- Skewers: metal or bamboo.
- Springform pan: One 9-inch round baking pan with removable sides for easy removal of baked cheesecakes, quiches, tortes, or cakes with crumb crusts.
- Wire cooling rack.
- Wire-mesh strainer: small.

Organizing Your Equipment

Organizing your pans and gadgets does not have to be rocket science. It simply means putting similar items together. When you need a wooden spoon or spatula, you can go directly to the large utensil drawer rather then roaming around the kitchen, opening drawers and rifling through the foil and Saran Wrap boxes to find the tool you need.

Place all of your pots and pans in the same cupboard, perhaps one of the lower cupboards near the stove. Place the baking pans in one area of the cupboard and the saucepans and skillets in another area.

Place large utensils such as whisks, large stirring spoons, spatulas, tongs, and ladles in one drawer. Place smaller utensils such as the bottle opener, corkscrew, measuring spoons, citrus zester, vegetable peelers, pastry brush, and meat thermometer in another drawer. If you find that you do a lot of baking and start collecting pastry bags and pastry tips, rolling pins, cookie cutters, and other baking items, you will want to create an area specifically just for your bakeware.

Just remember, keep similar items together. Measuring cups are easier to find if not stuffed in the same drawer as the dishtowels. As you spend more time in your kitchen you will begin to get an idea of your own needs and what works for you.

2

FOOD ESSENTIALS FOR YOUR PANTRY

A well-stocked pantry makes cooking more enjoyable and saves time and money. A pantry contains food items that are used frequently, or in large quantities, on hand for quick access. Stocking your pantry may seem overwhelming, but remember that most of these items last for months, and will only appear on your shopping list one or two at a time when they need to be replenished. With the basics already in your cupboard, your weekly shopping will be reduced to recipe and meal-specific items.

The basic pantry lists are a suggested starting place. What each person likes to cook or keep on hand depends on individual taste. If smothering everything you eat in A1 Steak Sauce is your thing, then be sure to add A1 Steak Sauce to the list. If you realize that you go through an item rather quickly, watch for sales and stock up.

Organizing Your Pantry

Organizing a pantry is easy and a matter of individual taste. Try putting similar items together. Place baking ingredients such as the sugars, flours, baking soda, and baking powder in one area; canned beans, vegetables, and fruits together; and salad dressings, oils, and vinegars together. Take it a step further by organizing within each area; for example, all canned fruits in one row and all vegetables in another. When replenishing the pantry, place the new items in the back and the older items in the front.

Be sure to read labels closely, as many items must be refrigerated after opening. Items in the *Basic Cupboard Pantry* list marked with an asterisk (*) must be refrigerated after opening. Transfer any unused portion of canned food into a covered container and refrigerate. Do not store unused foods in the can for any reason.

caution

Rinse or wipe off the top of the cans before opening, as dirt and bacteria that have gathered there during transport and warehouse storage may taint food.

Basic Cupboard Pantry

Baking Ingredients

- All-purpose white or whole-wheat flour
- Baking powder
- Baking soda
- Chocolate: unsweetened squares or semi-sweet morsels (chocolate chips)
- Cocoa powder, unsweetened
- Cornstarch
- Cornmeal
- Honey
- Sugars: white granulated, powdered (confectioners'), and brown
- Vanilla extract
- Yeast, dry active

Canned, Packaged, or Jarred Foods

- Beans, canned: black, pinto, red kidney, and garbanzo*
- Bread crumbs: unseasoned
- Broths, canned or in cartons: beef and chicken*
- Capers*
- Couscous
- Dried fruits: raisins and cranberries
- Nuts: almonds, walnuts, pine nuts, and pecans
- Olives: black pitted and kalamata*
- Pasta, dried: spaghetti, linguine, penne, and angel hair
- Peanut butter*
- Pickles*
- Preserves: fruit jam, chutney, and marmalade*
- Rice: long grain white, brown, wild, basmati, and Arborio
- Tomatoes, canned: whole plum, chopped tomatoes, and tomato paste (tube or can)*

Sauces, Oils, and Flavorings

- Asian hot chili paste*
- Horseradish*
- Ketchup*
- Mustards: Dijon and whole grain*
- Extra virgin olive oil
- Peanut oil
- Sesame oil*
- Soy sauce*
- Maple syrup
- Salt: Kosher or sea salt
- Salsa, jarred*
- Tabasco sauce
- Wine: dry sherry, dry burgundy, and dry white
- Worcestershire sauce
- Vinegars: red wine, white wine, rice wine, balsamic, and cider

Basic Refrigerator Pantry

- Butter, unsalted
- Eggs
- Mayonnaise
- Milk
- Sour cream

Basic Freezer Pantry

- Individually frozen berries
- Individually frozen vegetables: artichoke hearts, corn, petite peas, pearl onions, and whole leaf spinach
- Individually frozen chicken breasts
- Individually frozen shell-on raw shrimp

Basic Cheese Guide

Cheese is very versatile and, like eggs, can be eaten alone or as an ingredient in any meal. Cheese can be grated into scrambled eggs, sliced for a sandwich or as a snack, cubed in a salad, shredded in a casserole, or used as a garnish for pasta. The range of cheeses available at the grocery store now include cheeses that were once found only in specialty cheese shops, opening up a world of cooking and eating possibilities.

Cheese is made from cow, goat, or sheep's milk, usually without preservatives. The sharpness, flavor, and texture of a cheese are dependent upon how it is made and how long and where it is ripened or aged. Cheeses are classified as ripened or unripened, and then by consistency. Unripened cheeses, such as ricotta, cream cheese, and mascarpone, are classified only as soft or firm, while ripened or aged cheeses are classified as soft, semi-soft, firm, very hard, and blue-vein mold.

The harder the cheese, the longer it can be stored in the refrigerator. Soft, unripened cheeses usually carry a "use by" date on the packaging. Harder cheeses should be packed in an airtight plastic container after opening and may be stored in the coldest part of the refrigerator for several weeks.

With the exception of cottage cheese and ricotta, cheese can be frozen in an airtight container; however, changes in texture are likely. Thaw frozen cheese, unopened, in the refrigerator and use as soon as possible.

The general rule of thumb is that 4 ounces of cheese, except hard cheeses, yields 1 cup of shredded or grated cheese. For hard cheeses like Parmesan or Romano, figure 3 ounces of cheese to 1 cup of grated.

Cheese should be cooked at a low temperature, 325° to 350° F, for only short periods of time. High heat can cause the fats in the cheese to separate, making the cheese tough and stringy. To add cheese to sauces, grate or shred the cheese and add it during the last few minutes of cooking, stirring gently. The cheese will melt quickly and blend easily.

Pairing wine with cheese is a matter of personal taste, but generally the goal is to balance the flavors. Standard pairings are light and fruity wines with mild cheeses and assertive wines with strongly flavored cheeses. A hearty, robust Bordeaux or Cabernet would overpower a lighter cheese like Jarlsberg or Edam, but it will stand up nicely to the flavors of a Double Gloucester or Parmesan. Seeking professional advice from your local wine merchant is a great way to learn about wine and make a new friend.

If you are serving cheese on its own, it is very important to serve it at room temperature for maximum flavor. An inexpensive cheese at the right temperature can taste like you hocked your wedding ring to buy it. Conversely, an expensive cheese will be under-appreciated if served right from the refrigerator and not allowed to reach its full potential.

The chart below lists some of the most readily available gourmet cheeses on the market. Many specialty cheese stores and markets set out cheese samples to encourage tasting. Most are happy to give you a nibble at the cheese counter; however, cheeses that come straight from the refrigeration case cannot be fully appreciated until they approach room temperature. Use the guide below and start tasting.

TABLE 2.1   Basic Cheese Chart

Cheese (Country of Origin)	Characteristics	Serving Suggestions
Brie (France)	Soft cheese with an edible, thin rind; creamy yellow interior softens and becomes spreadable when fully ripened; mild to pungent buttery flavor.	Allow to ripen (soften) to room temperature and serve in small wheels or wedges on a cheese board with a knife for spreading on crackers or breads. Excellent for dessert with fruit.
Camembert (France)	Soft cheese with edible, thin rind; creamy yellow interior softens and becomes spreadable when fully ripened; mild to pungent buttery flavor that grows stronger with age.	Allow to ripen (soften) to room temperature and serve in small wheels or wedges on a cheese board with a knife for spreading on crackers or breads. Excellent for dessert with fruit.
Cheddar (England)	Firm cheese with a creamy, smooth texture; ivory to orange in color; mild to very sharp with a nutty flavor; strengthens with age.	Sliced on a cheese board, in sandwiches, or for snacks; grated or shredded for cooking.

TABLE 2.1   Basic Cheese Chart

Cheese (Country of Origin)	Characteristics	Serving Suggestions
Double Gloucester (England)	Firm cheese with a smooth, rich texture; orange color; mellow cheddar flavor.	Sliced on a cheese board, in sandwiches, or for snacks; grated or shredded for cooking.
Edam (Netherlands)	Firm cheese usually sold coated in red wax; creamy yellow interior with slightly nutty flavor.	Sliced on a cheese board, in sandwiches or salads, or with fruit for dessert.
Emmenthaler (Switzerland)	Firm cheese (this is the original Swiss); natural rind, light yellow interior with large holes; sweet, nutty flavor; slightly salty.	Sliced on a cheese board, in sandwiches or salads; grated or shredded for cooking; melts well.
Feta (Greece)	Soft cheese made from goat's or sheep's milk; pickled in brine; white, flaky texture; sharp, salty, tangy flavor.	Crumbled on a cheese board, served with Greek olives; crumbled in salads and for cooking.
Fontina (Italian)	Semi-soft to firm cheese, sometimes sold with wax coating; yellow interior; slight nutty flavor with hint of salt.	Sliced on a cheese board or in sandwiches; grated or shredded for cooking.
Gorgonzola (Italy)	Semi-soft cheese, moist but sometimes crumbly; creamy white interior marbled with blue-green veins; tangy strong flavor; most pungent of the blue cheeses.	Sliced or crumbled on a cheese board; classic dessert with fruit and dark breads; crumbled in salads or salad dressings, on steaks or baked potatoes.
Gouda (Netherlands)	Semi-soft to firm cheese sometimes sold in wax-coated flattened rounds; yellow interior; mild, mellow flavor.	Sliced on a cheese board, with fruit for dessert, in sandwiches, or for snacks; grated for cooking.
Gruyère (Switzerland)	Firm cheese, similar to Emmenthaler; light yellow interior with small holes; buttery, nutty flavor.	Sliced on a cheese board or with fruit for dessert; grated or shredded in quiche, sauces, and fondues.
Jarlsberg (Norway)	Firm cheese with smooth texture; light yellow interior; buttery, slight nutty flavor.	Sliced on a cheese board or in sandwiches, and salads; grated or shredded for cooking; melts well.
Mascarpone (Italy)	Soft cream cheese with a rich, smooth texture; mild flavor.	Used in cooking sweet and savory dishes for a creamy texture. Add herbs to make a rich dip; essential in making tiramisu.

TABLE 2.1 Basic Cheese Chart

Cheese (Country of Origin)	Characteristics	Serving Suggestions
Monterey Jack (USA)	Semi-soft to firm cheese produced in large wheels; creamy white texture; mild flavor strengthens with age.	Sliced on a cheese board, in sandwiches, or for snacks; grated or shredded for cooking.
Mozzarella (Italy)	Slightly firm cheese with creamy white, slightly rubbery texture; delicate flavor; also imported fresh, made from buffalo milk; sold in small bags with liquid to keep it moist.	Fresh only, sliced in tomato salads with fresh basil and balsamic vinegar; domestic and imported are good for pizza and other Italian dishes.
Parmesan (Italy)	Hard cheese with tan or black coating; creamy white to light yellow with a slightly granular, brittle texture; sharp, sweet flavor; Parmesan is the best available.	Sliced or crumbled on cheese board or with fruit for dessert; grated or shredded for cooking and garnish. Pre-grated, packaged cheese has an inferior flavor.
Ricotta (Italy)	Soft, unripened cheese with a moist, grainy texture; rich and slightly sweet.	Used in cooking sweet and savory dishes.
Romano (Italy)	Hard cheese made from sheep's milk with a tan or black coating; creamy white to light yellow interior with a slightly granular, brittle texture; sharp, sweet flavor; Romano-Reggiano is the best available.	Sliced or crumbled on cheese board or with fruit for dessert; grated or shredded for cooking and garnish. Pre-grated, packaged cheese has an inferior flavor.
Roquefort (France)	Semi-soft cheese made from sheep's milk; moist but sometimes crumbly; creamy white interior marbled with blue-green veins; pungent, very salty flavor.	Sliced or crumbled on a cheese board; classic dessert with fruit and dark breads; crumbled in salads or salad dressings.
Stilton (England)	Semi-soft cheese; moist but sometimes crumbly; creamy white interior marbled with blue-green veins; very strong, tangy flavor; can be very expensive.	Sliced or crumbled on a cheese board or with fruit and nuts for dessert; use in cooking sauces, quiches, and soups.

Guide to Basic Herbs and Spices

Herbs and spices are the keys to the aircraft, taking ordinary foods on a worldwide journey. The history of civilization can be traced through the history of trading herbs and spices, and we are fortunate to live in a time when a global assortment of herbs and spices are as close as our cupboards. When cooking with herbs and spices, remember to keep it simple, especially when first experimenting with a new herb or spice, because it is necessary to taste and identify all the flavors in your dish. To get a good taste of a new herb or spice on its own, mix it with a little unsalted butter. Let it sit to fully develop its flavor, spread it on a piece of white bread, and taste.

The basic herbs and spices, such as basil, oregano, tarragon, thyme, parsley, rosemary, cayenne, cinnamon, and, of course, salt and pepper, should be enough to get you started. Purchase additional herbs and spices when they are called for in a recipe. Even dried herbs are best when fresh; the full aroma of dried herbs and spices should rise up to meet your nose when the container is opened. It is best to purchase small quantities of herbs and use them completely within a year.

For maximum flavor, crush dried herbs between your fingertips just before adding them to your dish. Pepper and other whole spices, such as nutmeg, are best freshly ground or grated; a pepper mill is a must-have tool and a nutmeg grater is very useful.

Fresh-grown herbs bring bright flavors and color to your dishes and should be purchased as close to use as possible. They are fragile and perish quickly. Wrap the leafy tops of fresh herbs in a paper towel, place the stems in a small amount of water, and store them in the refrigerator for 2 to 5 days. If you discover that you frequently use a particular fresh herb, consider growing your own.

note

To substitute dried herbs or spices for fresh, 1 teaspoon of dried = 3 teaspoons of fresh.

TABLE 2.2   Herb and Spice Chart

Name and Forms	Characteristics	Suggested Uses
Allspice—spice **(Whole berries or ground)**	Flavor and aroma of cinnamon with nutmeg and clove.	Use in spice cakes, cookies, and fruit pies; chutneys, relishes, barbecue sauces, or pickles; stews, chili, ham, corned beef, baked winter squash, and sweet potatoes.
Anise—spice **(Whole seeds or ground)**	Flavor of licorice.	Use in cookies, cakes, breads, and fruit dishes.
Basil—herb **(Fresh sprigs or crumbled dried leaves)**	Very aromatic, sweet, slightly licorice taste.	Excellent in egg or tomato dishes, pasta sauces, pizza, soups, and in other Italian foods.

TABLE 2.2   (continued)

Name and Forms	Characteristics	Suggested Uses
Bay leaf—herb (**Large dried whole leaves**)	Pungent, slight woodsy flavor.	Adds depth to soups, stews, pot roasts, braised meats, and gravies. Remove leaves before serving.
Capers—spice (**Small, olive-green pods packed in salt or vinegar**)	Pungent, briny flavor.	Adds a tangy snap to potato and pasta salads, pasta sauces, tomato and eggplant dishes, sautéed meats, chicken, and fish.
Caraway—spice (**Dried whole seed**)	Nutty with a slight licorice flavor.	Use to bake rye bread and flavor dips, eggs, coleslaw, potatoes, cabbage, green beans, winter squash, and vegetable salads.
Cardamom—spice (**Dried whole seeds or ground**)	Aromatic with hints of cinnamon, ginger, and lemon.	Use to flavor cakes, cookies, pastries, breads, stews, winter squash, and Indian foods such as curry.
Cayenne—spice (**Dried whole pods or, more commonly, ground; also called ground red pepper**)	Very hot pepper with a burnt red color.	Use in dishes to add heat. Add to sauces, stews, curries, chili, eggs, cheese, and Mexican dishes.
Celery Seed—spice (**Dried whole seeds**)	Taste and aroma of celery.	Use in salads such as potato, tuna, or coleslaw; also great in a Bloody Mary cocktail.
Chervil—herb (**Fresh sprigs or dried crumbled leaves**)	Delicate herb with a light licorice-parsley flavor.	Due to its delicate flavor, add at completion of cooking to cream sauces, soups, fish, chicken, green beans, and peas. Add to green salads, dressings, egg salads, and fresh tomato dishes.
Chive—herb (**Long tubular stalk, either fresh, or minced, then dried or frozen**)	Delicate onion-garlic aroma and flavor.	Great in scrambled eggs, cream sauces, baked potatoes, cottage cheese, dips, and with sautéed fish and vegetables. Also a flavorful garnish.
Cilantro—herb (**Fresh sprigs or dried crumbled leaves**)	Fresh, mild, sweet-peppery flavor; too much can impart a soapy taste.	Essential in Mexican, Latin American, and Asian cooking. Use in salsas, soups, stir-fries, curries, rice, fish, shellfish, and chicken dishes.
Cinnamon—spice (**Dried whole sticks (rolled tree bark) or ground**)	Very aromatic, sweet, and mildly hot flavor.	Often used in combination with nutmeg and cloves in cakes, cookies, breads, puddings, and fruit pies, especially apple. Use in meat stews, rice dishes, chili, and many Mediterranean recipes.

TABLE 2.2   (continued)

Name and Forms	Characteristics	Suggested Uses
Clove—spice (**Dried whole buds or ground**)	Strong fragrance with a pungent, sweet flavor.	Traditional winter holiday spice in gingerbread, cookies, cakes, fruit pies; buds used to stud hams. Add to curries, sauces, winter vegetables, and sweet potatoes.
Coriander—spice (**Dried whole seeds or ground**)	Nutty, lemon-flavored dried seeds of the cilantro plant.	Use in baked goods, puddings, curries, relishes, and to season sweet pickles.
Cumin—spice (**Dried whole seeds**)	Very aromatic with a slightly hot, nutty, earthy flavor.	An essential ingredient in most chili and curry powders. Great in stews, chili, beans, chutneys and dips; sautéed vegetables, meats, chicken, fish, and cheese dishes.
Dill—herb (**Dried whole seeds, fresh sprigs, or dried crumbled leaves**)	Leaves, fresh or dried, have slight tangy licorice flavor; seeds are pungent and nutty.	Use to season pickles, in breads, potato salad, rice dishes, sauerkraut, cabbage, tomatoes, eggs, yogurt sauces, chicken, and fish, especially salmon.
Fennel—herb (**Dried whole seeds**)	Strong licorice flavor.	Use in Italian dishes, sausage, stews, soups, fish, and in Scandinavian baked goods.
Ginger—spice (**Fresh whole root, partial root, dried root, crystallized, preserved, or ground**)	Very aromatic with a tangy, sweet, spicy flavor.	Use fresh, grated or sliced in dipping sauces, marinades, or sautés; great with fish, chicken, pork, and vegetables. Use dried in cakes, cookies, fruit pies, and gingerbread. Use crystallized or preserved in baked goods and candies.
Lemon grass—herb (**Fresh or dried stalks**)	Leaves of stalk have lemony, woody flavor.	Essential ingredient in Indonesian cooking. Use in soups, dressings, marinades, and with fish, chicken, and shellfish.
Marjoram—herb (**Fresh sprigs, dried whole, or crumbled leaves**)	Delicate oregano-mint aroma and flavor.	Use in soups, sauces, salads, vegetables, meat, chicken, or fish dishes.
Mint—herb (**Fresh sprigs, dried crumbled leaves, or ground**)	Slightly sweet, cooling, menthol flavor.	Essential in many Middle Eastern dishes such as tabbouleh, yogurt sauces, and lamb. Use in fish, soups, salads, vegetables, fruit salads, candies, jellies, hot or cold teas, and in cocktails such as juleps and mojitos.

TABLE 2.2 (continued)

Name and Forms	Characteristics	Suggested Uses
Mustard—spice (Dried whole seeds or ground)	Brown, yellow, or white seeds with a spicy, nutty flavor.	Use in seasoning pickles, in sauces, dips, eggs, salad, cheese dishes, and dressings.
Nutmeg—spice (Whole seed or ground)	Aromatic, sweet, slightly spicy, nutty flavor. For best flavor, purchase the whole seed and grate as needed.	Use in eggnog, cakes, cookies, pies, pastries, puddings, applesauce, cheese dishes, cream sauces, chili, stews, braised meats, rice dishes, beans; and with vegetables such as Brussels sprouts, spinach, carrots, and cauliflower.
Oregano—herb (Fresh sprigs, dried whole leaves, crumbled leaves, or ground)	Pungent, sweet, earthy, slight mint aroma and flavor.	Essential ingredient in Italian, Greek, and Mexican cooking. Often combined with basil. Great in tomato sauces, eggs, stews, soups, and chili. Use with vegetables such as zucchini, peppers, and eggplant.
Paprika—spice (Dried ground capsicum pepper)	Hungarian paprika is the most flavorful with flavors ranging from hot to sweet.	Essential in Hungarian goulash. Use in stews, dips, sauces; with fish, shellfish, chicken; and in potato and egg salads.
Parsley—herb (Fresh sprigs or dried crumbled leaves)	Fresh sweet, celery flavor and aroma. The two most common varieties are curly parsley and Italian flat leaf parsley, which has a stronger flavor.	Versatile herb that flavors almost any dish: soups, beans, cream sauces, tomato sauces, green salads, grain salads, salad dressings, egg, rice and potato dishes, vegetable dishes, chicken, fish, shellfish, and meats. Curly parsley is popular as a garnish.
Pepper—spice (Whole dried black, white, pink or green; berries or ground)	Hot, biting, pungent flavor.	Freshly ground black pepper enhances almost any savory dish; white pepper is used in light colored dishes where black flecks are unappetizing.
Rosemary—herb (Fresh tiny ranches or whole, dried, needle-like leaves)	Very aromatic with pine-lemon aroma and flavor.	Excellent with grilled, broiled, or roasted meats, chicken, potatoes, or vegetables. Thicker branches are sometimes used as skewers for kabobs or brochettes. Use in baking breads, rolls, and stuffing mixtures.
Saffron—spice (Dried whole stigmas or ground— whole is best quality)	Fragrant with a slightly bitter flavor. Too much imparts a medicinal taste.	Small amount (1/8 to 1/4 teaspoon) adds color and flavor to rice dishes such as paella and risotto, cream soups, sauces, and fish dishes such as bouillabaisse. Bake into cakes, cookies, and breads.

TABLE 2.2 (continued)

Name and Forms	Characteristics	Suggested Uses
Sage—herb (**Fresh sprigs, dried whole leaves, dried crumbled leaves or ground**)	Very aromatic with a slightly musky, bitter flavor.	Great in poultry stuffing, or with poultry, pork, stews, soups, beans, omelets, and cheese dishes.
Savory—herb (**Fresh sprigs or crumbled dried leaves**)	Aromatic peppery flavor and aroma.	Use in bread stuffing, meatloaf, chicken, and cheese dishes; with peas and cauliflower. Excellent with dried and green beans.
Tarragon—herb (**Fresh sprigs, dried whole leaves or dried crumbled leaves**)	Sweet, slight licorice taste.	Excellent with fish, shellfish, chicken, carrots, mushrooms, and in potato salad. Excellent paired with mustard in salad dressings, sauces, mayonnaise, and vinaigrettes.
Thyme—herb (**Fresh sprigs or dried crumbled leaves**)	Aromatic, tiny leaves have strong, slight lemony, tea-like flavor.	Excellent in soups, stews, sauces, stuffing, cheese dishes, salad dressings, beans, mushrooms, potatoes, zucchini, fish, shellfish, poultry, and lamb.
Turmeric—spice (**Dried ground**)	Slightly musky, bitter flavor.	Essential in curry powders, mustard, and Indian cooking. Adds flavor and bright yellow color to egg, rice, and tofu dishes.
Vanilla bean—spice (**Whole, dark, long, slender pods with tiny seeds inside or pure extract**)	Very aromatic with pleasantly bitter-sweet aroma and flavor.	Essential to flavor most sweet foods such as cakes, cookies, pastries, custards, ice cream, puddings, sweet sauces, and frostings.

Spice Blends

Available for purchase in most grocery stores, these basic spice blends are some-times called for in recipes, but more often they are handy replacements for a group of individual herbs and spices. As herbs and spices can sometimes be pricey, the beginning cook can save money by purchasing a blend rather than all of the herbs and spices individually. The *Spice Blends Chart* details the individual herbs and spices contained in each blend to assist you in your purchase.

TABLE 2.3   Spice Blends Chart

Spice Blend	Ingredients and Suggested Uses
Bouquet Garni	A blend of parsley, rosemary, thyme, and bay leaf, tied into cheese-cloth and used to flavor soups and stews. The cheesecloth bundle is easily removed before serving.
Curry Powder	A blend of turmeric, coriander, cumin, black pepper, cayenne, ginger, and fenugreek used in Indian cooking.
Fine Herbs	A blend of chives, chervil, tarragon, and parsley used to flavor soups, sauces, and eggs.
Five Spice Powder	A blend of cinnamon, fennel, cloves, star anise, and white pepper used to flavor Asian dishes, beans, poultry, and meats.
Herbs de Provence	A blend of thyme, rosemary, savory, basil, marjoram, tarragon, and lavender flowers used to flavor soups, sauces, eggs, and fish and chicken dishes.
Italian Seasoning	A blend of oregano, basil, marjoram, thyme, and rosemary used in tomato sauces, salad dressings, on pizza, with pasta, and in cheese dishes.
Mexican Seasoning	A blend of ground chili peppers, garlic powder, onion powder, cumin, oregano, and bay leaf used to add spicy heat and flavor to Mexican dishes, sauces, vegetables, and eggs.
Poultry Seasoning	A blend of thyme, sage, marjoram, rosemary, black pepper, and nutmeg used to flavor poultry and stuffing and to season gravies and sauces.
Seafood Seasoning	A blend of celery salt, dry mustard powder, cayenne, ground bay leaves, nutmeg, cloves, ginger, and paprika used to flavor all types of seafood and seafood dishes.

3

GLOSSARY OF TERMS AND TECHNIQUES, CONVERSIONS AND EQUIVALENTS

Just like any specialty area, cooking has a vocabulary all its own. You will see terms like these in almost any recipe, so make sure that you know exactly what the recipe is asking you to do before you jump in and start cooking.

Glossary

Al dente: Italian term meaning "to the tooth." Used to describe the texture of pasta or other foods, such as blanched vegetables, that are cooked just until tender but slightly firm to the bite.

Bake: To cook, covered or uncovered, by dry heat, usually in an oven. When baking, it is important to preheat the oven first. Do not crowd the oven. Air must be allowed to circulate freely to ensure that the food cooks evenly. When meat, poultry, or vegetables are baked uncovered, it is called *roasting*.

Barbecue: To cook meat, poultry, fish, or vegetables on a grill placed over an intense heat created with charcoal, gas, or wood.

Baste: To spoon, brush, or drizzle barbecue sauce, pan drippings, or a marinade over meat, poultry, vegetables, or fish while grilling or roasting. A bulb baster is specifically designed for this purpose. Basting moistens, adds flavor, and enhances the finished appearance. If basting with pan drippings, check occasionally to ensure juices are not evaporating. If the pan drippings are evaporating, add a small amount of liquid such as stock, wine, or water to the pan. Brushing or basting roasting vegetables with oil or melted butter creates a browned crispy surface.

Batter: A thin or slightly thick liquid mixture usually containing flour, eggs, liquid, and a raising agent such as baking powder. This mixture can be poured, dropped from a spoon, or used as a coating for fried foods.

Beat: To mix foods by stirring vigorously in a quick, even, circular motion, lifting the mixture up and over with each stroke. This incorporates air into the mixture and makes it light and fluffy. Use a wooden spoon or a fork to beat. Most often used for eggs, but also a useful method to create a smooth consistency and remove lumps in sauces or custards. This also can be done with an electric mixer.

Bind: To add an ingredient, such as an egg, cream, or butter, to thicken and hold the other ingredients together.

Blanch: To immerse food, usually fruits or vegetables, very briefly in boiling water, either to help loosen the skin or to cook slightly to preserve color and flavor. To loosen the skin on fruits such as tomatoes, nuts, or peaches, immerse the fruit in boiling water for 20 seconds and then plunge into cold water. Remove, let the fruit cool slightly, and then remove the skin. Blanching before freezing stops the enzyme action that destroys the fresh flavor, color, and texture of fruits and vegetables. Immerse in boiling water 1–3 minutes, remove, and plunge into ice water to stop the cooking process and then freeze.

Blend: To thoroughly combine two or more ingredients with a wire whisk, spatula, fork, spoon, or electric mixer to a desired consistency.

Blind Bake: To bake an empty pastry shell so that it is well cooked and crisp. The pastry dough is placed in a pie or quiche pan and lined with parchment paper or aluminum foil. Dried beans or baking marbles are placed on the paper or foil to ensure the pastry retains its shape as it bakes. The weights and lining are then removed and the pastry is cooked a bit longer to complete the baking.

Boil: To bring the temperature of water to 212°F, at sea level, which causes bubbles to constantly rise and break on the surface. Small bubbles will start to form along the inside edge of the pot, gradually increasing in size and intensity. Large bubbles rapidly rising and breaking on the agitated surface indicates a full, rapid, or rolling boil. Covering the pan will speed this process. Food, such as potatoes or pasta, are placed in water that is not yet at a boil, or already boiling, and cooked for a determined amount of time according to the recipe instructions. Medium bubbles rising less intensely with a less agitated surface are known as a "slow boil."

Bone: To remove the bones from meat, poultry, or fish. A thin, flexible boning knife is often used for this process.

Braise: The technique of browning meats or vegetables on the stove top in a small amount of fat and then transferring them to the oven to slowly cook in a few inches of liquid. This cooking technique tenderizes and flavors foods and is especially appropriate for tough cuts of meat. A heavy, tightly-lidded, steep-sided pan such as a Dutch oven is a great pot for braising because it completely surrounds the food and cooks it evenly.

Bread: To dredge or coat with bread or cracker crumbs, usually after first dipping food into a beaten egg or other liquid so that the crumbs will adhere. Breading will seal in moisture and create a crispy crust when the food is cooked.

Brochette: Meat, fish, or vegetables threaded on a skewer and baked, broiled, or grilled.

Broil: To cook food under intense direct heat, usually under a gas or electric oven broiler. A quick, easy, and healthy method of cooking meats, poultry, fish, or vegetables as the high heat seals in the moisture while browning the outside and creating a tender inside. The broiler must be preheated, the food lightly brushed with oil (due to the intense heat), and placed 4–6 inches from the heat source. Barbecuing produces the same result, with the heat source on the underside of the food.

Broth: A liquid created by cooking meat, poultry, fish, or vegetables, or a combination of those foods, in water.

Brown: To cook food quickly at a high heat, usually in a skillet with a small amount of fat, to seal in the moisture and to give food an appetizing, rich, brown color on the surface. A very hot oven or a broiler also will brown foods.

Bruise: To partially crush an aromatic food, such as garlic, to release flavors before adding to a recipe. Press down on the garlic with the flat side of a knife blade, applying pressure with the palm of your hand.

Butterfly: To split food, usually meat, down the center, removing any bones and cutting almost all the way through. The two halves are laid open flat to resemble a butterfly or a book, creating a larger, thinner piece of meat suitable for stuffing.

Caramelize: To melt sugar over low heat, without burning, until it dissolves into a liquid state creating a golden or dark brown syrup. Also refers to sautéing onions or other vegetables over medium-high heat until their sugars break down and caramelize, resulting in a brown color and rich flavor.

Chiffonade: French for "made of rags." Vegetable or large herb leaves, such as basil, are stacked, rolled into a tight cylinder, and cut across the stem, which creates strips or ribbons when unrolled. Most often used as a garnish.

Chill: To refrigerate food or place it in ice or ice water until cold.

Chop: To use a knife to coarsely cut food more than one time, into small or large, non-uniform pieces.

Clarify: To clear a cloudy liquid, such as stock, by adding raw egg whites or eggshells and simmering for 10–15 minutes. This attracts and holds the impurities in the liquid. After cooling, the liquid is gently poured through a fine wire sieve (strainer) or cheesecloth to strain out the residue.

HOW TO CLARIFY BUTTER

Many recipes will ask you to use clarified butter without explaining the term. Just as the glossary explains, clarifying butter means making the butter clear by separating and discarding the milk solids. This creates a golden liquid with a much higher smoking point than regular butter. Unsalted butter is slowly melted over a low heat without stirring. As the water evaporates, the milk solids separate and sink to the bottom of the pan. Any impurities rise to the surface and the butter fat, in the middle, becomes clear. The pan is removed from the heat and the foam is skimmed off the top with a spoon. Carefully pour or ladle the clarified butter into another container, discarding the milk solids left behind.

Coat a spoon: To dip a spoon into egg-based custards and sauces to test for doneness. The food is done if an even film, thin to thick depending on the recipe instructions, is left on the spoon and a clear path is left when your finger is drawn across the coating.

Core: The center of a fruit or vegetable that holds the stem and seeds. To core is to remove this area with a small paring knife or *corer*, a tool designed specifically to remove the core from an apple or pear, leaving a cylindrical hole through the center.

Cream: To thoroughly blend a softened ingredient, such as butter or shortening, into itself or other ingredients, such as sugar. Use the back of a spoon against the side of the bowl to blend and eventually create a smooth, light and fluffy texture.

Crimp: To press two pastry edges together, sealing them, and forming a raised, decorative edge that holds in the filling. To crimp, place the thumb and side of folded index finger over the pastry edge at a 45° angle and gently pinch, continuing all around the edge, creating a diagonal ridge on the rim. Do not pinch too hard as you are only shaping the dough, not stretching it. Another method is to create a "V" with the thumb and index finger of your left hand placed on the pastry rim facing out. Gently press the dough up and out with the "V", while pressing in toward the "V" with the index finger of your right hand. This creates a little scallop that continues all around the edge. You also can press the two pastry edges together with the tines of a fork to create a flat, but sealed edge.

Cube: To cut food into small, square pieces ranging in size from 1/4-inch to 1 1/2-inches—larger than a dice, more uniform in shape and size than a coarse cut.

Curdle: Caused by overcooking, too much heat, or agitation. An egg- or cream-based mixture will separate into a liquid that contains small, solid particles.

Cut: To divide food one or more times with a knife into small or large pieces.

Cut-In: To mix a solid fat, such as butter or shortening, into a dry ingredient with a pastry blender, two table knives, or the fingers, until particles are the desired size, usually the size of coarse bread crumbs. A pastry blender is made for this purpose and is rocked back and forth through the mixture until the fat is distributed as desired. Two table knives are drawn back and forth in opposing directions, cutting the solid into the dry ingredients. Fingers are the choice of professional chefs, in a method referred to as *rubbing in*, in which the fat is rubbed into the flour using the tips of the fingers.

Dash: A measuring term referring to a very small quantity, usually between 1/8 and 1/16 of a teaspoon, or one or two quick shakes, as in "a dash of hot sauce."

De-beard: To remove the beard from a mussel prior to cooking.

Deep fry: To rapidly cook foods by submerging them in a deep pot of very hot oil. It is essential to use an oil that can be heated to a high temperature without smoking. Oils with a high smoke point are corn, grapeseed, safflower, and peanut oil. Fill the pan no more than halfway with oil since a higher level can be dangerous and many house fires are started by deep-fat pans catching fire. Heat the oil to just below the smoking point. With tongs, or a small wire basket on a long handle made for deep frying, place the foods, such as potatoes for French fries, breaded onion rings, or battered calamari, into the hot oil and deep fry. The recipe directions will give the length of time for cooking. When done, carefully lift the food out of the pan with tongs or a wire basket and transfer to paper towels to drain. This cooking method is most suited to less delicate foods that have been coated with batter or breading to protect them from the high heat.

De-glaze: To add wine, broth, or water to the bottom of a hot roasting or sauté pan in order to loosen the drippings or browned bits deposited while cooking a food, usually meat or poultry. As the liquid heats, scrape the bottom of the pan to release the browned bits. Stir these into the liquid to create the beginnings of a sauce to be seasoned and reduced to the desired consistency or used to make gravy.

Degrease: To carefully skim the fat off the surface of a liquid, such as a soup or stew, with a spoon. Alternately, you may chill the liquid to solidify the fat for easy removal.

De-vein: To remove the dark vein (the intestinal tract) which runs down the back of a shrimp. Shell the shrimp, cut a lengthwise slit along the outside curve of the back, and remove the vein. Rinse well under cold water. In smaller shrimp, the vein can be eaten. However, the vein in larger shrimp contains grit and should be removed.

Dice: To cut into equal-sized, 1/4-inch to 1/2-inch cubes. Smaller and more precise than a chop, while larger and more precise than a mince. Recipes will call for a fine, medium, or large dice when it matters what the vegetables look like, or that they cook in approximately the same amount of time.

HOW TO DICE FOODS

Wash or peel fruit or vegetable as directed in the recipe. Create a flat surface to keep the food from slipping while cutting. Do this by either cutting it in half or cutting a small piece off one side. Hold the fruit or vegetable with your fingertips curled under and knuckles out resting against the side of the knife blade. With the tip of your blade on the cutting board, pump your knife up and down, cutting the fruit or vegetable into slices, while slowly moving your fingertips backward and exposing more area for slicing. Turn the knife perpendicular and slice through the fruit or vegetable the other way making sure you have even pieces to the desired thickness.

- **How to dice carrots, potatoes and celery:** These are easier to handle if you cut them in half lengthwise and lay the flat side of one half down on the board before cutting. To dice carrots, quarter lengthwise and then make crosswise cuts to the desired dice size.

- **How to dice a pepper:** These are easy to handle by cutting in half lengthwise, through or next to, the stem. Remove the stem and seeds, and then place the pepper skin side down on the cutting board. Gently flatten the pepper with the heel of your hand, which spreads the pepper and creates a flat cutting surface. Follow the dicing instructions above.

- **How to dice an onion:** Cut the onion in half lengthwise, cutting down through the stem and root. Place the flat side of an onion half on the cutting board and trim off the stem end. Make horizontal cuts parallel to the cutting board through the onion half, but not through to the root end. Leaving the root end intact makes it easier to cut the onion. The width between the cuts will determine the size of the diced pieces. Make lengthwise cuts, starting just short of the root end, again to help keep the onion together. Turn the onion and cut crosswise, perpendicular to the previous cut and stop where the cuts stop. Discard the end.

Dilute: To thin the consistency or weaken the flavor of a sauce or stock by adding more liquid.

Dot: To scatter small bits of an ingredient, usually butter, over the surface of a food.

Drain: To remove or pour off liquid from food, such as cooked pasta or potatoes, through a colander or strainer. Fat can be drained from a skillet after cooking meat. Food such as bacon or fried chicken also can be placed on paper towels to drain. The towels will absorb the fat from the surface of the food.

Dredge: To coat food lightly but completely with dry ingredients such as flour, cornmeal, or bread crumbs in preparation for frying to help brown the food and seal in moisture. Food can be dragged through the dredging ingredients or shaken in a plastic or paper bag with the dredging ingredients. Always shake off excess dredging ingredients before browning. Baked or fried sweet items, such as donuts, are sometimes dredged with sugar and spices, such as cinnamon.

Drippings: The melted fat, juices, and browned bits left in a roasting or sauté pan by meat or poultry as it cooks. Fats are often skimmed from the pan, and the remaining drippings are used to make a sauce or gravy.

Drizzle: To slowly pour liquid in a fine stream over the surface of a food.

Dust: To lightly sprinkle a food, before or after cooking, with dry ingredients, such as flour, sugar, or spices. The dough, rolling pin, and the work surface are dusted with flour before rolling or kneading pastry to prevent it from sticking to any of the surfaces. A plate may be dusted with cocoa powder before setting a slice of cake or dessert on it to enhance the presentation.

Emulsify: To combine liquids that normally do not combine easily into one mixture, such as oil and vinegar. The presence of a third ingredient, called an *emulsifier*, is required to stabilize and sustain the pairing. Emulsifiers include mustard, eggs, and milk.

Entrée: The main dish of a meal.

Fillet: A piece of meat, chicken, or fish that has had all of the bones removed so only the flesh remains. To *fillet* is to cut the meat, chicken, or fish from the bones.

Flake: To gently break into small thin pieces, usually with the tines of a fork. Commonly refers to the texture of cooked fish which flakes easily.

Flambé: To drench food in brandy or liqueur and ignite with a match. The food bursts into a dramatic, flaming display while the alcohol burns off.

Flute: To make decorative indentations around the edge of pastry. See *Crimp*.

Fold: To gently incorporate one mixture with another through repeated, gentle turning-over motions by lifting from underneath without beating or stirring. A rubber spatula is generally used.

Fricassee: To cook food, usually chicken, by browning in butter, and then gently cooking with vegetables, all of which are covered in liquid. This results in a thick stew, often flavored with wine.

Fry: To cook foods in, but not submerged in, hot fat in a skillet over high heat until browned and very crispy. Oil with a high smoke point is ideal for this method of cooking. The thicker the food, the more oil you will need. Preheat the oil in the skillet to a high heat, and then add the food, such as battered chicken pieces, breaded pounded meat, chicken cutlets, breaded fish, or breaded vegetables. The outside cooks at once, preventing the food from absorbing too much oil. Once the food is cooked on one side, gently turn it with tongs or a spatula to the other side, taking care not to splash the hot oil on yourself. When the food is done, remove it with a spatula and transfer to paper towels to absorb any excess oil. This method works best with less delicate foods often dipped in batter or breaded first, such as breaded pork chops or thick fish fillets.

Garnish: To add fresh herbs, edible flowers, fruits, or small vegetables to a completed dish to enhance the flavor or the look.

Glaze: To coat the surface of a food with a thin liquid mixture to give it a smooth, glossy finish. Savories are usually brushed with egg before baking to create a rich, golden-brown finish. Sweet pastries can be brushed with water or milk, and then sprinkled with sugar to give them a crackly sweet finish. Meat, such as ham, often is glazed with a coating of mustard and syrup or brown sugar applied after the ham is partially cooked to achieve a sweet, browned crust.

Grate: To rub a solid food, such as cheese, vegetables, citrus skins, nutmeg, or chocolate, against the coarse, serrated holes of a grater to create shreds of food. These shreds will range in size according to size of the holes in the grater. A food processor can be used for this purpose as well, especially if you have a large quantity of food to prepare. A box grater offers four different sized grating surfaces from a fine zest-like grate to large slices.

Gratin: A food, most often potatoes or green vegetables, topped with grated cheese or bread crumbs, drizzled with oil or dotted with butter and baked in a shallow gratin dish until the inside is soft and the top is browned and slightly crunchy.

Grease: To rub a light coat of fat, usually butter or oil, on the inside of a baking dish to prevent sticking while the food cooks.

Grease and dust: A baking pan is dusted with flour after greasing it to prevent batter from sticking to the pan while baking. Smear a light coat of fat, usually butter or oil, on the inside bottom and sides of the baking pan. Add 1 or 2 tablespoons of flour and shake the pan back and forth so that flour scatters over the sides and bottom of the pan, allowing a fine dusting of flour to adhere to the grease. Gently tap the pan against your hand to loosen any clumps. Discard the flour that does not stick.

Grill: To cook food on a rack over a very intense heat created by charcoal, gas, or wood to brown the outside of the food and seal in moisture. Grilling can be done under intense heat, as in broiling, or on a very hot surface (iron works best). When this is done on the stove-top it is usually called "searing."

HOW TO GRILL MEAT

Before grilling wet or marinated food, pat it dry with a paper towel. Dry meat will brown better than wet meat. Brush or rub meat with a small amount of oil to add flavor and prevent meat from sticking to the grill.

Seasoning meat with a salt-spice rub mixture helps to brown the outside of the meat while grilling. This rub should be added immediately before cooking because salt draws the juices out of meat. Shake off excess dry rub and brush the surface of the meat with oil, to prevent burning and to encourage browning.

Preheat the grill so the meat sears quickly, locking in moisture. Reduce the heat to medium and complete the grilling to your preference.

tip

If using a gas grill, leave the heat on for a few minutes after removing the cooked meat. This will burn off any bits that are sticking to the grill rack. Let the grill cool slightly and use the grill brush to clean off charred bits. This leaves the grill clean for the next use. A grill brick is an excellent tool to have if you do a lot of grilling. Before turning the grill on or lighting charcoals, run the brick over the rack to thoroughly clean any residue or fat that may be left from the last use.

Hull: To ready berries, usually strawberries, for use by plucking out the stem and leaves.

Husk: To pull back and remove the leaves covering an ear of corn. It is best to also remove the silk strands found between the leaves and the ear of corn.

Julienne: To cut food, usually vegetables, into narrow, matchstick sized strips, often of a uniform length.

Knead: To work dough on a lightly floured surface until it is elastic and smooth. The dough is pushed with the heels of the hands. The sides are folded toward the center, and then the dough is pushed out and worked again with a gentle but firm downward and outward motion. This is repeated for the length of time specified in the recipe instructions. Kneading develops the gluten in the flour so it will hold its shape when rising.

Leaven: To add a leavening agent, such as yeast, baking powder, or baking soda. This causes the mixture to rise while baking and lightens the texture of the finished product.

Line: To cover the bottom of a baking dish or pan with parchment or waxed paper before adding food to prevent sticking.

Marinate: To soak foods, usually meats and poultry, in a marinade in order to tenderize it and add flavor. A marinade is made with a combination of vinegar, citrus juice, wine, oil, and seasonings such as garlic or herbs. Marinating times vary from 20 minutes to a few days. Do not allow foods to sit in marinades made with citrus for longer than an hour as the citrus actually begins to "cook" the food. Dry marinades are a mix of spices and herbs and are usually called a *rub*.

Mash: To crush cooked foods, usually root vegetables, using a fork, potato masher, or electric mixer. Butter and milk often are added to create a smooth, creamy consistency. Other flavors such as roasted garlic, gorgonzola cheese, or fresh minced herbs can be added.

Meringue: Egg whites and sugar beaten until stiff and slowly baked. Used as a topping for pie or to create dessert shells.

Mince: To cut or chop into teeny tiny pieces, a common preparation for garlic and herbs.

HOW TO MINCE

To mince garlic, place a garlic clove on a cutting board and cut off and discard the end that was attached to the garlic head. Place the flat side of the thick end of your knife over the garlic and hit the blade firmly with your hand or fist hard enough to smash the garlic and to loosen the skin of the garlic. Remove and discard the skin. Place the tip of the knife blade down on the cutting board and hold it down with one hand. Pump the handle up and down with your other hand, chopping into the garlic and moving the knife blade from right to left and back again. Scrape the garlic back into a little pile and repeat until the desired size of mince is achieved.

To mince herbs, place the tip of the knife blade down on the cutting board and hold down with one hand. Pump the handle up and down with your other hand, chopping into the herbs and moving from right to left and back again. Scrape the herbs back into a little pile and repeat until the desired size mince is achieved.

Mirepoix: The base aromatics for most traditional French cooking, pronounced mihr-PWAH. This mixture of diced carrots, onions, and celery sautéed in butter is used to season sauces, soups, and stews. A cornerstone of Cajun cooking, commonly referred to as *the holy trinity*, contains only onion, celery, and bell pepper.

Mise-En-Place: Translated, "to put in place" and pronounced MEEZahn-plahs. It means to have all ingredients prepared and ready to go before you start cooking. This is useful when cooking a recipe with many components, such as a stir-fry.

Mix: To stir ingredients together.

Pan-grilling: To cook foods, meat, or vegetables in a skillet over medium-high to high heat. This will brown the outside, sealing in moisture and juices, while cooking or melting the inside to the desired doneness. Food should be turned at least once to ensure even cooking.

Parboil: To partially cook a food in boiling or simmering water or broth. Similar to blanching, but the cooking time is longer.

Pare: To remove unwanted skins or rinds from fruits or vegetables with a small knife.

Peeling: To remove the skins from fruits or vegetables. For thick-skinned foods such as avocados or oranges, use a small knife. For thin-skinned vegetables such as carrots or potatoes, use a vegetable peeler.

Pinch: A measuring term referring to a very small, approximate amount of a dry ingredient, usually salt, pepper, or a spice that can be held between the tips of the thumb and forefinger.

Pit: To remove the seed from whole fruits or olives by cutting around the sides and pulling the seed away from the flesh.

HOW TO PIT AND PEEL AN AVOCADO

Cut the avocado in half lengthwise and twist the two halves apart. The pit will remain in one half. Lay the half with the pit on a flat surface and with a chef's knife, make a swift downward whack into the pit. Holding the knife in one hand and grasping the avocado with the other, twist the knife and the avocado in opposite directions. The pit will remain on the knife. Cut the skin lengthwise in four places and peel off in strips. If you plan on mashing the avocado, remove the pit, but do not peel. Simply scoop the avocado meat out of the skin with a tablespoon.

Poach: To cook food gently in simmering liquid so that the food retains its shape. Poaching is suitable for fish fillets, steak, chicken, vegetables, and eggs. The poaching liquids, such as wine, can impart flavor as well as absorb some of the flavors from the food being poached. This is ideal for creating a sauce. Fruit poaches well because it is tenderized by the slow simmering, but the fruit retains its shape and the flavored cooking liquid makes a nice sauce. Poached eggs are a healthy option because there isn't any fat involved in the cooking process. It is best to start food in warm liquid and slowly bring to a simmer.

Pound: To flatten or tenderize meat or chicken breasts between sheets of waxed paper with a heavy mallet to achieve a uniform thickness. Don't have a mallet? Improvise by using the bottom of a heavy skillet or the bottom of a beer bottle.

Preheat: To heat the oven to a specified temperature before adding the foods. Most recipes require preheating of the oven. The recipe will direct a cool oven if it should not be preheated.

Puree: To mash food, force it through a food mill, or process in a food processor or blender until it is smooth.

Reconstitute: To restore dried, condensed, or concentrated foods to their original state by adding, or soaking in, liquid.

Reduce: To thicken or concentrate a liquid, such as a sauce, stock, or wine, by rapidly boiling until evaporation decreases the original volume, thickening the liquid, and intensifying the flavor.

Render: To melt a solid animal fat over low heat, or to cook a piece of meat over low heat, until all fat melts away.

Roast: To cook, uncovered, by free-circulating dry heat in an oven. This is the same as baking but is used in reference to meats, poultry, vegetables, or fish. Large cuts of meat or poultry, vegetables such as potatoes, parsnips, beets, fennel, onions, eggplant, squash, garlic, and turnips, or a combination of meats and vegetables, are best suited for roasting. Place food(s) in a shallow roasting pan to allow the air to circulate and brown the food surfaces. Often meat is put into a very hot oven for a short period of time to seal in juices, and then the oven temperature is lowered to complete the cooking. The drippings collected in the bottom of the pan can be used to make a gravy or sauce to serve with the meat. A *roast* also refers to a cut of meat cooked by this method.

Roux: A mixture of melted fat or butter and flour, stirred constantly for a few minutes over low heat to remove the raw starch taste. Cooked until bubbly, the roux creates a base for thickening sauces and gravies.

Sauté: This is the French word meaning "to jump" which refers to moving the food around in the pan while cooking, either by stirring or shaking the pan. This method of sautéing is most often used to brown aromatic vegetables such as onions and garlic. The food is cooked quickly in a small amount of fat over high heat until lightly browned. A mixture of half olive oil and half butter is ideal for this method of cooking because the oil allows the butter to reach a high temperature without burning while still adding flavor. Thin, tender pieces of meat, poultry, fish, or vegetables are added to the hot fat and cooked on one side. The high heat seals the food keeping it moist and tender. The food is then turned and cooked on the other side until done. This process usually takes 5–10 minutes. The food is removed to a warming plate and a small amount of liquid such as wine or stock may be added to the pan to deglaze the pan and make a sauce.

Scald: To heat milk to just below the boiling point when tiny bubbles appear around the inside edge of the pan. This reduces the cooking time and adds flavor when making custards.

Score: To make thin cuts on the surface of foods before cooking. This helps to reduce the fat during cooking and the food cooks faster. Scoring also can be done for decoration, ease of cutting after cooking, or to help tenderize the food.

Sear: To brown the surface of meats quickly on all sides over high heat in a hot oven or under a broiler. This browns the meat and seals in the juices. Meat should not be turned until the underside is well browned to prevent sticking.

Season: To flavor foods with herbs, spices, salt, or pepper. To "adjust seasonings" is to taste during or after cooking and add needed seasonings.

Shred: To tear, cut, grate, or slice food into thin strips. Also refers to pulling apart very tender cooked meats with a fork.

Sift: To pass a dry ingredient, usually flour, through a sifter to eliminate lumps and to incorporate air, which lightens the texture. This also combines several ingredients that are passed through the sifter at the same time.

Simmer: To bring liquid, by itself or with other ingredients, to the point just below boiling over low heat. Gentle streams of small bubbles rise slowly, bursting before reaching the surface. A simmer is easy to maintain. If the liquid starts boiling, then the heat is too high and should be reduced. Simmering is a method of cooking where food, such as eggs, vegetables, fruit, meats, poultry, or fish, is placed in water, either cool or already simmering, and cooked for the amount of time specified in the recipe.

Skim: To remove fat, foam, or scum from the top surface of a liquid with a spoon or bulb baster. Hold a spoon parallel to the surface to be skimmed. Tip the spoon at a slight angle and dip the side edge of the spoon just under the surface of the fat or foam that floats on the top to the surface. Drag the spoon toward you until it is full of fat or foam. Discard and repeat.

Slice: To draw a knife down through a food making vertical cuts at a right angle to the cutting board. Slices can be cut at the desired thickness.

tip

Sift flour or sugar through a wire mesh strainer by gently tapping the edge of the strainer against the side of your other hand. Powdered sugar or flour will sift through the mesh leaving any hard bits behind. These hard bits can be smashed with the back of a spoon. Any bits that you can't smash should be discarded.

HOW TO SLICE AN ONION

Cut the onion in half lengthwise, cutting down through the root and stem. Place the flat side of one half onion on the cutting board and trim off and discard the root and stem ends. Remove and discard onion skin. Grasp the onion with the tips of your fingers that are folded back under your knuckles. Rest the flat side of the knife blade against your knuckles and raise and lower the knife, making vertical cuts, at a right angle to the cutting board. Cut down through the onion in the desired thickness of the slices.

Sliver: To cut foods into thin strips.

Smoke point: The stage at which heated fat or oil begins to emit smoke, harsh odors, and impart a bitter burnt flavor to foods. Oils or fats with a high smoke point are better suited for deep-fat and shallow-pan frying. Oils with a high smoke point

(441°–450°F) include corn, grapeseed, safflower, and peanut, which has the highest smoke point. Canola oil falls in the middle with a smoke point of 400°F. Butter (350°F) and olive oil (375°F) have a low smoke point and are not suited for frying. Butter added to an oil with a higher smoke point is ideal for sautéing because the butter adds flavor to the oil and protects the food from burning.

Snip: To cut herbs into small pieces with scissors.

Steam: To cook food, usually vegetables, on a rack or in a basket placed above a boiling liquid in a covered pan. There is no immersion in water, so most nutrients are retained, making this a very healthy method of cooking. A one- or two-tiered metal steamer placed into a covered saucepan will cook two or more vegetables at a time. The firmer vegetable should go into the bottom tier where the steam is hotter and more intense. The tender vegetable would go in the top tier, where the steam is slightly cooler. Collapsible wire steamers fit inside any sized pan. Fill a pan with a few inches of water, ensuring it is below the level of the steamer basket. Place the steamer into the pan, bring the water to a boil, add the vegetables to the basket, cover the pan, and steam for a determined amount of time or until vegetables are fork tender.

Steep: To place food in a liquid to soak for a given amount of time in order to infuse the liquid with flavor, such as tea leaves in hot water. This also can be to soften and infuse the food with the flavor of the liquids as with couscous in broth.

Stew: To cook meats (usually tougher cuts) and vegetables slowly in a covered pan that includes a simmering liquid, either on the stove top or in the oven. Meat, chicken, and/or vegetables are cut into small pieces and cooked in a large amount of liquid over a low heat for a long period of time, thickening the liquid as it reduces. Also refers to a completed dish cooked in this manner.

Stir: To blend a mixture together by gently moving it around and into itself with a spoon in a circular motion. Stirring is done to move foods around while cooking and to cool foods after cooking. Stirring is not the same as beating.

Stir-fry: To quickly sauté a combination of meat and/or vegetables in a hot skillet or wok. Cut the meats and vegetables into strips of approximately the same size so that they will cook evenly. Make sure all ingredients are prepared before you start as this is a very fast process. Heat a small amount of oil in the pan to a very high temperature that is below the smoking point. Stir-fry food in small quantities, taking care not to crowd the pan. If food is crowded, it will steam not fry. Sauté quickly while stirring constantly in a minimal amount of fat or liquid to a desired doneness. Food should be crisp, but tender and vivid in color. Seasonings and flavorings such as soy sauce, ginger, cilantro, garlic, and sesame oil may be added while cooking. Also refers to a completed dish cooked in this manner.

Stock: The strained liquid that results from the long, slow simmering of vegetables, meat, fish, and other seasonings in water. Browning bones and vegetables before adding to the cooking liquid produces a brown stock rich in flavor.

Strain: To pass or force a liquid mixture through a colander, sieve, or cheesecloth to remove solid particles. Food may be forced through a strainer with the back of a wooden spoon.

Stuff: To fill a food cavity of meat, fish, poultry, vegetables, pasta, bread, or fruits with another food. The stuffing is usually a mixture of foods such as bread, rice, cheese and vegetables, fruit and nuts, or cooked meats.

Sweat: To cook foods, usually vegetables, over low heat in a small amount of fat to draw out juices, to soften the food, and to develop flavor.

Temper: To moderate the temperature of a hot ingredient before gradually adding it to a cold mixture, or moderating the temperature of a cold ingredient before adding to a hot mixture. This reduces the possibility of the mixture separating or curdling. This is done by stirring a small amount of the cold ingredient into the hot mixture to reduce its heat. The moderate ingredient can now be combined successfully with the colder ingredient.

Tent: To loosely cover meat or poultry with aluminum foil.

Tests for doneness: To ascertain if a food is done. Different tests are used for different foods.

HOW TO TEST FOR DONENESS
Baked goods: Insert and remove a wooden toothpick into a baked food near the center, the part that cooks last. If only a few crumbs cling to the toothpick, then the food is done. Another indicator is when the edges of the baked food are beginning to pull away from the sides of the pan.

Fish: Near the end of the recommended cooking time, cut a small slit in the thickest part of the fish. If the flesh inside is slightly opaque, and has lost its wet look, remove the fish from the heat as it will continue cooking slightly. By the time you get it on the table, the inside flesh will be totally opaque and perfectly done.

Poultry: Near the end of the recommended cooking time, pierce the flesh of the thigh. If the juices run clear, then the poultry is done. If there is any pink in the juice, return the poultry to the oven and cook for another 10 minutes. Repeat this and test the meat again.

Toast: To brown, under or over a dry heat source such as an oven or toaster. Seeds, nuts, or spices may be toasted in the oven or in a skillet.

HOW TO TOAST NUTS
Place the nuts in a skillet over medium-low heat. Stir or shake the pan often as the nuts begin to brown. In the oven, place the nuts on a baking sheet in a 325°F oven for 5–10 minutes, checking often because they burn easily.

Toss: To mix ingredients, such as salad or pasta, lightly but quickly by lifting and turning with two large forks or spoons.

Truss: To secure poultry or meat with skewers or string after pulling into the desired shape. Trussing helps food to retain its shape during cooking. If poultry is stuffed, use skewers to close the cavity and lace together with twine to secure and keep stuffing inside.

Whip: To beat a lighter mixture, such as egg whites or whipping cream, with a wire whisk or electric mixer to incorporate air. This lightens and increases volume. Use a large bowl and move the wire whisk quickly and vigorously in a circular motion. If whipping cream, the best outcome results from using a chilled bowl and a chilled whisk or mixer beater. If whipping eggs, the best outcome results from using eggs at room temperature.

Whisk: To whip, beat, emulsify, or blend with a wire whisk until blended and smooth. Also refers to the looped, wire-handled utensil used to perform this task.

Zest: The outer peel of citrus fruit, not including any of the bitter white pith just under the surface. The peel is grated and used as a flavoring.

HOW TO ZEST A LEMON, LIME, OR ORANGE

Using a citrus zester, scrape the scalloped end of the zester over the fruit to remove the top layer of the fruit peel. If you are using a grater, run the fruit over the finest holes of the grater while applying light pressure. The zest will be forced through the holes and accumulate under the grater.

Weight and Measurement Conversions

1 pinch = less than 1/8 teaspoon (dry)

1 dash = 3 drops to 1/4 teaspoon (liquid)

3 teaspoons = 1 tablespoon = 1/2 ounce (liquid and dry)

2 tablespoons = 1/8 cup = 1 ounce (liquid and dry)

4 tablespoons = 1/4 cup = 2 ounces (liquid and dry)

5 1/3 tablespoons = 1/3 cup = 2.6 ounces (liquid)

8 tablespoons = 1/2 cup = 4 ounces (liquid or dry)

10 tablespoons + 2 teaspoons = 2/3 cup

12 tablespoons = 3/4 cup = 6 ounces (liquid or dry)

16 tablespoons = 1 cup = 8 ounces = 1/2 pound

16 tablespoons = 48 teaspoons

32 tablespoons = 2 cups = 16 ounces = 1 pound

64 tablespoons = 32 ounces = 1 quart = 2 pounds

1 cup = 8 ounces (liquid) = 1/2 pint

2 cups = 16 ounces (liquid) = 1 pint

4 cups = 32 ounces (liquid) = 2 pints = 1 quart

16 cups = 128 ounces (liquid) = 4 quarts = 1 gallon

1 quart = 2 pints (dry)

Common Cooking Abbreviations

Teaspoon: tsp. (t.)

Tablespoon: Tbsp. (T.)

Cup: C.

Ounce: oz.

Pint: pt.

Pound: lb.

Quart: qt.

Oven Temperature Chart

Description	American Standard
Very cool	225°F
Cool	275°F
Moderate	350°F
Hot	425°F
Very hot	475°F

Food Yield Equivalents Chart

Shopping for ingredients listed in a recipe can be frustrating. When the recipe calls for 1 cup of sliced apples, how many apples do you buy? Sometimes it is awkward for a recipe to call for anything other than the measurement needed. Instead of 1/4 cup of diced onions, the recipe might call for 1/2 of 1 small onion diced to hopefully resemble something such as 1/4 cup, but that's like having to say "the artist formally known as Prince"—it just isn't as much fun.

The chart shown in Table 3.1 can assist in decrypting ingredient quantities needed for your recipe; however, remember that because fruits and vegetables are not perfectly uniform, the measurements are approximations. With most recipes, and certainly the ones in this book, a slight difference does not make a difference.

THE **CULINARY** INSTITUTE of MICHIGAN

Table 3.1 Food Yield Equivalents Chart

Meat and Eggs	Weight or Count	Measure or Yield
Bacon	8 slices cooked	1/2 cup crumbled
Egg, whole	1 large	1/4 cup
Eggs, whole	9 medium	1 cup
Eggs, whites	8–11	1 cup
Eggs, yolks	12–14	1 cup
Dairy	**Weight or Count**	**Measure or Yield**
Butter	1 pound	2 cups
Butter	1 stick	1/2 cup
Sour Cream	8 ounces	1 cup
Cheese (semi-firm and firm)	4 ounces	1 cup shredded
Cheese (hard)	3 ounces	1 cup grated
Whipping cream	1 cup	2 cups whipped
Fruits and Vegetables	**Weight or Count**	**Measure or Yield**
Apples	1 medium	1 cup sliced
Bananas	3 medium	2 1/2 cups sliced; 1 cup mashed
Beans, green or wax	1 pound	3 to 3 1/2 cups cut
Bell pepper	1 medium	1 cup chopped
Cabbage, raw	1 pound	4 cups shredded
Carrots	2 medium 1 1/2 medium	1 cup sliced 1 cup shredded
Cauliflower	1 pound	3 cups florets
Celery	2 medium stalks	1 cup sliced
Cherries	1 pound	3 cups whole or 2 1/2 cups pitted
Corn	2 medium ears	1 cup kernels
Cranberries	1 pound	4 cups
Cucumber	1 small to medium	1 cup chopped
Dates, pitted	1/2 pint	3 cups chopped
Dates, not pitted	1 pound	1 1/2 cups chopped
Frozen fruit	10 ounce package	1 1/4 cups
Frozen vegetables	9 to 10 ounce package	2 cups thawed vegetables
Green bell pepper	1 large	1 cup diced
Lemon	1 medium	2 to 3 tablespoons juice 2 teaspoons grated rind
Lettuce	1 pound head	6 1/4 cups torn

Table 3.1 (continued)

Fruits and Vegetables	Weight or Count	Measure or Yield
Lime	1 medium	1 1/2 to 2 tablespoons juice 1 1/2 teaspoons grated rind
Mushrooms, fresh	1/2 pound fresh or 3 ounces dried	3 cups sliced
Onion	1 medium	1/2 cup chopped
Orange	1 medium	1/3 to 1/2 cup juice 2 tablespoons grated rind
Peaches	2 medium	1 cup sliced
Pears	2 medium	1 cup sliced
Peas in the pod	1 pound	1 cup shelled
Potatoes	1 pound	3 to 4 medium russet potatoes
Potatoes	6 medium	4 cups 1/2-inch diced or 1 3/4 cup cooked and mashed
Raisins, seedless	1 pound	3 cups
Scallions (green onions)	9 (with tops)	1 cup sliced
Strawberries	1 quart	4 cups sliced
Tomato	1 medium	1 cup chopped
Zucchini	1 medium	2 cups sliced

Grains, Beans, Rice, and Pasta	Weight or Count	Measure or Yield
Beans, dried	1 pound	6 cups cooked
Macaroni	4 ounces dried (1 cup)	2 1/4 cups cooked
Oats, quick-cooking	1 cup	1 3/4 cups cooked
Rice, long-grain	1 cup uncooked	3 to 4 cups cooked
Rice, converted	1 cup uncooked	3 to 4 cups cooked
Rice, wild	1 cup uncooked	3 cups cooked
Spaghetti, uncooked	7 ounces	About 4 cups cooked

Nuts	Weight or Count	Measure or Yield
Almonds	1 pound shelled	3 1/2 cups nutmeats
Pecans	1 pound shelled	4 cups nutmeats
Walnuts	1 pound shelled	4 cups nutmeats

Table 3.1 (continued)

Miscellaneous	Weight or Count	Measure or Yield
Bread	2 slices	1 cup soft crumbs
Chocolate, baking	1 square	1 ounce
Chocolate chips (morsels)	6 ounce package	1 cup
Cocoa	1 pound	4 cups
Crackers, graham	14 squares	1 cup fine crumbs
Crackers, saltine	28 squares	1 cup finely crushed
Flour, all-purpose	1 pound	4 cups, un-sifted
Flour, cake	1 pound	4 3/4 to 5 cups sifted
Flour, whole wheat	1 pound	3 1/2 cups un-sifted
Fresh-ground pepper	6 grinds of pepper mill	1/4 teaspoon
Milk, sweetened condensed	14-ounce can	1 1/4 cups
Salt, coarse or kosher	1 ounce	2 tablespoons
Salt, table	1 ounce	1 1/2 tablespoons
Sugar, brown	1 pound	2 1/2 cups firmly packed
Sugar, granulated	1 pound	2 cups
Sugar, powdered (confectioners')	1 pound	4 cups sifted
Yeast	1/4 ounce package	2 1/2 teaspoons

4

GETTING A
MEAL ON THE TABLE

Constructing a balanced menu, choosing the right recipes, shopping for the ingredients, preparing the food, and getting it all on the table at the same time can be an intimidating experience. The following guidelines take the mystery out of these tasks and provide information to help you in planning and execution.

Meal Planning Guidelines

A Balanced Plate

Plan a plate of contrasting colors and textures and consider how flavors work with each other. Poached white fish with cauliflower and mashed potatoes is boring in appearance and the food textures are too similar to be interesting. However, serving broccoli with couscous and topping the fish with a cool fruit salsa easily brings the plate alive with a deliberate variance of flavor, color, and textures.

A balanced dinner should include at least one protein, a few vegetables, and no more than one starchy dish. Bread and fruit make nice additions.

- Protein suggestions are meat, chicken, fish, shellfish, eggs, beans, or cheese.
- Starchy dish suggestions are potatoes, pasta, rice, beans, or corn.
- Vegetable suggestions are green leafy vegetables and root vegetables.

Balance strong or spicy flavors with a milder accompaniment—such as *Southwestern Chili* (page 134) topped with a dollop of sour cream and served with warmed flour tortillas. Do not mix pungent ethnic foods such as *Indian Lamb Curry* (page 132) with *Thai Noodle Salad* (page 151).

Plan the meal as a whole so that the flavors of the appetizer do not conflict with the entrée. Guacamole and chips are not a good beginning to *Spaghetti Bolognese* (page 261). Instead choose *Crostini* (page 321) and *Herb Roasted Garlic* (page 323). A light dessert is lovely following a heavy meal while a rich dessert balances a light meal.

Do not overdo one cooking technique, for example deep-frying, by serving *Fried Chicken* (page 219) with French fried potatoes and breaded fried zucchini sticks followed by fried apple fritters. Fried chicken served with steamed green beans and a dessert of frozen yogurt is much more palatable.

Planning Your Time

Getting everything on the table at the same time can seem like magic to the beginning cook. It can be tricky even for an experienced chef and that is why planning in recipe selection and overall menu choices is important. Consider the following when designing a meal:

- Choose recipes that do not require each of the foods to be cooked at the last minute, such as a sautéed chicken breast, *Mashed Potatoes* (page 269), and *Country Skillet Gravy* (page 298).
- Do not choose more than one recipe that requires extensive preparation.

- Include a couple of dishes that can be made ahead of time such as a *Quick Pasta Primavera Salad* (page 159) to go along with your *Grilled Cilantro-Lime Swordfish* (page 226).

- Include dishes that can be cooked at the same time using the same preparation method, such as roasting root vegetables along with a chicken.

- Choose a dish that can be assembled and slow-cooked, such as *Chicken Cacciatore* (page 213). This frees up your time to prepare side dishes while your entrée cooks without requiring much attention.

- Make desserts and salad dressings ahead of time.

- Do not choose dishes that require baking at different temperatures, such as *New Mexican Frittata* (page 71) at 350°F and *Biscuits* (page 79) at 450°F.

- Do not attempt more than one new recipe at a time. It is best to try a recipe once before making it for guests!

- Know your time and energy limitations and choose recipes that work within those boundaries. A complex recipe with a lengthy cooking time is best attempted during a leisurely weekend, not when you are tired after a hard day at work.

- Base your schedule on when you will serve the meal and work backwards, writing out a step-by-step plan if necessary.

Meal Planning and Shopping for the Week

It is most economical as far as both time and money to plan meals in advance. Shopping for several meals at once takes about the same amount of time as shopping for a single meal. Frequent trips to the store are inconvenient, tiring after work, and often result in more money spent on impulse buying.

Plan multiple meals by choosing recipes that allow you to use leftovers from one meal as a main ingredient in the next. Leftover grilled chicken can be used the following day sliced for a sandwich, in a salad, or added to a soup or pasta dish.

Choose a few recipes for entrées, but allow some flexibility in the choice of accompanying fruits and vegetables. When at the grocery store, let the season, and what looks fresh, dictate these choices. Include a variety of produce, meats, chicken, fish, and grains to ensure you are getting a broad range of nutrients and vitamins.

Read the recipes thoroughly and make a complete list of all items needed. Check the pantry and refrigerator to see if you already have the item on hand. Consolidate the quantities of like items that you will buy on your grocery list to save time while shopping.

When writing a shopping list, group all similar items together: dairy with dairy, meat with meat, produce with produce. When you are in that section, it saves time and energy to have all the items needed listed together.

Read the Recipe

Read a recipe in its entirety before you get started to avoid any unpleasant surprises. Discovering that the cheesecake you had planned for dessert takes 4 hours to cool is not something you want to learn while you are throwing it together an hour before your guests arrive. Read a recipe more than once, to make sure that you understand all of the steps, have all the necessary tools or are able to improvise, and have all the ingredients on hand or added to your grocery list.

Altering a recipe to suit your individual taste is what cooking is all about. However, it is suggested that you follow the recipe as stated the first time you make it, then add, modify, or delete as desired.

The recipes in this book are written in a particular order and include:

- **Recipe**: name and information, such as history of the dish, tips for preparation, or serving suggestions.
- **Ingredients**: a complete list of all ingredients needed to complete the recipe. Page numbers referring to particular recipes are listed next to an ingredient item requiring prior preparation.
- **Equipment**: a detailed list of all cookware and kitchen tools needed to complete the recipe. Improvising is encouraged and several suggestions are listed later in this chapter.
- **Methods**: A list of techniques and methods required to complete the recipe. For more detailed explanations, check Chapter 3, "Glossary of Terms and Techniques, Conversions and Equivalents."
- **Quantity**: the number of servings you can expect the recipe to produce.
- **Preparation**: Step-by-step instructions of all the work needed to prepare the ingredients for cooking.
- **Cooking Directions**: Step-by-step instructions of all cooking needed to complete the recipe.
- **Variations**: a listing of food items, flavoring, and spices that may be added and deleted to create variances in the completed recipe.
- **Pantry/Refrigerator Check**: a list of ingredients that may already be on hand. If these items are not on hand, add them to your shopping list.
- **Shopping List**: a list of all ingredients that are not in your pantry, but are needed to complete the recipe.

Improvise

Learning to improvise in the kitchen is part of learning how to cook. Beginning cooks usually start out with only a few kitchen tools and add to their arsenal as the need arises. If you find yourself constantly reaching for a particular tool that you do not currently own, watch for sales and buy one. Let your pots and pans do double duty—a medium skillet works the same as a large skillet, just sauté your food in batches. If you don't have a small mixing bowl, use a small pan or cereal bowl. Here are some other suggestions for improvising tools used by many cooks.

- For a rolling pin, use a wine bottle.
- For a meat mallet, use the bottom of a beer bottle or heavy skillet.
- For a sifter, use a wire mesh strainer.
- For cheesecloth, use paper towels or coffee filters.
- For a double boiler, use a saucepan with a stainless steel mixing bowl set into it, making sure that the mixing bowl sits 2 inches above the boiling water.
- For a colander or strainer, hold the lid of the pan tightly over the ingredients, just back a fraction of an inch from the edge of the pan. Tilt the pan at a 90° angle to pour off the unwanted liquid. Be careful when using this method as it is easy to slip and lose the entire dish.
- For a strainer to strain citrus fruit, place your cupped hand, with your fingers almost touching each other, over a small bowl. Squeeze the citrus fruit and allow the juice to flow through your fingers while catching the seeds.
- For a ladle, use a coffee cup.
- For a wire whisk, use a fork.

5

EGGS AND OTHER BREAKFAST FARE

An old culinary legend says that the many pleats in a chef's hat represent the multitude of ways he can prepare an egg. The most versatile and probably most important food in the kitchen, eggs are good on their own at any time of the day, as well as for adding flavor, richness, and color to many other dishes. Pastries, breads, sauces, mayonnaise, ice cream, pastas, and many casseroles would be lacking with the omission of the all-around good egg.

Eggs are the cornerstone of the breakfast menu, either by themselves or as an ingredient in most morning fare. The recipes in this section will teach you about eggs: How to perfectly fry, scramble, poach, or boil an egg and then how to create *Eggs Benedict* (page 61), flavored scrambles, omelets, and frittatas. With these skills you can become your family's short-order breakfast cook, and let someone else play the role of dishwasher while you relax with the morning paper.

Egg Facts

Salmonella is a type of bacteria found in contaminated eggs. Though extremely rare, if you consume a contaminated egg, the effects can be serious. To lower the risk, discard any eggs with a cracked shell, and always refrigerate eggs and products containing raw egg at temperatures no greater than 40°F.

note

White and brown eggs are identical in taste and nutritional value.

Eggs are passed before "an intense light" and then graded according to freshness. USDA Grade AA is the highest and Grade A is only slightly lower. Grade B eggs are used commercially and are not found in grocery stores.

All graded eggs carry an expiration date of 30 days or less from the day they are packed. If you can't find an expiration date, look for a three-digit code that reveals the day of the year the eggs were packaged. 365 indicates they were packaged on December 31st, while 007 indicates a packaged date of January 7th, not that they were inspected by James Bond.

HOW OLD IS THAT EGG?

To tell the age of an egg, fill a deep bowl with water and gently drop in an egg.

- The egg sinks to the bottom and lies on its side: Fresh.
- The egg stays on the bottom at a 45° angle: 3 to 5 days old.
- The egg stays on the bottom and stands straight up: 10 to 12 days old.
- The egg floats to the top: Too old to eat, so throw it away.

The older the egg, the runnier and clearer the white becomes, which can make it harder to work with and easier for the yolk to break.

How to Break an Egg

Always break each egg in a small cup and then transfer it to the work bowl. This prevents a bad egg or bits of shell from spoiling the other ingredients.

1. Grasp the egg in one hand.

2. Gently but firmly tap the egg against the rim of a small glass bowl or measuring cup to crack, but not shatter, the egg.

3. Hold the egg firmly with both hands, thumbs at the crack, and gently open the egg over the bowl. The egg will fall out of the shell and into the bowl.

4. If pieces of the shell happen to fall into the bowl along with the egg, simply remove them by using the tip of a teaspoon.

note

1 large egg is equivalent to about 1/4ᵗʰ cup and 1 small egg is equivalent to 1/6ᵗʰ of a cup.

How to Separate an Egg

Never pass the egg between two broken shell halves to separate the yolk from the white. Bacteria can live on the outside of the eggshells and the egg could become contaminated.

1. Place a small funnel over a measuring cup.

2. Crack the egg against a hard rim and break over the funnel.

3. The white will drain into the measuring cup and the yolk will remain stuck in the top of the funnel.

BOILED EGGS

Timing is everything and two distinct schools of thought exist on this subject. Professional chefs will tell you to start eggs in cold water, bring the water to a boil, and then start the timing. This can be difficult and it chains you to the stove. The other way is to bring the water to a boil, gently drop in the eggs, turn the heat down to a simmer, and start the timer. Try it both ways to determine what works best for you.

The freshness of the egg that has been boiled will determine how easy or hard it will be to peel. A fresh egg is much harder to peel then an old egg, but most of us don't plan ahead and allow eggs to age just for boiling. We just boil eggs when we want boiled eggs, using the eggs that are currently hanging around in the refrigerator. The closest we get to planning for old eggs is that nagging stab every time we open the refrigerator and think, "Gosh, I really need to use those eggs." As a last resort before throwing them out, we boil the lot and make egg salad.

How to Peel Hard Boiled Eggs

1. Gently tap a cooled egg on a hard surface, cracking the shell on all sides.

2. Place the palm of your hand over the egg and, exerting a slight pressure, roll it around on the hard surface to loosen the shell.

3. Insert a teaspoon between the egg and shell, rotating the egg. Peel the shell from the egg and discard, or dry the shells and crush them for use in the garden.

Eggs Cooked in the Shell: Hard- and Soft-Boiled

The versatile egg is great all by its basic self. Hard-boiled eggs are inexpensive snacks in their own little packages. Soft-boiled eggs are the breakfast of royalty, served upright in an eggcup, a little egg holder that looks like half of an egg on a pedestal. Tap around the top, cracking and removing the top third of the shell, and then serve with crumpets or toasted French bread.

tip

If you are boiling eggs to use as deviled eggs, stirring the water while cooking will keep the yolks centered.

Ingredients

6 eggs

Equipment

Medium saucepan, slotted spoon, timer (or use the timer on your stove or microwave), colander

Methods

Boiling, simmering (see Chapter 3, "Glossary of Terms and Techniques, Conversions and Equivalents")

Quantity

6 eggs

Cooking Directions

1. Fill a medium saucepan 2/3 full of water. Place the pan over high heat and bring the water to a boil.

2. When the water comes to a boil, gently lower the eggs into the pan with the slotted spoon. Immediately reduce the heat slightly to a gentle boil or simmer. (A rolling boil will knock the eggs about and increase the likelihood of cracking.)

3. Begin timing:

   - **4 minutes:** Soft-boiled—white just cooked, yolk runny.
   - **6 minutes:** Soft-boiled—yolk is soft cooked, not runny.
   - **10 minutes:** Hard-boiled—both yolk and white are cooked through.

4. When the eggs are done to your liking, remove them to a colander and run under cold water. This cools the eggs and halts the cooking process.

Pantry/Refrigerator Check

Eggs

tip

Add a few drops of food coloring to the water when boiling eggs. The shells will take on a slight hue. This will make it easy to tell the difference between hard-boiled eggs and uncooked eggs in your refrigerator.

Poached Eggs

Tender and delicate, poached eggs are lovely solo on buttered toast or as the sturdy basis for the elegant brunch stars, Benedict or Florentine. Adding vinegar and salt to the water and breaking the egg into a small dish before gently slipping it into the simmering water will keep the egg white together and prevents those long, ropey strands. Use 1 tablespoon of vinegar and 1/2 tablespoon of salt for every 8 cups of water.

Ingredients

8 cups water

1 tablespoon vinegar

1/2 tablespoon salt

4 eggs

Equipment

Medium saucepan, small dish, slotted spoon, timer (or use the timer on your stove or microwave)

Methods

Simmering, poaching (see Chapter 3)

Quantity

4 eggs

tip

The more eggs you add to the water, the more the temperature of the water will drop, and the longer it will take to poach the eggs.

Cooking Directions

1. Place water, vinegar, and salt in the saucepan and bring to a gentle simmer over medium-low heat.

2. Break 1 egg into a small dish and carefully slide the egg into the simmering water. Repeat with the remaining eggs. It is handy to have all the eggs broken into 4 separate dishes for even cooking.

3. The eggs will drop to the bottom and then float back up to the top of the water.

4. Simmer for 3 to 4 minutes as the white sets around the yolk and becomes opaque.

5. Remove the eggs with a slotted spoon and carefully blot dry with a paper towel. Serve immediately.

Pantry/Refrigerator Check

Eggs

Vinegar (cider or white wine)

Salt

Eggs Benedict

This dish is so fun because once you get the hang of it you can wow your family by creating your own signature Benedict. Poached eggs are the only constant—think crab on a crumpet with Mornay sauce, bacon on a biscuit with country gravy, or smoked salmon on a bagel with a sour cream and caper sauce.

Ingredients

2 tablespoons fresh chives, minced

2 English muffins

2 tablespoons unsalted butter

4 slices Canadian bacon

4 *Poached Eggs* (page 59)

1 cup *Hollandaise Sauce* (page 294)

Nonstick cooking spray

Equipment

Large nonstick skillet, chef's knife, cutting board, table knife

Methods

Mincing, pan grilling (see Chapter 3)

Quantity

2 servings

Preparation

1. Wash chives, pat dry, and mince.

Cooking Directions

2. Separate the English muffins, toast to golden brown, spread with butter, and set at the back of the stove top to keep warm.
3. Spray the skillet with cooking spray and sauté the Canadian bacon over medium heat, until just slightly brown on each side. Remove to a warm plate.
4. While the eggs poach, prepare plates by placing two toasted English muffin halves, cut sides up, on each plate.

5. Top each muffin half with 1 slice of Canadian bacon.

6. Place 1 poached egg on top of each piece of Canadian bacon.

7. Top each egg with 1/4 cup Hollandaise Sauce.

8. Garnish each with a sprinkle of minced chives and serve immediately.

Variations

Eggs Florentine
Replace the Canadian bacon with 1 cup spinach sautéed with 1 tablespoon shallots.

Pantry/Refrigerator Check

1 stick unsalted butter

Eggs

Nonstick cooking spray

Shopping List

1 bunch or package fresh chives

Canadian bacon

English muffins

Fried Eggs

Fried eggs are the cornerstone of the all-American, stick-to-your-ribs breakfast of bacon and eggs with potatoes and toast. Fried eggs make great sandwiches and are a New Mexican specialty on enchiladas. When frying eggs, use oil, butter, or animal fat (even if you are using a nonstick pan). Season with salt and pepper while cooking for the best flavor. Breaking the eggs into a small dish before gently slipping them into the hot oil will eliminate broken yolks and any eggshells from finding their way into the pan. It is messy and difficult to fish eggshells out of hot oil. Eggs with broken yolks can be reserved for another purpose, or change the breakfast menu and make scrambled eggs.

Ingredients

4 tablespoons butter, bacon fat, or vegetable oil

2 eggs

Salt and freshly ground black pepper to taste

1 teaspoon water (for steaming method)

Equipment

Large skillet, metal or hard plastic spatula

Methods

Pan frying, basting, steaming (see Chapter 3)

Quantity

1 serving

tip

If you are cooking the eggs in bacon fat, eliminate the salt.

Cooking Directions

1. Place the skillet over medium heat and add the butter, bacon fat, or oil. Do not allow the butter to turn brown. When the foaming subsides, reduce the heat to medium-low.
2. Break the eggs into a small cup and slip them into the skillet.
3. Sprinkle the eggs with salt and pepper.
4. Cook according to desired method and doneness.

For Sunny-side-up Eggs

The *basting method* works best with at least 3 tablespoons of fat. Tilt the pan so that the fat collects at one side. Use a spoon to scoop up the hot fat and pour it over the egg. This cooks and sets the top of the egg. Cook the egg to desired doneness and remove to a warm plate with spatula.

To use the *steaming method,* reduce heat to low, add water to skillet and cover immediately. The egg is done when the white is cooked over and around the yolk. Remove the egg to a warm plate with a spatula.

For Over Easy, Medium or Hard Eggs

Once the white is cooked and set, flip the egg and cook on the second side according to the times listed below. When the egg is done, remove to a warm plate.

- **Over easy:** 20 to 30 seconds
- **Over medium:** 1 minute
- **Over hard:** 2 minutes

Variations

- Fry bacon in a skillet and remove all but 4 tablespoons of the bacon fat. Cook the eggs according to the above instructions.

Pantry/Refrigerator Check

Butter, bacon, or vegetable oil

Eggs

Salt

Ground black pepper

Basic Scrambled Eggs

Scrambled eggs benefit from adding a small amount of water for moisture, a small amount of butter and cream for flavor, and a slow, low-heat cooking process. Constant stirring will create a creamy texture with soft curds while less frequent stirring will produce eggs with a firm texture and larger curds. Additions are endless, either stirred in or as a topping. For basic scrambled eggs, allow three eggs per person. If there are additions, plan for two eggs per person. The opposite of hard-boiled, the fresher the eggs, the better the flavor.

Ingredients

3 eggs

1 tablespoon water

Salt and freshly ground black pepper to taste

2 tablespoons unsalted butter

Equipment

Small skillet, medium bowl, whisk or fork, wooden stirring spoon

Methods

Whisking, sautéing (see Chapter 3)

Quantity

1 serving

Preparation

1. Break eggs into a small cup and transfer them to a medium bowl.
2. Using a fork or whisk, break the eggs and blend just until the yolks and whites are combined and smooth.
3. Add water, salt and pepper and whisk once or twice to combine with the eggs.

Cooking Directions

4. Place the skillet over medium heat and add butter.
5. When the butter is melted, pour the eggs into the skillet.
6. Turn the heat down to low.

7. As the mixture begins to thicken and set, constantly stir with a wooden spoon or the back of a fork, moving the egg mixture from the bottom and sides of the skillet.

8. Eggs are done when soft, slightly moist, and creamy. If you like your eggs less creamy, cook longer and stir less.

9. Remove the eggs from the heat while still slightly underdone, as they will continue to cook.

Variations

■ Add 1 tablespoon fresh minced herbs or 1 teaspoon dried spices such as basil, tarragon, or parsley along with the salt and pepper in step 3.

■ Add 3 tablespoons grated cheese, crumbled bacon, chopped ham, leftover steamed vegetables, cooked potatoes, or chopped olives during step 7.

■ Top with 3 tablespoons grated cheese and 1 tablespoon salsa and serve wrapped in a warmed flour tortilla after step 9.

Pantry/Refrigerator Check

Eggs

Salt

Black pepper

1 stick unsalted butter

Aegean Scramble

Tasty with the flavors of the Mediterranean, this is just one example of the many ways to dress up scrambled eggs. Spoon eggs into a toasted pita half and serve with *El Greco Salsa* (page 308).

tip

Fast track this recipe by using ready-to-eat, packaged baby spinach, pitted olives and crumbled feta.

Ingredients

8 eggs

4 tablespoons water

1/4 teaspoon salt

1/4 teaspoon freshly ground black pepper

2 tablespoons kalamata olives

1/4 red bell pepper

1/4 cup fresh spinach

2 tablespoons unsalted butter

1 teaspoon dried oregano

1/4 cup crumbled Greek feta cheese

Equipment

Large skillet, large bowl, chef's knife, cutting board, whisk or fork, wooden stirring spoon

Methods

Pitting, chopping, whisking, sautéing (see Chapter 3)

Quantity

4 servings

Preparation

1. Break the eggs into a small cup and transfer to a large bowl.
2. Using a fork or whisk, break the eggs and blend just until the yolks and whites are combined and smooth.
3. Add water, salt, and pepper and whisk once or twice to combine with eggs.
4. Pit and chop the kalamata olives.
5. Wash the red bell pepper. Cut in half lengthwise, remove the stem and seeds and coarsely chop.
6. Wash the spinach and pat dry.

Cooking Directions

7. Place the skillet over medium heat and add the butter.

8. When the butter is melted, pour the eggs into the pan.

9. Turn the heat down to low.

10. As the mixture begins to thicken and set, constantly stir it with a wooden spoon or the back of a fork, moving the egg mixture from the bottom and sides of the skillet.

11. Add all remaining ingredients and continue cooking to desired doneness. Remember, stirring more produces smaller and softer curds, whereas stirring less allows the egg mixture to set on the bottom of the skillet longer, creating larger and firmer curds.

12. Eggs are done when soft, slightly moist, and creamy. If you like your eggs less creamy, cook longer and stir less.

13. Remove the eggs from the heat while still slightly underdone, as they will continue to cook.

Variations

Mexican Scramble

Omit the olives, feta, and spinach. Add to the eggs at step 11: 1/4 cup grated Monterey Jack cheese, 3 tablespoons canned chopped green chilies, 3 tablespoons chopped fresh tomatoes and 1/2 teaspoon cumin. Serve with salsa.

Cajun Scramble

Omit the olives, feta, and spinach. Add to the eggs at step 11: 1/2 cup crumbled cooked Andouille sausage, 3 tablespoons sliced green onions, and 1/4 coarsely chopped green bell pepper.

Pantry/Refrigerator Check

Eggs

Salt

Ground black pepper

Dried oregano

1 stick unsalted butter

1 10 oz. can kalamata olives

Shopping List

1 red bell pepper

1 bunch fresh spinach

2 oz. Greek feta cheese

Basic Omelet

Omelets bring to mind little late-night French dinners and sunny weekend breakfasts, and add just plain old panache to anyone's cooking repertoire. Practice making this basic omelet first, then try filling one with crab, shallots, and sour cream for a special brunch or just use up leftovers for an easy Wednesday night supper. Be sure to use a nonstick pan—it makes all the difference.

Ingredients

3 eggs

2 teaspoons water

Salt and freshly ground black pepper to taste

Butter

Equipment

Small nonstick skillet, medium bowl, whisk or fork, measuring spoon, plastic or hard rubber spatula

Methods

Whisking, pan-frying (see Chapter 3)

Quantity

1 serving

Preparation

1. Break eggs into a small cup and then transfer to a medium bowl.
2. Using a fork or whisk, break the eggs and blend just until the yolks and whites are combined and smooth.
3. Add water, salt, and pepper and whisk once or twice to combine with the eggs.

Cooking Directions

4. Place the skillet over medium-high heat and add the butter.
5. When the butter is melted and foamy, pour the eggs into the skillet, reduce the heat to medium-low and let cook for about 10 seconds.
6. As the eggs start to bubble, use the spatula to carefully gather the edge of the omelet to the center, tipping the skillet slightly to allow the uncooked eggs to flow to the side of the skillet and underneath the cooked portion.

7. Repeat, tipping the skillet to different sides and gathering the eggs to the center until most of the uncooked eggs have disappeared. This will take no more than 30 seconds to one minute.

8. To fold in half, tilt the skillet slightly away from you, slip the spatula partially under the edge nearest the handle, and fold (or flip) half of the omelet over onto the other half.

9. For a classic rolled omelet, slide the spatula around the edge of the omelet to ensure it is not sticking. Tilting the skillet away from you, use the spatula to roll the edge of the omelet toward the center, folding the top third over onto the middle third, as you would fold a letter. Shake the skillet to loosen the omelet, place the edge of the skillet onto a plate, slide the last third of the omelet onto the plate, and flip or roll the omelet onto itself. This is absolutely much easier than it sounds.

Variations

For Creamier Omelet

At step 3 add 2 teaspoons fresh minced herbs and 2 tablespoons of cream, reducing the water to 1 teaspoon.

For Filled Omelets

Add fillings at the end of step 7, before folding the omelet. Endless varieties can be created. Try a delicate mix of 2 tablespoons grated gruyère cheese, 1 tablespoon chopped ham, and 1 tablespoon chopped grilled asparagus. The classic Denver omelet is filled with 2 tablespoons of the following: chopped onion, green bell pepper, and ham. Top this with salsa to create a Spanish omelet.

Pantry/Refrigerator Check

Eggs

Salt

Black pepper

1 stick unsalted butter

New Mexican Frittata

This dish is wonderful for a brunch or light supper. In either case, add fresh fruit and cornmeal muffins to the table for a satisfying meal.

Ingredients

1/4 small onion

1 small fresh Anaheim chili

1/2 cup Monterey Jack cheese

6 eggs

2 tablespoons half and half

1/2 teaspoon salt

1/2 teaspoon freshly ground black pepper

1/4 teaspoon red chili powder

2 tablespoons unsalted butter

Equipment

10-inch ovenproof skillet, medium bowl, chef's knife, cutting board, measuring cup, measuring spoons, cheese grater

Methods

Chopping, grating, sautéing, baking (see Chapter 3)

Quantity

4 servings

Preparation

1. Preheat oven to 350°F.
2. Peel the onion and chop.
3. Wash the chili, cut in half lengthwise, remove the stem, seeds, and white veins, and coarsely chop.
4. Grate the cheese.
5. In a medium bowl, whisk the eggs with the half and half, cheese, salt, pepper, and chili powder.

Cooking Directions

6. Place the skillet over medium-low heat and melt the butter.

7. Add the onions and chili. Sauté for about 5 minutes until softened.

8. Pour the egg mixture over the onions and chili and then place the skillet in the center of the preheated oven.

9. Bake for about 45 to 50 minutes until it puffs and a table knife inserted in the center comes out clean.

caution

Chili oil is very hot and transfers easily to the skin. DO NOT touch your eyes with your fingers after cutting the chilies.

Variations

Add any of the following delicious combinations for a change of flavors:

- 3 tablespoons chopped sun-dried tomatoes, packed in oil, 1/2 cup grated mozzarella cheese, and 2 tablespoons minced fresh basil

- 1 small cooked red potato, chopped, 1/2 cup grated cheddar cheese, and 2 tablespoons minced fresh thyme

- 1/4 cup minced leeks, 1/2 cup grated gruyére cheese, and 1/4 cup sliced ham

- 1/4 cup chopped fresh spinach, 1/4 cup chopped white onion, 3 strips cooked crumbled bacon, 1/2 cup grated Swiss cheese, and 1/2 teaspoon ground nutmeg

- 1 medium chopped cooked russet potato, 1/4 cup canned chopped green chilies, 1/2 cup grated cheddar cheese, and 1 tablespoon minced fresh cilantro

Pantry/Refrigerator Check

1 stick unsalted butter

Eggs

Salt

Black pepper

Red chili powder

Shopping List

1/2 pint half and half

1 small onion

1 small fresh Anaheim chili

2 oz. Monterey Jack cheese

Home Fries

This recipe makes it easy to prepare a big country-style breakfast. By roasting the potatoes in the oven, you free up time and stove top space to use for cooking bacon, eggs, and toast. Add your own twist with garlic, green onions, fresh chilies, lemon pepper, or curry powder.

Ingredients

3 medium russet potatoes

1/2 green bell pepper

1/2 red bell pepper

1 medium onion

3 tablespoons extra virgin olive oil

1 teaspoon freshly ground black pepper

1 teaspoon salt

1 teaspoon Hungarian paprika

1 teaspoon dried thyme

tip

Fast track this recipe by using frozen, cut-up potatoes and bell peppers and season with a bottled grilling spice.

Equipment

Nonstick baking sheet, chef's knife, cutting board, metal or hard plastic spatula

Methods

Chopping, roasting (see Chapter 3)

Quantity

4 servings

Preparation

1. Preheat the oven to 475°F.
2. Wash the potatoes, quarter lengthwise, and chop each into about six pieces.
3. Wash the peppers, cut in half lengthwise, remove the top stem and seeds, and coarsely chop.
4. Peel the onion, cut in half, and coarsely chop.
5. Place the chopped potatoes and peppers on a baking sheet, drizzle with oil, sprinkle with spices, and toss to coat well.

Cooking Directions

6. Place the baking sheet into the preheated oven.

7. Cook for 25 to 30 minutes, occasionally turning with a spatula to ensure even browning.

8. Remove from the oven and serve while hot.

Variations

- When cooked, transfer the potatoes to a baking dish, top with 1/2 cup grated cheddar or Monterey Jack cheese and return to the oven until the cheese is melted.

Pantry/Refrigerator Check

Extra virgin olive oil

Black pepper

Salt

Hungarian paprika

Dried thyme

Shopping List

3 medium russet potatoes

1 green bell pepper

1 red bell pepper

1 medium onion

Buttermilk Pancakes

Homemade pancakes are so simple to make with ingredients you already have on hand. Top cooked pancakes with butter and warm maple syrup, powdered sugar, or *Ginger-Pear Topping* (page 371).

Ingredients

4 tablespoons unsalted butter

2 cups all-purpose white flour

1 teaspoon baking soda

1 1/2 teaspoons baking powder

1/2 teaspoon salt

1 teaspoon white sugar

2 eggs

2 cups buttermilk

1 tablespoon canola oil

Equipment

Large nonstick skillet, large bowl, 2 small bowls, measuring cup, measuring spoons, wire whisk or fork, wooden stirring spoon, wide spatula, ladle

Methods

Mixing, pan grilling (see Chapter 3)

Quantity

About 12 4-inch round pancakes

Preparation

1. Preheat the oven to 200°F.
2. In a small bowl, melt the butter in the microwave oven for 30 seconds on high.
3. In a large bowl, mix the flour, baking soda, baking powder, salt, and sugar. Make a well in the center of dry ingredients.
4. In a small bowl, whisk together the eggs and buttermilk.
5. Pour the egg-buttermilk mixture into the center of the dry ingredients. Slowly mix until just blended.
6. Add the melted butter and stir until just blended. Do not over mix—lumps are expected.

Cooking Directions

7. Place the skillet over medium-high heat and add the oil. Tip the skillet to coat the bottom with oil.

8. Ladle 1/2 cup of batter into the skillet. The batter will spread, so work in batches to avoid crowding the pancakes. Keep the pancakes from touching.

9. Cook the pancakes until they are slightly puffed, drying at the edges with small bubbles forming and breaking on the surface, about 2 minutes per side. The underside will be golden brown.

10. Flip the pancakes with a spatula and cook until puffed and springy in the center, about 2 more minutes.

11. Transfer to a platter and place in the oven to keep warm.

Variations

■ Add 1/2 teaspoon cinnamon, nutmeg, or powdered ginger during step 3.

■ Add 1/2 cup fresh berries, chopped bananas, or chocolate chips and chopped nuts during step 6.

Pantry/Refrigerator Check

1 stick unsalted butter

All-purpose white flour

Baking soda

Baking powder

Salt

White sugar

Eggs

Canola oil

Shopping List

Buttermilk

Banana Nut Muffins

Make an extra batch and freeze these muffins. When you are short on time, pop one in the microwave for a warm home-baked breakfast.

Ingredients

3 ripe bananas

1/2 cup chopped walnuts

1/2 cup white sugar

1/2 cup brown sugar

1/4 cup canola oil

1/2 cup unsweetened applesauce

1 egg

1 cup whole wheat flour

1 cup all-purpose white flour

2 teaspoons baking soda

2 tablespoons vanilla extract

3 tablespoon buttermilk

1/4 teaspoon nutmeg

1/2 teaspoon cinnamon

Nonstick cooking spray

tip

Do not stir the batter too much or the muffins will be tough and not rise as well as they should. Stir until the ingredients are well-mixed and then stop.

Equipment

12-muffin tin pan, chef's knife, cutting board, large mixing bowl, masher or fork, wooden stirring spoon, large tablespoon

Methods

Mashing, stirring, baking (see Chapter 3)

Quantity

12 muffins

Preparation

1. Preheat the oven to 350°F.

2. Mash the bananas and place in a large mixing bowl.

3. Chop the walnuts.

4. Add the sugars, oil, applesauce, and egg to the mashed bananas and stir until just mixed.

5. Add the flour and baking soda to the banana mix, stirring until just combined.

6. Add the vanilla, buttermilk, nutmeg, cinnamon, and nuts and stir well to blend.

Cooking Directions

7. Lightly spray the inside of the muffin cups and over the top area with nonstick cooking spray. If you do not have nonstick cooking spray, pour a tablespoon of oil on a paper towel and wipe the insides and top of each cup. Oiling the top of the muffin tin will prevent muffins from sticking if they puff over the top of the cups.

8. Fill each muffin cup 3/4 full with batter.

9. Bake for 25 to 30 minutes. Muffins are done when a toothpick inserted near the center comes out clean. Cool in the tin for 5 minutes, then remove the muffins and finish cooling them on a wire rack.

Variations

■ Add 1/2 cup raisins, currants, or dried chopped apples during step 4.

Pantry/Refrigerator Check

White sugar

Brown sugar

Canola oil

Unsweetened applesauce

Eggs

Whole wheat flour

All-purpose white flour

Baking soda

Vanilla extract

Ground nutmeg

Ground cinnamon

Nonstick cooking spray

Shopping List

3 ripe bananas

1/2 pint buttermilk

2 oz. walnuts

Biscuits

Homemade biscuits are simple to make with ingredients that one usually has on hand. This recipe is a classic and has been used for generations to create one of the original comfort foods. For savory or sweet biscuits, see variations that follow. Serve at breakfast with eggs, bacon, and home fries.

Ingredients

2 cups all-purpose white flour

3 1/2 teaspoons baking powder

1/2 teaspoon salt

5 tablespoons unsalted butter

3/4 cup milk

Equipment

Nonstick baking sheet, large bowl, measuring cup, measuring spoons, strainer or sifter, pastry blender or 2 table knives

Methods

Dusting, sifting, cutting in, kneading, baking (see Chapter 3)

Quantity

8 to 12 biscuits

Preparation

1. Preheat the oven to 450°F.
2. Clean an area of the kitchen counter and scatter or "dust" with 1 tablespoon of flour.
3. Over a large bowl, sift together the flour, baking powder and salt, mixing well to blend.
4. Cut the butter into small pieces and cut-in to the flour mixture using a pastry blender, 2 table knives, or your finger tips until the mixture resembles coarse crumbs.
5. Make a well in the middle of the flour mixture and pour the milk into the well.
6. Gently stir the dough with a fork until it forms a mass.
7. Gather the dough with clean hands, form into a ball, and place it on the floured surface.

8. Knead the dough, pulling the edges to the center and pushing it into itself about 10 times. The dough will feel light and soft but not sticky.

9. Roll or pat the dough into a 1/2-inch thick circle.

10. With a 2-to 3-inch round cookie cutter, jar rim or drinking glass rim, cut out circles as close together as possible.

11. Transfer the biscuits to an ungreased baking sheet, arranging them about 1 inch apart for crispy-sided biscuits or close together for soft-sided biscuits.

12. Gather the remaining dough, form into a ball, pat into a circle 1/2-inch thick, and cut into biscuits. Transfer to the baking sheet.

Cooking Directions

13. Place in a preheated oven and bake for about 15 minutes, until the biscuits are puffed and golden and the tops are browned.

Variations

Sweet Biscuits

Reduce the flour to 1 3/4 cups and add 2 tablespoons of sugar. Add 1/4 teaspoon cinnamon or 1 teaspoon orange zest during step 5. If desired, brush tops of biscuits with butter and sprinkle with sugar after they have baked.

Savory Herbed Pepper Biscuits

Add 1 tablespoon fresh minced herbs and 1/2 teaspoon freshly ground black pepper, and substitute buttermilk for regular milk during step 5.

Pantry/Refrigerator Check

All-purpose white flour

Baking powder

Salt

1 stick unsalted butter

Milk

6

BASIC SANDWICHES

Because necessity is the mother of invention, the creation of the sandwich was inevitable. Named after John Montagu, the Fourth Earl of Sandwich, the dish was concocted by his cook in the mid-1700s when the Earl ordered a meal that he could eat without leaving the gaming table. Alas, the chef remains nameless, but his creation has taken on a life of its own.

The Anatomy of a Great Sandwich

Sandwiches have no set rules and can be morphed to suit all occasions. They are equally good hot or cold, open-faced or closed, large or small, fancy or informal. You will find sandwiches on all menus, at any time of the day, in the form of elegant, bite-sized hors d'oeuvres on up to large, sloppy breakfast, lunch, or dinner entrées.

The key ingredients remain constant: not lettuce, tomatoes, and mustard, but rather, creativity and quality of contents. A sandwich is a great place for a beginning cook to experiment with the pairing of flavors and develop a creative flair. Practice crafting imaginative sandwiches variations of the classics; add bananas or chopped apple to peanut butter, or use honey instead of jelly. Trade in tuna with the predictable chopped pickles for a tuna with sliced olives and a hint of lemon.

In the sandwich world, all parts have equal importance—a truly democratic affair. The success of your sandwich depends not only on your creativity, but also on the quality of your ingredients. How disappointing to be served a delicious Cajun turkey sandwich filled with garlic cheddar cheese on a Dutch crunch roll to find only that the lettuce is wilted or the tomatoes are hard and tasteless!

A quick stroll through the local supermarket will net a bounty of quality items for a most incredible sandwich. No longer restricted to Wonder Bread, Skippy peanut butter and grape jelly (not that there's anything wrong with that)—today we can purchase bakery-fresh, hearty wheat and nut breads; grind our own peanut butter to the desired consistency of crunch; and use a jam or jelly that is made from fruits grown locally or imported from halfway around the world. Most supermarkets have a deli department, or deli case, that carries a large assortment of meats and cheeses such as Italian spiced roast beef, mesquite smoked turkey, Black Forest ham, smoked cheddar, imported Swiss, dilled Havarti, and jalapeño Jack.

Let your artistic culinary imagination run wild. Here are a few ideas for great sandwiches:

- Smoked ham and thin sliced red onion with spicy mustard on dark rye bread
- Ripe tomato, cucumber, provolone cheese, and alfalfa sprouts with garlic-mayonnaise on a French baguette
- Grilled chicken breast with roasted red peppers and basil-pesto on a sourdough roll
- Bacon, butter lettuce, and ripe tomato with Monterey Jack cheese and avocado on toasted hearty multi-grain bread
- Cream cheese, sliced fresh strawberries, and chopped pecans on toasted cinnamon bread
- Roasted pork, green apple slices, chopped arugula, and herbed butter on walnut-raisin bread

- Smoked salmon and asparagus tips with dill mayonnaise on a pumpernickel bagel
- Double-decker club of roasted vegetables and warm brie on English muffin-type bread
- Sliced roast beef, sun-dried tomato cream cheese, and chopped basil in a spinach wrap
- Tuna salad with capers and olives topped with slivered iceberg lettuce on a fresh croissant
- Roasted turkey breast with cranberry sauce on thick country potato bread
- Sliced lamb, chopped red onion, fresh parsley, and feta cheese with yogurt dressing in a pita half

The Basic Sandwich

The following are some examples of an infinite number of sandwich combinations. Mix and match, pick and choose, and throw a dart. You can't miss! For a quick party, purchase a variety of foods from each category and set them out on cutting boards, in baskets, bowls, or whatever you have, and let everyone become their own Earl of Sandwich.

Ingredients

The following sections describe the basic ingredients that can go into any sandwich.

Assorted Breads

If possible, consideration should be taken to match the bread choices to the type of sandwich. Rye is great with ham or corned beef, but gross with peanut butter and strawberry jam. Use fresh bread or, if slightly stale, toast immediately before assembling the sandwich. Here are some breads to choose from:

- Sliced breads: white, sourdough, hearty whole grain, oat bread, rye, pumpernickel

- Rolls or baguettes: hard or soft, French, Dutch crunch, Kaiser, sourdough, honey-wheat

- Flatbreads: focaccia, ciabatta, pita, corn or flour tortillas, wraps

caution

Avoid extra-thick slices of bread because they are hard to eat.

Spreads

The spread protects the bread from becoming soggy and adds moisture to the sandwich. It also helps to keep ingedients, like the tomatoes, from slipping out. Your choice of spreads is limited only by your imagination. Fillings such as tuna or chicken salad contain spreads so there is no need to use additional spread on your sandwich. Spreads can be simple and hang out in the background like plain mayonnaise; or they can bring a special flavor and texture to the sandwich, like chili-cumin cream cheese. Here are some spreads to choose from:

- Mayonnaise and butter, plain or with additives: garlic, curry, fresh herbs, spices, honey

- Cream cheese, plain or with additives: fruits, vegetable, spices, fresh herbs

- Mustards, plain or with additives: dijon, garlic, Cajun spiced, wine infused

- Oils and vinaigrettes: *Lemon Mustard Vinaigrette* (page 167), *Orange-Pecan Vinaigrette* (page 166); suggested for rolls or baguettes only
- Vegetable and herb spreads: hummus, tapenade, pesto, caponata, guacamole
- Nut and seed butters: peanut, almond, cashew, sesame tahini
- Jams, jellies, fruit preserves, savory and sweet chutneys, pickle and fruit relishes

Filling

The filling is the meat and potatoes of the sandwich; in fact, you can use meat and potatoes if you so desire! Here are some fillings to choose from:

- Deli-style sliced meats: spiced roast beef, corned beef, pastrami, smoked turkey, peppered turkey, rosemary-spiced ham, sliced chicken breast, salami, mortadella
- Sausages: kielbasa, gourmet chicken and turkey with Italian, Cajun, and Mexican spices, garlic pork
- Cheeses: plain and with additives: garlic cheddar, jalapen[td]o Jack, herbed Havarti, smoked Gouda, Swiss, Muenster, Brie, Edam, provolone, fontina, Gorgonzola
- Grilled or roasted vegetables: roasted eggplant, red pepper, zucchini, onion, portobello mushroom
- Salads: tuna salad, chicken salad, salmon salad, egg salad, tofu salad

tip

Last night's leftovers make an excellent sandwich because the flavors have expanded and gotten to know each other. You might even find yourself stashing a slice or two of the meatloaf to star in tomorrow's lunch.

Garnishes

On a sandwich or on the plate, garnishes are the finishing touch. Putting a little thought into matching the garnish to the sandwich will reward your effort. Ripe tomatoes don't add much to a hot pastrami sandwich, but pickles add a compatible twang. The tomatoes are a welcome bit of moisture and freshness with roast beef or sliced chicken. Side garnishes can add to the enjoyment of a sandwich as well, and some pairings are naturals. Serve tortilla chips with tacos, potato salad with roast beef, vinegar and salt kettle chips with tuna salad, or pita chips and hummus with roasted lamb. Here are some garnishes for the sandwich to choose from:

- Lettuce or sprouts: romaine, green leaf, red leaf, butter lettuce, iceberg lettuce, alfalfa or clover sprouts
- Onions: red or Spanish, white and green; thinly sliced, raw, or caramelized

- Ripe tomatoes: red beefsteak, yellow heirloom, hothouse, Roma, yellow pear, cherry tomatoes

- Peppers: hot or sweet

- Pickles: dill or sweet

- Olives: green or black

Here are some garnishes for the plate to choose from:

- Salads: potato, green leaf, coleslaw, fruit, pasta

- Chips: potato—all flavors and varieties, tortilla chips, vegetable chips, pita chips, bagel chips, crackers

- Vegetables: carrots, celery, zucchini spears, cucumber spears

Curried Chicken Salad Croissant

When cooking chicken breasts for dinner, cook a couple of extra breasts to use in this great salad the next day. Try this salad mounded into a split croissant with butter lettuce. Serve it with fresh, tangy coleslaw as a counterpoint to the creamy consistency of the filling.

Ingredients

1/2 small rib of celery

1 green onion

1 teaspoon lemon juice from 1 lemon

2 cooked chicken breasts

1 tablespoon of chopped mango chutney

2 butter lettuce leaves

1/4 cup mayonnaise

1/4 teaspoon dijon mustard

1/4 teaspoon garlic salt

1/2 teaspoon curry powder

Dash cayenne pepper

2 croissants

Equipment

Mixing bowl, chef's knife, cutting board, wire mesh strainer, measuring cup, measuring spoons, rubber spatula

Methods

Slicing, cubing, chopping, mixing (see Chapter 3, "Glossary of Terms and Techniques, Conversions and Equivalents")

Quantity

2 sandwiches

Preparation

1. Wash celery, trim ends, and thinly slice.
2. Peel tough outer leaves from the green onion, trim roots, trim tough tops, and slice.
3. Squeeze the lemon through a small strainer and discard seeds.

4. Cut chicken into small cubes.

5. Coarsely chop chutney.

6. Wash lettuce leaves and pat dry.

Assembly Directions

7. In a medium bowl, mix together all the ingredients, except the croissants and butter lettuce. Gently stir with a rubber spatula to combine.

8. Cut the croissants in half horizontally.

9. Mound 1/2 of the chicken salad into a croissant half, and top with a lettuce leaf and the other croissant half. Repeat with the remaining salad and croissant.

Variations

■ At step 7 add 2 tablespoons of nuts, raisins, or chopped fruit such as green apples or pears.

Pantry/Refrigerator Check

Mango chutney

Mayonnaise

Dijon mustard

Garlic salt

Curry powder

Cayenne pepper

Shopping List

1 bunch green onions

1 small head celery hearts

2 chicken breasts

1 lemon

2 croissants

1 head butter or red leaf lettuce

Grilled Albacore Tuna Melt

What could be more delicious than a grilled tuna melt? You can tailor the ingredients to match your personal tastes, but this recipe will give you a tasty place to start.

Ingredients

1 6 oz. can albacore tuna, packed in water

2 teaspoons lemon juice from 1 lemon

1 green onion

3 tablespoons mayonnaise

1 teaspoon curry powder

1 teaspoon capers

4 pieces sliced sourdough bread

2 slices Monterey Jack cheese

4 teaspoons softened unsalted butter or mayonnaise

Equipment

Small skillet with lid, can opener, knife, cutting board, measuring spoons, table knife, metal or hard plastic spatula, medium bowl

Methods

Chopping, pan-grilling (see Chapter 3)

Quantity

2 sandwiches

Preparation

1. Drain the liquid from the tuna. This is easily accomplished by opening the can with a can opener and instead of taking the lid off, pushing it down on the tuna and tilting the can at an angle over the sink. The liquid will flow from the can and the drained tuna will remain.

2. Squeeze the lemon over a small strainer and discard seeds.

3. Wash green onion, trim roots, trim tough tops, and slice.

4. In a medium bowl, mix the mayonnaise with the curry powder.

5. Add the tuna, capers, green onion, and lemon juice, mixing to combine.

6. Spread 1/2 of the tuna mixture over one slice of bread, top with one slice of cheese, and cover with the other bread slice. Spread 1 teaspoon of butter or mayonnaise on the outside of the top slice of bread.

Cooking Directions

7. Preheat the skillet over medium heat.

8. Place the tuna sandwich, buttered side down, in the skillet.

9. Butter the top slice of bread, cover the pan and cook for 1 to 2 minutes or until the bottom slice of bread is golden brown. Check by lifting a corner of the sandwich with the spatula.

10. Carefully flip the sandwich with a spatula.

11. Uncover and cook for 1 to 3 minutes, until the bottom slice of bread is golden brown.

12. Transfer the sandwich to a warmed plate. Garnish with a dill pickle or black olives.

13. While the first sandwich is grilling, prepare the second sandwich.

14. Repeat the grilling instructions for the second sandwich.

Variations

- At step 4 omit curry and add 2 teaspoons of fresh- minced herbs, or 2 tablespoons of chopped black olives.

Pantry/Refrigerator Check

1 6 oz. can albacore tuna, packed in water

Mayonnaise

Monterey Jack cheese

1 stick unsalted butter

Curry powder

Capers

Shopping List

1 bunch green onions

1 lemon

Sliced sourdough bread

Croque Monsieur (Grilled Ham and Cheese Sandwich)

A traditional French Croque Monsieur includes layers of jambon de Paris (ham) and Swiss Gruyère, covered in rich béchamel sauce and encased in toasted white bread, then topped with more béchamel and grated Gruyère. It is served hot from the oven. The cheese is golden-brown and melts over the sides with a scrumptious, creamy center. To make a Croque Madame, the Monsieur is topped with an egg. The following version is easy, but rich and almost as good as an afternoon in Paris. For a lovely lunch, serve with a small green salad dressed with *Orange-Pecan Vinaigrette* (page 166).

Ingredients

2 teaspoons softened unsalted butter, divided

2 pieces sliced French bread

2 slices Gruyère or Swiss cheese

3 thin slices cooked ham

1/2 teaspoon dijon mustard

Equipment

Small skillet with lid, measuring spoon, table knife, metal or hard plastic spatula

Methods

Pan-grilling (see Chapter 3)

Quantity

1 sandwich

Preparation

1. Preheat skillet over medium heat.

Cooking Directions

2. Spread 1 teaspoon softened butter on 1 slice of bread, and place with buttered side down in the preheated skillet.

3. Layer 1 slice of cheese, all of the ham, the dijon mustard, and then the remaining slice of cheese on the bread in the skillet.

note

The skillet may also be placed in a 325°F oven to melt the cheese, if desired.

4. Butter the remaining slice of bread and place on top of the layers, buttered side up.

5. Cook for 1 to 3 minutes or until the bottom slice is golden brown and the cheese begins to melt. Check by lifting the corner of the sandwich with a spatula.

6. Carefully flip the sandwich with a spatula.

7. Cook for 1 to 3 minutes, until the bottom slice is golden brown. If the bread is browning, but the cheese is not melting, turn the heat to medium-low and cover the skillet.

8. Transfer the sandwich to a warmed plate and serve.

Variations

■ Substitute smoked or garlic cheddar for Gruyère, or use challah bread or a croissant.

Pantry/Refrigerator Check

Dijon mustard

1 stick unsalted butter

Shopping List

2 slices Gruyère or Swiss cheese

3 slices good quality deli ham

Sliced French bread

Hot Reuben Sandwich

There are a few theories as to the origin of the Reuben sandwich in the early 1900s. Some say Reuben Kulakofsky created the Reuben at the Blackstone Hotel in Omaha, Nebraska. Others believe it was invented in Manhattan at Reuben's Delicatessen on 58th Street. This deli staple can easily be made at home and it is especially good served with crisp dill pickles and a side of potato salad.

tip

Fast track by using purchased Russian or Thousand Island dressing.

Ingredients

2 slices rye bread

2 tablespoons *Russian Dressing* (page 171), divided

6 slices corned beef

2 tablespoons jarred sauerkraut

1 slice Swiss or Gruyère cheese

Equipment

Table knife, aluminum foil

Methods

Oven heating

Quantity

1 sandwich

Preparation

1. Preheat the oven to 400°F.

2. In the following order, top 1 slice of bread with:

   1 tablespoon Russian dressing

   3 slices corned beef

   2 tablespoons sauerkraut

   3 slices corned beef

   1 slice cheese

3. Spread the remaining bread slice with the remaining dressing and place on top of the sandwich.

Cooking Directions

4. Wrap the sandwich in foil and place in the oven for about 10 minutes, until the cheese melts and the sauerkraut is hot.

5. Remove the sandwich from the foil, slice in half and serve warm.

Pantry/Refrigerator Check

Russian dressing

Aluminum foil

Shopping List

Rye bread

6 slices corned beef

1 slice Swiss or Gruyère cheese

1 small jar sauerkraut

The Best Basic Burger

Making an incredible hamburger that tastes like the ones from your favorite diner is easy—the key is in the crafting. Lightly toast the buns and place the meat directly on the bottom bun so the savory juices are absorbed. Moisten and flavor the top bun with mayonnaise and mustard. Layer the following in order on top of the meat to build a truly classic, perfect hamburger: thinly sliced red onion, thinly sliced ripe tomato, and crisp red leaf lettuce. For added flavor, melt a slice of cheese on the meat and add a couple of slices of crisp cooked bacon. See variations following the recipe for more suggestions.

Ingredients

1 ripe tomato

1/2 red onion

4 to 8 tender red leaf lettuce leaves

2 pounds ground beef chuck or beef round

1/4 teaspoon ground black pepper

2 teaspoons butter

1 tablespoon extra virgin olive oil

4 hamburger buns

1/4 teaspoon salt

4 tablespoons mayonnaise

4 teaspoons dijon mustard

Equipment

Large heavy-bottomed skillet, medium bowl, chef's knife, serrated knife, cutting board, measuring spoons, table knife, metal or hard rubber spatula

Method

Slicing, mixing, pan-grilling, toasting (see Chapter 3)

Quantity

4 hamburgers

Preparation

1. Wash the tomato and slice it into 1/2 inch-thick slices.
2. Cut the onion in half lengthwise, trim the ends, peel, and thinly slice one half. Store the unused half in a resealable plastic bag for later use.
3. Wash the lettuce leaves and pat dry.
4. Place the meat and pepper in a medium bowl and mix with clean hands until just combined. Over-mixing can make the burger tough.
5. Divide the meat into 4 portions and form each into a patty about 3/4-inch thick.

Cooking Directions

6. Preheat the broiler.
7. Place a skillet over medium-high heat and heat the butter and oil until melted and sizzling.
8. Place the hamburger patties in the skillet and cook 4 to 5 minutes per side, depending on desired doneness. The USDA (United States Department of Agriculture) suggests an internal temperature of 160°F. Use an instant-read thermometer. Also check for doneness by cutting into the burger. The inside should be slightly pink.
9. Place the hamburger buns on the rack in the preheated broiler. Toast 3 to 4 minutes until lightly browned, checking occasionally to avoid burning.
10. Remove the buns from the broiler and place, open-faced, on individual plates.
11. Lightly salt the hamburgers, remove from the pan, and place each on the bottom half of the bun.
12. Top the burger with red onion, sliced tomato, and lettuce leaves, in that order.
13. Spread the mayonnaise, mustard, or any favorite condiments on the top half of the bun, and place on top of lettuce.

Variations

■ At step 4 add any of the following: 2 tablespoons minced onion, minced garlic, or fresh herbs.

■ At step 8 after turning the burger, top with a slice of Jack, cheddar, or Swiss cheese, or 1 tablespoon of crumbled Gorgonzola or Stilton cheese.

■ At step 11 place the burger on the bun and top with 2 crisp cooked bacon strips, 1 tablespoon canned chopped green chilies, sautéed mushrooms, roasted red peppers, or chili con carne.

■ At step 12, after layering the sliced tomato, add fresh avocado, alfalfa sprouts, or basil leaves.

■ At step 13 spread the top bun with gourmet flavored mustard, pesto, chutney, or relish.

Pantry/Refrigerator Check

1 stick unsalted butter

Extra virgin olive oil

Ground black pepper

Salt

Mayonnaise

Dijon mustard

Shopping List

2 pounds ground beef chuck or beef round

4 hamburger buns

1 ripe tomato

1 small red onion

1 head red leaf lettuce

7

Soups and Stews

The great thing about soup is that soup has so many wonderful qualities. The basic steps are simple, so it's easy to make and it's hard to wreck. It's also good for us, it's inexpensive, the varieties are endless, it's fancy and it's casual, it's a great way to use up leftovers, and it makes us feel better when we are sick, blue, overworked, lovesick, or missing home.

Soup Basics

There are many categories of soups. Consommé, bisque, chowder, and bouillon are the names of a few soups, but basically soup boils down to two types: broth-based soups and cream-based soups. The cream soup is actually just a broth-based soup that is puréed or contains cream.

The following steps are absolutely necessary for making soup, both broth- and cream-based. The recipes then expand on these basic steps. As in all cooking, the end result reflects the quality of the ingredients. Choose a soup you think you might like and follow the recipe exactly the first time. Get familiar with the methods and skills used, and then try it again. Let your imagination, or the leftovers in your refrigerator, guide your experimentation.

Follow these steps to make a basic broth-based soup:

1. Create a base flavor by sautéing aromatic vegetables, such as garlic and/or onions, in unsalted butter, oil, or bacon drippings over medium heat for 10 minutes. Add garlic 3 minutes before the onions are done to avoid overcooking and bitterness.

2. Add coarsely chopped vegetables, such as carrots and celery, and sauté for about 10 minutes over medium heat until tender.

3. Add liquid, such as chicken, beef, or vegetable stock, and add dried herbs, salt, and pepper. Bring the ingredients to a boil, quickly reduce the heat, and simmer the soup while covered for about 20 minutes.

4. Add more vegetables such as zucchini, green beans, corn, chard or spinach. You can also add cut-up meats, cooked beans, small-sized pasta, egg noodles, or leftovers. Simmer the soup for another 5–20 minutes depending on what you have just added.

5. If you want to add fresh herbs do so about 5–10 minutes before the soup finishes cooking.

6. Taste and adjust the seasonings with salt and fresh-ground pepper.

Follow these steps to make your favorite vegetable cream-based soup:

1. Create a base flavor by sautéing aromatic vegetables, such as onions or shallots, in unsalted butter and oil over low heat for 10 minutes, taking care that you do not brown the vegetables.

2. Add your favorite vegetable (coarsely chopped) along with chicken stock and dried herbs, and simmer until tender. The time it needs to cook depends on the vegetable.

3. If adding fresh herbs, do so about 5–10 minutes before the vegetables are tender.

4. Purée small batches of the soup in a food processor or blender.

5. Return the soup to the pot, stir in the cream, and then heat, but do not allow the soup to boil.

6. Taste and adjust the seasonings with salt and fresh-ground pepper.

Soup Rules

Following a few rules will help you create better soups, but even if you ignore all of them, your soup will most likely taste just fine:

- Add fresh herbs near the end because herbs lose their flavor and bright fresh color after about an hour's worth of cooking.
- Never allow cream or milk to boil because it burns easily, and burned milk smells and tastes foul and will ruin your soup.
- Garlic cooks quickly and when it burns, it imparts a bitter flavor. If sautéing garlic with another item, such as onions, always add garlic a couple of minutes before the end of the sautéing process to avoid overcooking.
- Boiling soup dissipates flavors, so watch the pot as it comes up to a boil and quickly reduce the heat to a simmer. If you have an electric stove, remove the pot for a minute until the heating unit cools.
- Use unsalted butter because salted butter will sometimes separate when melting and it can add a bitter taste to your soup.

Soup Tips

These tips are also worth keeping in mind as you prepare your soups:

- If you happen to over-salt your soup, try adding a can of whole peeled tomatoes or 1/2 teaspoon of brown sugar, depending on the soup. If those flavors won't work with your soup, thinly slice half an apple or a small potato, add to the soup, and then simmer for 5 minutes. Remove the apple or potato and discard. This helps absorb the excess salt.
- If you happen to have gone overboard on the garlic (if that is possible), put some parsley flakes in a piece of cheesecloth or a tea ball and let it hang in the soup for 10 minutes. The garlic is attracted to the parsley. Discard the parsley.
- If you have excess fat floating on top of your soup, place a piece of white bread on top of the soup. The bread will absorb the fat in just a few seconds. Remove the bread before it starts to fall apart, and discard.
- Soup and stew flavors can be enhanced by adding more of the herbs and spices called for in the recipe, or with a small addition of salt, pepper, nutmeg, chili powder, chili paste, Asian fish sauce, truffle oil, sundried tomatoes, or dijon mustard. You can also add a splash of balsamic vinegar, soy sauce, wine, sherry, lemon or lime juice, Liquid Smoke, or a bottled browning and seasoning sauce such as Kitchen Bouquet.

Chicken Stock

This is one of the basic recipes in a cooking arsenal. However, unless you are trying to impress the in-laws or your Martha Stewart-type neighbor, you probably won't make this often. Homemade stock (or broth) is always better because you control the quality of the ingredients, and you have the satisfaction of knowing you made it yourself. However, these days you can buy good quality stock in 1-quart containers. It's wise to have quality stock on hand, either store bought or homemade.

Ingredients

1 whole chicken

2 medium carrots

2 celery ribs, leaves included

1 large white onion

2 cloves garlic

4 sprigs of fresh thyme

1/2 bunch of fresh parsley

4 quarts (16 cups) cold water

1 bay leaf

1 teaspoon whole black peppercorns

1 teaspoon salt

Equipment

Large stockpot with lid, chef's knife, cutting board, measuring cup, measuring spoons, large spoon, large strainer, cheesecloth

Methods

Cutting, boiling, simmering, skimming, straining (see Chapter 3, "Glossary of Terms and Techniques, Conversions and Equivalents")

Quantity

3 quarts

tip

If your large stockpot has a metal pasta-cooking insert, put all of your stock ingredients in the insert and then into the liquid. When the stock is done, just remove the insert that contains the bones, meat, and vegetables. This saves the time of fishing for bits and pieces.

Preparation

1. Remove the giblets (the heart, liver, and gizzard) from inside the chicken. Check that the kidneys (small, dark red, and about the size of marbles) have been removed from the end cavity near the tail. If not, scoop them out with your fingers.

2. Cut the chicken into quarters and rinse well.

3. Wash the carrots, peel, and cut into chunks.

4. Wash the celery and cut into large chunks.

5. Peel and cut the onion into quarters.

6. Peel the garlic and crush it with the side of a knife, blade side away from you.

7. Wash the thyme and parsley, and tie together with kitchen string.

Cooking Directions

8. Place the chicken and vegetables in a large stockpot and cover with cold water.

9. Add the thyme, parsley, bay leaves, peppercorns, and salt.

10. Slowly bring the water to a boil over medium-high heat.

11. When the stock boils, immediately reduce the heat to medium-low, cover the pot, and gently simmer for 2–3 hours.

12. Frequently skim the impurities off the top with a large spoon.

13. Transfer the pot from the stove top and allow to cool slightly.

14. Remove the chicken to a cutting board to cool and then separate the meat from the skin and bones. Discard the skin and bones, and then store the reserved meat in the refrigerator.

15. Strain the stock into another pot through a fine sieve or a strainer lined with cheesecloth. Discard the vegetables.

16. Cool the reserved stock immediately by putting the pot into a bowl filled with ice. Because bacteria form quickly, it is important to cool and refrigerate the stock as soon as possible.

17. Refrigerate for up to one week or freeze for up to one month.

Variations

■ Use the carcass of a roasted chicken (from a previous dish) instead of a whole chicken.

Pantry/Refrigerator Check

Salt

Black peppercorns

Bay leaves

Shopping List

1 whole chicken (about 4 pounds)

2 medium carrots

1 head of celery

1 large white onion

1 head of garlic

1 bunch fresh thyme

1 bunch fresh parsley

Chicken Noodle Soup

This is a realist's version of a classic comfort food. If you have time, you can make your own stock and use the chicken meat you reserve. However, for speed and ease, we use canned stock and chicken breasts cooked along with the soup.

Ingredients

1 medium yellow onion

2 medium carrots

2 celery ribs, leaves included

2 garlic cloves

3 tablespoons minced fresh parsley

2 tablespoons fresh lemon juice from 1 lemon

4 boneless, skinless chicken breasts

3 tablespoons canola oil

1 tablespoon dried thyme

1 bay leaf

2 quarts chicken stock (8 cups)

1 1/2 cups dried wide egg noodles

1 teaspoon salt

1/2 teaspoon fresh-ground black pepper

tip

Fast track this recipe even further by using bagged chopped vegetables and a roasted chicken purchased at the grocery store. The deli departments of most grocery stores roast chickens and you can smell them roasting a mile away. Discard the skin and bones, and then add the succulent roasted chicken and all the juices to your soup. Only your grocer will know that you didn't spend the day at home slaving over a hot stove.

Equipment

Large stockpot with lid, chef's knife, cutting board, vegetable peeler, strainer, measuring cup, measuring spoons, wooden stirring spoon

Methods

Dicing, peeling, mincing, sautéing, boiling, simmering (see Chapter 3)

Quantity

6 to 8 servings

Preparation

1. Peel and dice the onion.
2. Wash the carrots and peel if desired. Quarter lengthwise and dice into 1/2-inch pieces.

3. Wash the celery, trim ends, half lengthwise, and dice into 1/2-inch pieces.

4. Peel and mince the garlic.

5. Wash the parsley and pat dry. Pull the leaves from the stems, and mince. Set aside.

6. Squeeze the lemon juice through the strainer, and discard the seeds.

7. Clean the chicken breasts and cut in half lengthwise.

Cooking Directions

8. Heat the oil over medium-low heat in a stockpot.

9. Add the onion, carrots, celery, garlic, thyme, and bay leaf, and sauté for 8–10 minutes. Stir occasionally until the vegetables are softened but not browned.

10. Add the chicken stock and chicken breast pieces.

11. Cover the pot, increase the heat to medium, and slowly bring to a boil.

12. When the soup boils, immediately reduce the heat to medium-low, remove the lid, and simmer for 30 minutes. Carefully remove the chicken pieces, transfer to a cutting board, and shred the meat by hand. Return the meat to the pot.

13. Add the egg noodles and simmer for 5 minutes, or until tender.

14. Add the lemon juice, fresh parsley, salt and pepper.

Variations

- At step 9 omit the dried thyme, and add 3 tablespoons fresh thyme at step 14.
- At step 14 add 1 cup of leftover cooked vegetables.
- Substitute 2 peeled and chopped russet potatoes for egg noodles and add them 15 minutes into cooking at step 12.
- At step 13 add 1/2 cup uncooked rice and omit the egg noodles. Simmer for an additional 10 minutes.

Pantry/Refrigerator Check

Canola oil

Dried thyme

Bay leaves

Salt

Black pepper

2 quarts chicken stock

Wide egg noodles

Shopping List

1 lb. boneless, skinless chicken breasts

1 medium yellow onion

2 medium carrots

1 head of celery

1 head of garlic

1 bunch fresh parsley

1 lemon

Minestrone

Minestrone is the Italian word for "to hand out." The monks used to keep a big pot of this classic soup over the fire to hand out to hungry travelers. Vegetables were added according to what was in season. The recipe below should be a guide for you and is a great way to use up vegetables like zucchini, green beans, celery, and even broccoli and cauliflower. This warming and healthy after-school snack can also become a hearty dinner by adding a salad and a basket of garlic bread. Place a small bowl of grated Parmesan cheese on the table so everyone can garnish their own soup.

Ingredients

1 large yellow onion

4 cloves fresh garlic

2 medium carrots

1/2 head green cabbage

1 medium russet potato

1 15 oz. can red kidney beans

1 15 oz. can cannellini (white kidney beans)

1/4 cup extra virgin olive oil

2 tablespoons unsalted butter

1 tablespoon dried basil

2 tablespoons dried oregano

1 teaspoon salt

1 teaspoon fresh-ground black pepper

2 28 oz. cans whole plum tomatoes in juice

2 quarts (8 cups) chicken stock

2 tablespoons tomato paste

1/2 cup dried elbow macaroni

1/2 cup grated Parmesan cheese

Equipment

Large stockpot with lid, chef's knife, cutting board, vegetable peeler, measuring cup, measuring spoons, wooden stirring spoon, colander

Methods

Chopping, mincing, core, shredding, peeling, slicing, sautéing, stirring, boiling, simmering (see Chapter 3)

Quantity

6 to 8 servings

Preparation

1. Peel and chop the onion.
2. Peel and finely mince the garlic.
3. Peel and coarsely chop the carrots.
4. Cut the cabbage in half, core, and finely shred. Wrap and reserve the remaining half for later use.
5. Peel the potato, quarter lengthwise, and cut into 1/2-inch thick slices.
6. Drain the beans in a colander and rinse. Set aside.

Cooking Directions

7. Heat the oil and butter over medium heat in a large stockpot.
8. Add the onion, carrots, basil, oregano, salt, and pepper, and sauté for 8 minutes. Stir occasionally to prevent sticking.
9. Add the garlic and sauté for an additional 3 to 5 minutes, until the garlic is softened.
10. Pour the tomatoes into a bowl and crush them by hand. Add the tomatoes, with their juice, to the stockpot.
11. Add the chicken stock, tomato paste, cabbage, and potato. Increase the heat and bring to a boil.
12. When the soup boils, immediately reduce the heat, cover the pot, and simmer over medium heat for 15 minutes.
13. Add the drained beans and pasta, and then simmer for an additional 15 to 20 minutes, until the pasta is just cooked.
14. Taste and adjust the seasoning, adding more salt and pepper if needed.

Variations

- At step 7 add 2 tablespoons of pesto.
- At step 8 use 3 tablespoons of fresh chopped basil and 1/4 cup of fresh chopped oregano instead of the dried herbs.
- At step 13 add 1 diced zucchini or 1 can of drained garbanzo beans.

Pantry/Refrigerator Check

Extra virgin olive oil

1 stick unsalted butter

Dried basil

Dried oregano

Salt

Black pepper

1 6 oz. can tomato paste (or resealable tube)

2 28 oz. cans whole plum tomatoes in juice

1 15 oz. can red kidney beans

1 15 oz. can cannellini (white kidney beans)

2 quarts chicken stock

Elbow macaroni or other small pasta

Shopping List

1 large yellow onion

1 head of garlic

2 medium carrots

1 small head green cabbage

1 medium russet potato

1 1/2 oz. Parmesan cheese

Gazpacho

Take advantage of abundant, inexpensive summer produce to make this favorite soup. When it is too hot to cook, whip up a batch of *Gazpacho,* served icy cold. Topped with a dollop of sour cream and chopped cilantro, the presentation is beautiful and inviting. Serve with crusty French bread or as the first course to a summertime barbecue.

Ingredients

1 large red bell pepper

1 large yellow bell pepper

1 large cucumber

5 green onions

1 large white onion

2 large ripe tomatoes

2 tablespoons chopped fresh cilantro

1/2 cup red wine vinegar

1/2 cup extra virgin olive oil

2 cups tomato juice

1/4 teaspoon cayenne pepper

1/2 teaspoon fresh-ground black pepper

1/2 teaspoon salt

2 dashes Tabasco (optional)

Equipment

Chef's knife, cutting board, medium bowl, measuring cup, measuring spoons, whisk, rubber spatula, blender or food processor, glass or plastic container with tight fitting lid, wooden stirring spoon

Methods

Chopping, whisking, puréeing, blending (see Chapter 3)

Quantity

8 servings

Preparation

1. Wash the red and yellow peppers. Cut in half, remove the seeds, and chop into 6–8 large pieces.

2. Peel and chop the cucumber into 6–8 large pieces.

3. Wash the green onions, cut off the root end, and any tough upper greens, and chop into 4–6 large pieces.

4. Peel and chop the white onion into 6–8 large pieces.

5. Wash and chop the tomatoes into 6–8 large pieces.

6. Wash the cilantro. Leave whole or coarsely chop into 6–8 large pieces.

Assembly Directions

7. In a medium bowl, whisk together the vinegar, oil, tomato juice, cayenne pepper, black pepper, and salt.

8. In a blender or food processor, in small batches, blend the vegetables into a rough purée, adding the vinegar-oil mixture to keep the blades running smoothly. Do not purée completely as gazpacho should be a little crunchy.

9. Empty the puréed soup into a large non-reactive (glass or plastic) container that has a lid.

10. Continue blending the vegetables and vinegar-oil mixture in small batches until all vegetables are puréed.

11. Season with Tabasco to taste.

12. Cover tightly and chill for at least 4 hours. If the container does not have a tight fitting lid, then cover securely with plastic wrap.

Variations

- Use other combinations of vegetables, all red or all green.
- At step 7 add 3 tablespoons vodka.
- Garnish the soup with chopped avocado and/or crumbled bacon.
- Make a fruit gazpacho using strawberries, cantaloupes, apples, nectarines, and grapes with raspberry vinegar. Use your imagination!

Pantry/Refrigerator Check

Red wine vinegar

Extra virgin olive oil

2 11.5 oz. cans tomato juice

Cayenne pepper

Black pepper

Salt

Tabasco (optional)

Shopping List

1 large red bell pepper

1 large yellow bell pepper

1 large cucumber

1 bunch green onions

1 large white onion

2 large ripe tomatoes

1 bunch fresh cilantro

French Onion Soup

This soup is the perfect combination of both elegance and ease. The most difficult task is slicing all those onions! Theories for preventing watery eyes while slicing onions range from impaling a balled-up piece of white bread on the tip of your knife to wearing goggles. Placing the onion in the freezer for 10 minutes, or in the refrigerator for 1 hour, before slicing actually seems to work.

Ingredients

8 medium white onions

6 thick slices crusty French bread

1 1/2 cups grated Gruyère or Swiss cheese

4 tablespoons unsalted butter

2 tablespoons extra virgin olive oil

1/2 cup sherry

2 quarts (8 cups) beef stock

1 bay leaf

1/2 teaspoon salt

1/2 teaspoon fresh-ground black pepper

tip

Fast track the process by purchasing packaged large croutons and using preshredded Swiss cheese.

Equipment

Large saucepan, chef's knife, cutting board, grater, measuring cup, measuring spoons, wooden stirring spoon, 6 ovenproof soup bowls, baking sheet, ladle

Methods

Slicing, toasting, grating, sautéing, deglazing, boiling, simmering, broiling (see Chapter 3)

Quantity

6 servings

Preparation

1. Peel and thinly slice the onions. Set aside.

2. To make the croutons, cut the bread to fit inside the soup bowls. Toast and set aside.

3. Grate the cheese and set aside.

Cooking Directions

4. In a large saucepan, melt the butter and oil over medium heat.

5. Add the onions and sauté, stirring frequently until tender and dark caramel colored, about 25–30 minutes.

6. Add the sherry and deglaze the pan by stirring and scraping up the flavorful bits from the pan bottom.

7. Add the beef stock, bay leaf, salt, and pepper, and increase the heat to bring to a boil.

8. When the soup boils, immediately reduce the heat to medium-low and simmer for 30 minutes. Remove and discard the bay leaf.

9. Preheat the broiler, placing the rack so that the top of each soup bowl will be about 4 inches from the heat source.

10. Place 6 ovenproof soup bowls on a baking sheet. Ladle the soup into the bowls.

11. Float 1 crouton in each bowl of soup and top with a mound of grated cheese.

12. Carefully transfer the baking sheet to the oven. Watch closely because when the cheese starts to melt, it will melt and turn golden brown very quickly. It should take about 3 minutes for melting to start, depending on your broiler.

13. Remove from the oven and serve immediately.

Variations

- At step 4 add 1/4 cup good brandy or Cognac, and 2 teaspoons of fresh-chopped thyme.

Pantry/Refrigerator Check

1 stick unsalted butter

Extra virgin olive oil

Dry sherry

2 quarts beef stock

Salt

Black pepper

Shopping List

8 medium white onions

Crusty French bread

Gruyère or Swiss cheese

Lentil Soup

This hearty and healthy bean soup is full of good-for-you ingredients like spinach and root vegetables. Lentils do not need to soak before cooking, so you could Fast Track this recipe by using cubed cooked ham and ready-to-eat packaged spinach. You can say "soup's on" in less than 40 minutes!

Ingredients

1 pound bag French green lentils

1 medium white onion

2 medium carrots

2 medium celery ribs

2 garlic cloves

1 cup fresh spinach

1/4 cup extra virgin olive oil

5 cups chicken stock

5 cups water

1 meaty ham bone

2 teaspoons dried thyme

1 bay leaf

1/4 teaspoon salt

1 teaspoon fresh-ground black pepper

2 tablespoons dry sherry

Equipment

Large saucepan with lid, chef's knife, cutting board, measuring cup, wooden stirring spoon

Methods

Chopping, sautéing, boiling, simmering (see Chapter 3)

Quantity

6 servings

Preparation

1. Pour lentils onto a large plate. Pick through the beans, discarding small pebbles and extremely shriveled beans. Rinse the remaining beans.
2. Peel and chop the onion.
3. Peel the carrots, half lengthwise, and finely chop.
4. Wash the celery, trim the ends, cut the stalk in half lengthwise, and finely chop.
5. Peel and mince the garlic.
6. Wash the spinach.

Cooking Directions

7. Heat the olive oil over medium heat in a large saucepan.
8. Add the onion, carrot, and celery, and then sauté until almost softened, about 5 minutes.
9. Add the garlic and sauté for 3 minutes or until all vegetables are soft.
10. Add the chicken stock, water, ham bone, thyme, bay leaf, salt, and pepper, and then increase the heat to medium-high and bring to a boil.
11. When the soup boils, immediately reduce the heat to medium-low and simmer, partially covered, for 1 hour.
12. Carefully remove the ham bone from the soup and transfer to a cutting board. Remove the meat from the bone, discard the bone, and then return the ham to the soup.
13. Add the spinach and dry sherry, and then simmer for an additional 5 minutes.
14. Taste the soup and adjust the seasoning with salt and pepper.

Variations

- Omit the ham bone. At step 13, substitute 2 cups of precooked cubed ham. Reduce the simmer time in step 11 to 30 minutes.
- At step 13, add 3 tablespoons of minced fresh tarragon.

Pantry/Refrigerator Check

Extra virgin olive oil

5 cups chicken stock

1 pound bag French green lentils

Dried thyme

Bay leaf

Salt

Black pepper

Dry sherry

Shopping List

1 medium white onion

2 medium carrots

1 head celery

1 head garlic

1 bunch fresh spinach

1 meaty ham bone

Cream of Tomato Soup with Chiffonade Basil

A wintertime favorite with grilled cheese sandwiches, this soup is also a great way to use up extra summertime garden tomatoes. For a smoky flavor, try roasting the fresh tomatoes. See the Note in the variations that follow this recipe for easy roasting instructions. The garnish of sour cream topped with chiffonade basil creates a beautiful yet simple presentation.

Ingredients

2 medium onions

2 shallots

8 large fresh basil leaves

2 tablespoons extra virgin olive oil

4 tablespoons unsalted butter

2 28 oz. cans whole plum tomatoes with juice

4 cups chicken stock

1/2 teaspoon white sugar

1/2 teaspoon salt

1/2 teaspoon fresh-ground black pepper

1 1/2 cups heavy cream or whipping cream

8 tablespoons sour cream (optional)

Equipment

Large saucepan with lid, chef's knife, cutting board, measuring cup, measuring spoons, wooden stirring spoon, blender or food processor

Methods

Chopping, chiffonade, sautéing, boiling, simmering (see Chapter 3)

Quantity

6 to 8 servings

Preparation

1. Peel and chop the onions.
2. Peel and chop the shallots.
3. Wash the basil, dry, and pull the leaves from the stems. Stack the leaves in a neat pile, all facing the same way. Roll the leaf pile into a tight tube and slice crosswise. Set aside 2 tablespoons of chiffonade for garnish.

Cooking Directions

4. Heat the oil and butter over low heat in a large saucepan.

5. Add the onion and shallots, cover the pan, and sauté over low heat for about 15 minutes to soften but not brown, stirring occasionally.

6. Add the basil (except the reserved), and the tomatoes with their juices, chicken stock, sugar, salt, and pepper.

7. Increase the heat to a medium-low and simmer for 10 minutes.

8. Remove the saucepan from the heat and allow to slightly cool.

9. Transfer the soup, in small batches, to a blender or food processor, and then purée until smooth. As each batch is puréed, transfer it to a large bowl to make room for the next batch.

10. Return all puréed soup to the saucepan, stir in the cream, and then heat but do not allow the soup to boil.

11. Taste and adjust the seasonings with salt and pepper.

12. Ladle the soup into bowls and garnish with a dollop of sour cream and a sprinkling of basil chiffonade.

Variations

■ At step 3 add roasted fresh tomatoes in place of canned.

Pantry/Refrigerator Check

1 stick unsalted butter

Extra virgin olive oil

2 28 oz. cans whole plum tomatoes with juice

1 quart chicken stock

White sugar

Salt

Black pepper

Shopping List

2 medium onions

2 shallots

1 bunch fresh basil

1 pint heavy cream or whipping cream

note

To roast tomatoes, halve and seed 2 pounds of ripe tomatoes, and then place them cut-side down on a foil-lined baking sheet. Place the baking sheet under a broiler for 10–15 minutes, turning the tomatoes once the skin side is blackened. Let the tomatoes cool and remove the charred skin. If some charred spots remain, don't worry—it will add to the rustic look and flavor of the soup.

Potato Leek Soup

Most soups are versatile and this one is certainly no exception. For a rustic, chunky potato soup, omit the blending step. If you want to create the swanky chilled vichyssoise made famous by Chef Louis Diat in 1910 at the New York Ritz-Carlton Hotel, then just follow the instructions in the variations.

Ingredients

4 leeks

4 large russet potatoes

1/2 cup minced fresh chives

4 slices bacon

1 tablespoon extra virgin olive oil

3 cups chicken stock

3 cups water

1/2 teaspoon fresh-ground black pepper

1/2 cup heavy cream

1/2 cup sour cream

Equipment

Large saucepan, chef's knife, cutting board, measuring cup, wooden stirring spoon, blender or food processor, colander

Methods

Slicing, cutting, mincing, sautéing, boiling, simmering (see Chapter 3)

Quantity

6 to 8 servings

Preparation

1. Thoroughly clean the leeks. They are grown in sand, which is harder to loosen than regular soil. Trim the root and a few inches of the tough upper leaves. Cut each leek in half lengthwise, and then slice the leek across the stalks into 1/2-inch thick pieces. Separate the rings with your fingers into a large bowl of water that contains 1 tablespoon of vinegar. Swish the pieces around to flush out the gritty sand. Transfer the leeks to a colander and rinse thoroughly under cold running water, then drain well.

2. Peel the potatoes, quarter lengthwise, and cut into large uniform pieces.

3. Wash and finely mince the chives. Set aside.

Cooking Directions

4. Sauté the bacon until crisp over medium heat in a large saucepan. Transfer the bacon to paper towels to drain. Crumble the bacon and set aside. Spoon off the bacon fat but leave 1 tablespoon.

5. Add the oil to the pan and heat to medium-high.

6. Add the leeks, reduce the heat to medium, and sauté for 10 minutes to soften but not brown, stirring occasionally.

7. Add the chicken stock, water, potatoes, and pepper. Partially cover, reduce the heat to medium-low, and simmer for 20–30 minutes, until the potatoes are tender and offer no resistance when pierced with a fork. Remove the pan from the heat and allow to cool slightly.

8. Transfer the contents of the pan, vegetables and liquid, in small batches to a blender or food processor, and then purée until smooth. As each batch is puréed, transfer to a large bowl to make room for the next batch.

9. Return all puréed soup to the pan, stir in the cream, and heat, but do not allow to boil. If the soup is too thick, adjust by adding a small amount of warmed chicken stock.

10. Taste and adjust the seasonings with salt and fresh ground pepper.

11. Ladle into bowls and garnish with a tablespoon of sour cream, minced chives, and crumbled bacon.

Variations

Vichyssoise

Omit the bacon, substituting 2 tablespoons unsalted butter to sauté the leeks at step 5. At step 7 add the potatoes, 4 cups chicken stock, and 1 teaspoon salt, omitting the water and pepper. At step 9, substitute 1 cup of milk and 1 cup of half–and-half for the heavy cream. Chill the soup for at least 4 hours, and then add 1 cup of heavy cream. Stir to blend. Adjust the seasoning with salt and pepper. Garnish with minced chives.

Pantry/Refrigerator Check

Extra virgin olive oil

1 quart chicken stock

Black pepper

Shopping List

4 leeks

4 large russet potatoes

1/2 pound bacon

1/2 pint heavy cream

1 bunch fresh chives

4 oz. sour cream

Curried Carrot Soup

This easy to make soup frequently appears on dinner menus in better restaurants with good reason. The clean simple flavor is rich and sumptuous, the color deep and lush, yet the soup is actually quite light, perfect for a first course.

Ingredients

1 1/2 pounds carrots

1 medium onion

1 tablespoon extra virgin olive oil

2 tablespoons unsalted butter

4 cups chicken stock

1 cup water

1 tablespoon curry powder

1 teaspoon salt

1/2 cup heavy cream

1 teaspoon Hungarian paprika

tip

Fast track this recipe by using packaged peeled baby carrots.

Equipment

Large saucepan with lid, chef's knife, cutting board, measuring cup, measuring spoons, wooden stirring spoon, blender or food processor, large bowl

Methods

Peeling, chopping, sautéing, boiling, simmering (see Chapter 3)

Quantity

6 to 8 servings

Preparation

1. Peel the carrots, quarter lengthwise, and coarsely chop.
2. Peel and chop the onion.

Cooking Directions

3. Heat the olive oil and butter over medium heat in a large saucepan.
4. Add the onion and carrots, and then sauté for 10 minutes stirring occasionally to avoid sticking, until softened but not browned.

5. Add the chicken stock, water, curry powder, and salt, increase the heat to medium-high, and then bring to a boil.

6. When the soup boils, immediately reduce the heat to medium-low, partially cover, and simmer until the carrots are tender, about 15 minutes.

7. Transfer the soup in small batches to a blender or food processor, and then purée until smooth. As each batch is puréed, transfer to a large bowl to make room for next batch.

8. Return all puréed soup to the saucepan, stir in heavy cream, and then heat but do not allow to boil. If the soup is too thick, adjust by adding a small amount of warmed stock.

9. Taste and adjust seasonings with salt and fresh- ground pepper.

10. Ladle soup into bowls and garnish with a dash of paprika.

Variations

■ At step 5 omit the curry powder and add 2 tablespoons of minced fresh dill. Garnish with a sprinkling of minced fresh dill.

Pantry/Refrigerator Check

Extra virgin olive oil

1 stick unsalted butter

1 quart chicken stock

Curry powder

Salt

Hungarian paprika

Shopping List

1 1/2 pounds carrots

1 medium onion

1/2 pint heavy cream

New England Clam Chowder

Chowder is a Nor'eastern staple and the subject of an age-old East Coast feud. This version is the cream-based recipe and is Fast Tracked by using canned clams and bottled clam juice. The other version, *Manhattan Clam Chowder*, is a broth-based tomato soup. See variations to convert this recipe to *Manhattan Clam Chowder*. Both are great with oyster crackers.

Ingredients

3 slices bacon

1 large onion

2 ribs celery, with leaves

2 cloves garlic

4 small russet potatoes

3 tablespoons minced fresh flat leaf parsley

4 6 1/2 oz. cans chopped clams

2 tablespoons unsalted butter

1/4 cup all-purpose white flour

2 8 oz. bottles clam juice

1 teaspoon dried thyme

1 teaspoon fresh-ground black pepper

1 cup half-and-half

1 cup heavy cream or whipping cream

1 cup milk

1 teaspoon Tabasco sauce

Equipment

Large saucepan with lid, chef's knife, cutting board, vegetable peeler, measuring cup, measuring spoons, wooden stirring spoon, can opener

Methods

Dicing, mincing, sautéing, boiling, simmering (see Chapter 3)

Quantity

6 servings

Preparation

1. Cut bacon into 1-inch pieces.
2. Peel and dice the onion.
3. Wash the celery, trim ends, and chop ribs and leaves into a medium dice.
4. Peel and mince the garlic.
5. Peel and cut the potatoes into 1-inch dice.
6. Wash the parsley, dry, pull leaves from the stems, and chop.
7. Open the cans of clams and drain the juice into a small bowl to reserve.

Cooking Directions

8. In a large saucepan, sauté the bacon until it begins to brown over medium-low heat for about 3 minutes.
9. Add the butter, onions, and celery, and then sauté over medium-low heat for about 8 minutes until softened but not browned. Stir frequently.
10. Add the flour and cook while stirring constantly, for about 5 minutes.
11. Gradually add the reserved clam juice and bottled clam juice while whisking constantly.
12. Add the potatoes, thyme, and pepper, increase the heat to medium-high, and bring to a boil.
13. When the soup boils, immediately reduce the heat, partially cover, and then simmer for 15 minutes or until the potatoes are tender.
14. Add the clams, half-and-half, heavy cream, milk, and Tabasco sauce, and then simmer for 5 minutes to blend flavors, stirring frequently.
15. Season to taste with salt and pepper.

Variations

Manhattan Clam Chowder

At step 9 add 1/2 cup each (diced) of green bell pepper, carrots, and leeks. At step 12 add a 15 oz. can of whole crushed plum tomatoes. At step 14 omit the half-and-half, heavy cream, and milk, substituting 3 cups chicken stock along with the reserved clam juice.

Pantry/Refrigerator Check

Garlic

1 stick unsalted butter

All-purpose white flour

Dried thyme

Black pepper

1/2 pint milk

Tabasco sauce

Shopping List

1/2 pound bacon

1 large onion

1 head celery

4 small russet potatoes

1 bunch fresh flat leaf parsley

4 6 1/2 oz. cans chopped clams

2 8 oz. bottles clam juice

1/2 pint half-and-half

1/2 pint heavy cream or whipping cream

Beef Stew

Fast Track this recipe by purchasing precut stew meat and a bag of peeled baby carrots. Use leftovers to make a quick potpie by spooning leftover stew into individual casseroles and then covering with purchased pie crust or biscuits from a can or mix. Bake in a preheated 350°F oven until the tops are golden brown and the potpies are bubbly.

Ingredients

3 pounds stew meat

1 large onion

6 medium carrots

2 celery ribs

4 cloves garlic

8 red potatoes

4 tablespoons extra virgin olive oil, divided

Fresh-ground black pepper to taste

4 tablespoons all-purpose white flour

4 cups beef stock

2 tablespoons tomato paste

2 bay leaves

1/2 teaspoon salt

2 teaspoons dried thyme

2 tablespoons dried parsley

Equipment

Large, heavy-bottomed stockpot or Dutch oven, chef's knife, cutting board, vegetable peeler, measuring cup, measuring spoons, wooden stirring spoon

Methods

Chopping, cutting, mincing, sautéing, boiling, simmering (see Chapter 3)

Quantity

8 servings

Preparation

1. Cut the meat into 1-inch cubes (or use precut beef, if desired)
2. Peel and coarsely chop the onion.
3. Peel and cut the carrots into 2-inch pieces.
4. Wash and cut the celery into 1-inch pieces.
5. Peel and mince the garlic.
6. Wash the potatoes, cut in half lengthwise, and cut each piece in half.

Cooking Directions

7. Heat 2 tablespoons of the olive oil in a large heavy-bottomed pot over medium-high heat.
8. Add the beef in small batches, and do not crowd the pan. If the pan is too crowded, the meat will stew, not brown. Season the beef with pepper while browning. Remove the browned meat to a large bowl and continue until all the meat is browned.
9. Add the remaining 2 tablespoons of olive oil to the pan. Add the onion and celery, and then sauté for 8 minutes until softened and slightly browned. Stir occasionally to prevent sticking.
10. Add the garlic and sauté for 3 additional minutes.
11. Add all the browned beef, sprinkle with the flour, and sauté for about 5 minutes, stirring constantly.
12. Add the beef stock and deglaze the pan by stirring and scraping up the flavorful bits from the pan bottom.
13. Stir in the tomato paste, bay leaves, salt, thyme, and parsley, and then bring to a boil.
14. Cover the pot, reduce the heat and simmer for 1 1/2 hours, stirring occasionally.
15. Stir in the potatoes and carrots, then cover and cook for 30 minutes until the vegetables and meat are tender.
16. Remove the stew from the heat and serve while hot.

Variations

- Substitute parsnips or turnips for potatoes.
- At step 13 add canned tomatoes.
- At step 15 add fresh green peas.

■ For a more exotic stew, substitute other meats and spices. At step 8 substitute cubed pork for the beef. At step 13 omit the thyme and parsley and substitute 2 teaspoons cumin, 2 teaspoons dried oregano, and 1 teaspoon red chili pepper.

Pantry/Refrigerator Check

Garlic

Extra virgin olive oil

Black pepper

All-purpose white flour

Salt

1 quart beef stock

1 6 oz. can or resealable tube tomato paste

Bay leaves

Dried thyme

Dried parsley

Shopping List

3 pounds stew meat, preferably boneless beef chuck or beef shoulder (see *Best Cuts*, pages 176-177)

1 large onion

1 head celery

6 medium carrots

8 red potatoes

Indian Lamb Curry

Add a little spice to your life with this tasty lamb curry. It's even better the next day, so make sure you cook enough to have leftovers. Remember that good ingredients make good meals, so it is important to purchase a good quality curry powder. Serve over basmati rice and accompany with steamed asparagus.

Ingredients

1 large onion

1 Anaheim green chili pepper

1 tablespoon grated fresh ginger

3 pounds lamb shoulder or leg-of-lamb meat

2 tablespoons extra virgin olive oil

2 tablespoons unsalted butter

2 teaspoons curry powder

1/2 teaspoon ground cumin

1/2 teaspoon ground cardamom

1/4 teaspoon red chili powder

1 14 oz. can chopped tomatoes

1 cup beef stock

1 14 oz. can coconut milk

Equipment

Large saucepan, chef's knife, cutting board, measuring cup, measuring spoons, wooden stirring spoon

Methods

Chopping, slicing, grating, cutting, sautéing, boiling, simmering (see Chapter 3)

Quantity

6 servings

Preparation

1. Peel and coarsely chop the onion.
2. Wash the pepper, cut off the top, and halve lengthwise. Open each half, scrape out the seeds, and slice crosswise into 1/4-inch wide strips.
3. Peel the ginger with a paring knife and finely grate.
4. Cut the lamb into 1-inch thick chunks.

Cooking Directions

5. Heat the oil and melt the butter over medium-high heat in a large saucepan. Add the lamb and sauté for 5 minutes, stirring frequently.

6. Add the onion and Anaheim pepper, and then sauté, stirring occasionally for another 5 minutes.

7. Reduce the heat to medium and slowly add the spices, including ginger, to the lamb-onion mixture. If you add the spices too quickly, then they will dust up into your eyes. Sauté for a few minutes longer.

8. Stir in the tomatoes and sauté for 2 minutes.

9. Add the beef stock and coconut milk, stirring well to blend, and bring to a boil.

10. When the curry boils, immediately reduce the heat, cover the saucepan, and then simmer for 1 hour until the lamb is tender.

11. Taste and adjust the seasoning with salt.

Variations

- For hotter curry substitute a Serrano chili for the Anaheim chili in step 2.
- At step 4 substitute cubed chicken breast for lamb.
- At step 8 substitute 3 fresh-chopped tomatoes for canned.
- At step 11 add 1/4 cup mango chutney and 1/4 cup of orange marmalade along with diced boiled potatoes, cooked cauliflower, green peas, or lentils.

Pantry/Refrigerator Check

1 stick unsalted butter

Extra virgin olive oil

Curry powder

Ground cumin

Ground cardamom

Red chili powder

8 oz. beef stock

1 14 oz. can chopped tomatoes

1 14 oz. can coconut milk

Shopping List

1 large onion

1 Anaheim green chili pepper

3 pounds lamb shoulder or leg of lamb meat

1 small piece fresh ginger root

Southwestern Chili

Because this recipe takes advantage of canned beans, corn, chili, and tomatoes, it is only necessary to cook it for 30 minutes to allow the flavors to blend. It is ideal for a mid-week dinner! Add grated cheddar cheese, canned cut corn, or chopped green chilies to packaged cornbread batter and bake while the chili is cooking. Place bowls of grated cheddar or Jack cheese, sliced green onions, and sour cream on the table; and let everyone create their own masterpiece. Great served with warm flour tortillas.

Ingredients

1 large onion

3 cloves garlic

2 28 oz. cans whole plum tomatoes with juice

1 15 oz. can black beans

1 15 oz. can cut corn

1 4 oz. can chopped green chilies

2 tablespoons extra virgin olive oil

1 pound ground beef round

1 teaspoon ground cumin

1 teaspoon red chili powder

1 teaspoon ground coriander

1 teaspoon dried oregano

1 teaspoon dried cilantro

1/2 teaspoon salt

1/2 teaspoon fresh-ground black pepper

1 tablespoon tomato paste

Optional toppings:

1/2 cup sour cream

1/2 cup cheddar cheese

2 green onions

Equipment

Large stockpot or Dutch oven, chef's knife, cutting board, colander, large bowl, measuring cup, measuring spoons, wooden stirring spoon, strainer

Methods

Chopping, sautéing, stirring, boiling, simmering (see Chapter 3)

Quantity

10 servings

Preparation

1. Peel and coarsely chop the onion.
2. Peel and mince the garlic.
3. Pour the tomatoes with their juice into a large bowl and crush with clean hands.
4. Drain the beans in a colander, rinse, and then put into a large bowl. Set aside.
5. Drain the corn and green chilies, and then add to the large bowl of tomatoes.

Cooking Directions

6. Heat the olive oil over medium heat in a large saucepan.
7. Add the onions and sauté for about 5 minutes, until softened, stirring occasionally.
8. Add the garlic and sauté 2 more minutes.
9. Add the beef and sauté until browned, about 8 to 10 minutes, breaking up the beef with the back of a spoon so that no large pieces remain.
10. Add the tomatoes, corn, and green chilies, along with the juice, cumin, chili powder, coriander, oregano, cilantro, salt, and pepper, and then stir to mix.
11. Add the beans and stir to mix.
12. Add the tomato paste and stir to blend.
13. Cover the pot and simmer for 30 minutes.
14. While chili is cooking, grate the cheese, and clean and chop the green onions.
15. Taste and adjust the seasoning with salt and pepper.
16. Serve in bowls topped with any combination of sour cream, cheese, and green onions.

Variations

■ At step 9 substitute ground turkey or cubed pork for beef.

Pantry/Refrigerator Check

Garlic

Extra virgin olive oil

2 28 oz. cans whole plum tomatoes with juice

1 15 oz. can black beans

1 15 oz. can cut corn

1 4 oz. can chopped green chilies

1 6 oz. can or resealable tube tomato paste

Ground cumin

Red chili powder

Ground coriander

Dried oregano

Dried cilantro

Salt

Black pepper

Shopping List

1 large onion

1 pound ground beef round

Optional toppings:

4 oz. carton sour cream

2 oz. cheddar cheese

1 bunch green onions

8

SALADS AND DRESSINGS

When we think "salad" we generally think "greens," but with a few exceptions, a salad is actually any combination of chilled, balanced ingredients highlighted by a dressing. Because the flavors of the salad ingredients will not marry through cooking, the freshness of the ingredients is paramount because we will taste each individual flavor. When planning a menu keep this in mind and shop according to the season— you may even want to wait until you get to the produce section of your grocery store before deciding which salad ingredients you'll buy.

A few years ago, I attended a Christmas party where the hostess served Salad Caprese. This is a wonderfully simple salad of tomatoes, fresh buffalo mozzarella, and basil. The fresh ripe flavors of the few ingredients are essential to the success of the finished product. Unfortunately, it is hard to find ripe tomatoes in December; so the tomatoes in the salad were mealy and flavorless, resulting in a salad that was less than inviting. *Your salads will be only as good as the ingredients you use.*

Salad dressings complement the flavors of a salad and should not upstage the salad ingredients. When choosing a salad dressing for your salad, remember that it is an accessory and should be paired with the salad it will dress. Never use too much dressing and always dress your salad right before serving.

Every cook should have a good salad dressing recipe in their repertoire. Master the basic vinaigrette recipe in this book and then experiment, adding your favorite flavors to create your own signature salad dressing. Soon your friends will be begging you for the recipe!

A Big Salad

Think hors d'oeuvres tray meets bowl of lettuce and you have *A Big Salad*. This basic recipe is a good jumping off point for many variations, all suited to your tastes. You may delete, substitute, or continue adding foods until you can't fit anything else in the bowl. Thin strips of meat and cheese, firm bites of beans, succulent cherry tomatoes, tangy artichoke hearts, lush grates of zucchini, and crunchy nuts, all catch in the nooks and crannies of the bigger pieces of lettuce and create a salad full of flavors and textures. Bring it all together with a favorite dressing and you have a true feast.

Ingredients

note

Instead of deli meat, you could use 2 oz. baked tofu.

1 cup romaine lettuce

1 cup baby spring mix

5 cherry tomatoes

1/8 small cucumber

2 oz. Jack or provolone cheese

2 oz. one or more sliced deli meats: turkey, ham, roast beef, chicken breast

2 oz. thinly sliced salami

1/4 cup garbanzo beans

2 artichoke hearts

1/2 small zucchini

5 pitted black or kalamata olives

1/4 cup chopped walnuts

2 tablespoons your favorite dressing

Equipment

Medium bowl, chef's knife, cutting board, grater, measuring cup

Methods

Slicing, chopping, grating (see Chapter 3, "Glossary of Terms and Techniques, Conversions and Equivalents")

Quantity

2 servings

Preparation

1. Wash the lettuce, and pat dry.
2. Wash the tomatoes.
3. Wash the cucumber, peel if desired, and slice into 1/4-inch thick slices.
4. Cut the cheese into thin strips.
5. Cut the meats and salami into thin strips.
6. Drain and rinse the garbanzo beans.
7. Drain and chop the artichoke hearts.
8. Wash, dry, and grate the zucchini using the large holes of the grater.
9. Chop the walnuts.

tip

If you eat a lot of salads, purchase a $12 salad spinner.

Assembly Directions

10. Place all of the ingredients in a medium bowl, pour on the dressing and toss to coat evenly.

Variations

Cobb Salad

Shredded romaine lettuce, tossed with *Lemon-Mustard Vinaigrette* (page 167), topped with cubed roasted turkey, diced avocados, sliced celery, green onions, crumbled blue cheese, and crumbled crisp bacon.

Caesar Salad

Torn or cut romaine lettuce leaves, tossed with bottled Caesar salad dressing, topped with garlic croutons and shaved or grated Parmesan cheese.

Salad Niçoise

Layered red leaf lettuce, sliced *Seared Lemon-Tarragon Tuna* (page 224), steamed haricot verts or small green beans, cooked tiny red potato halves, ripe cherry or pear tomatoes, and Nicoise olives, drizzled with a *Red Wine Vinaigrette* (page 165).

Warm Spinach Salad

Spinach leaves tossed in a *Honey-Mustard Vinaigrette* (page 166) with an added touch of warm bacon drippings, topped with sliced hard-cooked eggs, thinly sliced red onion, and crumbled crisp bacon.

Pantry/Refrigerator Check

1 15 oz. can garbanzo beans

1 14 1/2 oz. can artichoke hearts in water or oil

1 can pitted black olives or kalamata olives

Shopping List

1 head romaine lettuce

1 bag packaged spring mix

5 cherry tomatoes

1 small cucumber

1 small zucchini

2 oz. Jack or provolone cheese

2 oz. cooked deli meat

2 oz. thinly sliced salami

2 oz. walnuts

1 bottle favorite dressing

Create Your Own Classic Big Salad

Choose from the following selections and create your own special salad:

- Lettuce selection: arugula, curly endive, bibb lettuce, red leaf, green leaf, escarole, frisee, radicchio, spinach, romaine, butter lettuce, iceberg lettuce, or a spring mix of greens

- Meats, fish, or poultry: sliced fried chicken breasts, grilled fish or steak, shrimp, chunked canned tuna, cold poached salmon, fresh crab, sliced roasted pork, chopped turkey breast, crumbled cooked bacon or prosciutto, sliced deli meats

- Rich cheeses: Asiago, Romano, herbed or smoked cheddar, Monterey Jack, Gorgonzola or blue cheese, goat's cheese, feta, Gruyère, Jarlsberg

- Savory additives: cannellini (white kidney beans), red kidney beans, jarred asparagus spears, roasted red peppers, canned green beans, marinated mushrooms, cooked potatoes, rice ·

- Sweet or fresh bits: apples, pears, oranges, grapefruit, mango, nectarines, dried cranberries, apricots

- Crunchy additions: toasted pumpkin seeds, pine nuts, hazelnuts, almonds, celery, jicama, raw broccoli, cauliflower, croutons

Greek Salad

In Greece you will find this on every summertime menu. With the addition of lettuce, it is called a green salad. When it is too hot to cook, serve this fresh salad along with *Couscous* (page 238) and grilled lamb chops.

Ingredients

1 medium cucumber

2 ripe tomatoes

1 small red onion

1 green bell pepper

2 tablespoons fresh oregano

1 tablespoon extra virgin olive oil

1 tablespoon red wine vinegar

Salt to taste

Fresh-ground black pepper

4 oz. feta cheese

10 kalamata olives

Equipment

Large serving bowl or platter, chef's knife, cutting board, measuring spoon

Methods

Slicing, coring, cutting, mincing (see Chapter 3)

Quantity

2 servings

Preparation

1. Wash the cucumber, trim ends, peel if desired, and slice into 1/4-inch thick slices.
2. Wash the tomatoes, cut in half, remove the cores, and cut into quarters.
3. Peel the onion, cut in half, and slice into 1/4-inch thick slices.
4. Wash the green pepper, cut in half, and remove the stem and seeds. With the inside up, cut into 1/4-inch wide slices.
5. Wash the oregano and pat dry. Pull the leaves from the stem and mince.

Assembly Directions

6. Arrange the vegetables on a platter or in a serving bowl.
7. Sprinkle the vegetables with vinegar and oil.
8. Season the vegetables with salt and pepper.
9. Crumble the feta over the salad and add the olives.
10. Sprinkle with the chopped oregano.

Variations

■ Add washed and torn red leaf, baby romaine, or butter lettuce leaves.

Pantry/Refrigerator Check

1 14 oz. can kalamata olives

Extra virgin olive oil

Red wine vinegar

Salt

Black pepper

Shopping List

1 medium cucumber

2 ripe tomatoes

1 small red onion

1 green bell pepper

1 bunch or package fresh oregano

4 oz. feta cheese

Grilled Tequila Chicken Salad

When making *Grilled Tequila-Lime Chicken* (page 203), double the recipe and freeze the extra chicken breasts for later use in this entrée salad.

Ingredients

4 *Grilled Tequila-Lime Chicken breasts* (page 203)

1/4 cup toasted pine nuts

8 cups romaine lettuce (about 2 heads)

1/2 red onion

1 cup ripe cherry tomatoes

2 ripe avocados

1/2 cup *Creamy Cilantro Dressing* (page 173)

tip

Fast Track by purchasing roasted chicken or marinated chicken breasts from the butcher to broil in the oven. Use packaged bagged lettuce and bottled dressing.

Equipment

Skillet, chef's knife, cutting board, measuring cup

Methods

Toasting nuts, slicing, pitting and peeling avocado (see Chapter 3)

Quantity

4 servings

Preparation

1. Cut each chilled chicken breast, on the bias, into 6 or 8 pieces.
2. Toast the pine nuts in the skillet over medium heat. Slide onto a plate to cool.
3. Wash the lettuce, dry, and tear or cut into bite-sized pieces.
4. Peel the onion, cut into half lengthwise, and thinly slice. Wrap the remaining half onion and store in the refrigerator for future use.
5. Wash and dry the tomatoes.
6. Cut each avocado in half, remove the seed, peel, and slice each into 8 slices.

Assembly Directions

7. Divide the lettuce equally between 4 dinner plates.

8. Arrange 6 to 8 chicken slices on top of the lettuce on each plate, fanning out from the center of the plate like the spokes on a wheel.

9. Place the avocado slices in between the chicken slices.

10. Divide the cherry tomatoes between the plates.

11. Drizzle 2 tablespoons of dressing over each salad and top with toasted pine nuts.

Variations

■ At step 3 use an assortment of lettuces or a spring mix.

■ At step 11 add 2 tablespoons of crumbled Mexican queso blanco (white cheese), and substitute *Red Chili Vinaigrette* (page 167) for *Creamy Cilantro Dressing* (page 173). Top the salad with toasted tortilla strips.

Pantry/Refrigerator Check

4 *Grilled Tequila-Lime Chicken breasts*

Creamy Cilantro Dressing

2 oz. pine nuts

Shopping List

2 heads romaine lettuce

1 small red onion

2 ripe avocados

1 small basket cherry tomatoes

Asian Slaw Salad

A crisp salad with a sweet-tart dressing, this is easy to make. You may also prepare it and store it covered tightly in the refrigerator for up to 3 days. Top the salad with packaged fried wonton strips for extra crunch.

Ingredients

1 medium head green cabbage

2 green onions

2 red bell peppers

1/2 cup slivered almonds

1/2 cup peanut oil

2 tablespoon sesame oil

3 tablespoons rice wine vinegar

2 tablespoons lime juice

1/4 cup white sugar

1 teaspoon salt

1 teaspoon fresh-ground black pepper

tip

Fast track by using purchased bagged sliced cabbage. Serve with *Grilled Cilantro-Lime Swordfish* (page 226) and crusty French bread.

Equipment

Skillet, paring knife, chef's knife, cutting board, large bowl, whisk, measuring cup, measuring spoons, small bowl

Methods

Chopping, slicing, toasting nuts (see Chapter 3)

Quantity

6 to 8 servings

Preparation

1. Remove the tough outer leaves of the cabbage. Cut the cabbage in half through the core. With a paring knife, cut out the hard, V-shaped core. With the cut-side down, start at one end and thinly slice the cabbage. Make a few cuts across the slices to create shorter pieces.

2. Wash the green onion, trim the root and tough upper greens, and thinly slice.

3. Wash the red pepper, cut in half, remove the stem and seeds, and slice.

4. Toast the almonds in the skillet over medium heat. Slide onto a plate to cool.

Assembly Directions

5. Combine the oils, vinegar, lime juice, and sugar in a small bowl. Whisk vigorously to blend and incorporate the sugar into the dressing.

6. Taste and adjust the seasoning with salt and pepper.

7. Mix the sliced cabbage, onions, red pepper, and almonds in a large bowl.

8. Pour the dressing over the vegetable mixture and toss to thoroughly coat.

9. For best flavor, refrigerate for 1 to 2 hours and toss before serving.

Variations

■ At step 1 add 1 cup grated carrots or substitute Napa cabbage for the green cabbage, green bell pepper for red bell pepper, and toasted sesame seeds for slivered almonds.

Pantry/Refrigerator Check

Peanut oil

Sesame oil

Rice wine vinegar

White sugar

Salt

Black pepper

Shopping List

1 medium head green cabbage

1 bunch green onions

2 red bell peppers

1 lime

4 oz. toasted slivered almonds

Mexican Bean and Corn Salad

This colorful salad makes a great addition to a Mexican-themed barbeque or patio party. The use of canned beans, corn, and chilies makes your prep time fast. You can alter the heat factor by using more or less of the Serrano chili. If Serrano chilies are unavailable, substitute fresh jalapeños or use canned chipotle chilies for a smoky flavor.

Ingredients

3 cloves garlic

1 Serrano chili

4 green onions

1/4 cup chopped fresh cilantro

6 oz. jalapeno Jack cheese

2 15 oz. cans black beans

1 15 oz. can red kidney beans

1 15 oz. can cut corn

3 tablespoons red wine vinegar

4 tablespoons extra virgin olive oil

2 teaspoons ground cumin

1 teaspoon dried oregano

1/2 teaspoon red chili powder

1 teaspoon salt

1 teaspoon fresh-ground black pepper

2 tablespoons fresh lime juice

1 4 oz. can chopped green chilies

Equipment

Small bowl, large bowl, chef's knife, cutting board, can opener, colander, whisk, wooden stirring spoon

Methods

Mincing, slicing, chopping (see Chapter 3)

Quantity

6 servings

Preparation

1. Peel and mince the garlic.
2. Wash the Serrano chili, cut in half lengthwise, remove the stem and seeds, and mince.
3. Wash the green onions, trim the root end and tough upper greens, and slice.
4. Wash the cilantro and pat dry. Pull the leaves from the stems, and coarsely chop.
5. Cut the Jack cheese into 1/2-inch slices.
6. Drain the canned beans and corn in a colander. Rinse and drain well.

caution

Chili oil is hot and transfers easily to the skin. Do not touch your eyes with your fingers after cutting the chili.

Assembly Directions

7. In a small bowl, whisk together the vinegar, olive oil, cumin, oregano, red chili powder, salt, pepper, garlic, Serrano chili, and lime juice.
8. In a large bowl, combine the beans, corn, green chilies, green onions, and cilantro.
9. Add the dressing and gently mix to combine.
10. Cover and refrigerate for 1 hour.
11. Remove from the refrigerator and bring the salad to room temperature.
12. Add the cheese and mix to combine and serve.

Variations

■ Add 1 chopped red, yellow, or green bell pepper, 12 pitted and chopped black olives, 1 sliced avocado, or 20 cherry tomatoes.

Pantry/Refrigerator Check

Garlic

Red wine vinegar

Extra virgin olive oil

Ground cumin

Dried oregano

Red chili powder

Salt

Black pepper

Shopping List

1 Serrano chili

1 lime

1 bunch green onions

1 bunch fresh cilantro

6 oz. jalapeno Jack cheese

2 15 oz. cans black beans

1 15 oz. can red kidney beans

1 15 oz. can cut corn

1 4 oz. can chopped green chilies

Thai Noodle Salad

This is a rich, satisfying salad with a creamy, tangy dressing. This salad works well served as a main entrée or a side dish. Take some to work for a special lunch-time treat. Always a hit at dinner parties, picnics, and barbeques, you will be asked for the recipe by everyone who tastes it. Serve immediately or store in the refrigerator covered tightly for up to 3 days.

Ingredients

3 garlic cloves

2 green onions

1/4 cup fresh cilantro

1/4 cup creamy peanut butter

1/4 cup soy sauce

1/4 cup rice wine vinegar

1/4 cup peanut oil

2 tablespoons sesame oil

1 teaspoon Asian hot chili paste

3 tablespoons white sugar

2 boneless, skinless chicken breasts

12 oz. dried linguine

Equipment

Large pot with lid, medium pot with lid, colander, large serving bowl, chef's knife, cutting board, wire whisk, wooden stirring spoon

Methods

Mincing, slicing, chopping, poaching (see Chapter 3)

Quantity

6 side servings

Preparation

1. Peel and mince the garlic.
2. Wash the green onions, trim the root end and tough upper greens, and slice.
3. Wash the cilantro and pat dry. Pull the leaves from the stems and coarsely chop.

Cooking Directions

4. Whisk together the peanut butter, soy sauce, vinegar, oils, chili paste, sugar, and garlic in a medium bowl until well combined. Set aside.

5. Place the chicken breasts in a medium pot, cover the chicken with water, and bring to a simmer. Cover the pot and poach the chicken for about 20 minutes, or until firm and white. To test for doneness, cut into the thickest part of the meat. If any pink remains, return the chicken to the pot and poach for an additional 3 to 5 minutes and test again.

6. Transfer the cooked chicken to a plate to cool.

7. While the chicken is poaching, place a large pot of water, covered, over high heat and bring to a boil.

8. Add the pasta to the boiling water and stir to submerge completely.

9. Cook the pasta, stirring occasionally, until tender but still firm, about 10 minutes. Check a noodle for doneness, and if it is still too firm, continue cooking and checking for a few more minutes. (See *How to Cook Pasta* page 237.)

10. Drain the pasta through a colander over the sink. Rinse the pasta under cold running water to cool the pasta and stop the cooking process.

11. Gently jiggle the colander to shake off excess water and transfer the pasta to a large bowl.

12. Cut or shred the cooled chicken into bite-sized pieces and add to the bowl with pasta.

13. Whisk the soy-peanut butter mixture once or twice to recombine if it has separated.

14. Pour the dressing over the pasta and chicken and toss to coat.

15. Add the green onions and cilantro and toss again.

caution

Overcooked chicken will become tough; time the chicken carefully.

Variations

- Add chopped peanuts.
- At step 5 substitute cooked shrimp or baked tofu for the chicken.
- At step 9 substitute rice noodles instead of linguine. Cook the rice noodles according to the package instructions.

Pantry/Refrigerator Check

Garlic

12 oz. dried linguine

Creamy peanut butter

Soy sauce

Rice wine vinegar

Peanut oil

Sesame oil

Asian hot chili paste

White sugar

Shopping List

1 bunch green onions

1 bunch cilantro

2 boneless, skinless chicken breasts

Tabbouleh

A traditional Middle Eastern dish, this salad is made with bulgur—whole-wheat kernels that are cooked, dried, and cracked. Bulgur can be found in the bulk section of the grocery store. The kernels need only to be reconstituted with boiling water, so this recipe requires no cooking. This colorful, healthy salad makes a nice lunch presentation when served on a large lettuce leaf. Great chilled or at room temperature.

Ingredients

1 cup bulgur (cracked wheat)

1 cup boiling water

3 large garlic cloves

2 ripe tomatoes

3 green onions

1/2 cup minced fresh parsley

2 tablespoons minced fresh mint

1/4 cup fresh lemon juice from 2 lemons

1/3 cup extra virgin olive oil

Salt

Fresh-ground black pepper to taste

tip

Fast Track this already quick, easy recipe by using dried parsley and mint.

Equipment

Large bowl, chef's knife, cutting board, strainer, measuring cup, measuring spoons, whisk, wooden stirring spoon

Methods

Mincing, chopping, slicing, whisking, mixing (see Chapter 3)

Quantity

6 servings

Preparation

1. Place the bulgur in a large bowl. Stir in 1 cup of boiling water and let sit until all the water is absorbed and the bulgur is tender, about 30 minutes.

2. Peel and mince the garlic.

3. Wash, core, and coarsely chop the tomatoes.

4. Wash the green onions, trim the root end and tough upper greens, and slice.

5. Wash the parsley and pat dry. Pull the leaves from the stems, and mince.

6. Wash the mint and pat dry. Pull the leaves from the stems, and mince.

Assembly Directions

7. Squeeze the lemon through a strainer into a small bowl, add the garlic and oil, and whisk to blend.

8. Add the tomatoes, green onions, parsley, and mint to the bulgur. Mix to combine.

9. Pour the oil mixture over the bulgur and stir gently to blend.

10. Taste and adjust the seasoning with salt and pepper.

11. Cover the bowl tightly with plastic wrap and refrigerate for at least 1 hour to blend the flavors.

Variations

■ Add 1/2 cup finely chopped cucumber.

Pantry/Refrigerator Check

Garlic

Extra virgin olive oil

Salt

Black pepper

Shopping List

8 oz. bulgur (sometimes labeled cracked wheat)

2 ripe tomatoes

1 bunch green onions

1 bunch fresh parsley

1 bunch or package fresh mint

2 lemons

Potato Salad

Many cooks have a strong opinion as to what makes a great potato salad. Recipes vary regionally and are enhanced or ruined, depending upon your opinion, by any number of additives from a very long list. Think of this basic recipe as a starting point. A list of suggested items follows, so add or delete to your liking and create your own signature dish. Better the next day, potato salad will keep, tightly covered, in the refrigerator for 3 to 4 days.

Ingredients

2 1/2 pounds russet potatoes (about 8 smallish potatoes)

3 hard boiled eggs (page 57)

2 ribs celery with leaves

1 small red onion

3/4 cup chopped fresh parsley

1/4 cup red wine vinegar

1/2 teaspoon salt

1/2 teaspoon fresh-ground black pepper

3/4 cup mayonnaise

3 tablespoons dijon mustard

1/4 teaspoon celery seed

caution

As potato salad contains mayonnaise and eggs, it is not safe to leave the salad out. After everyone is served, cover and place the salad in an ice chest or back in the refrigerator.

Equipment

Large saucepan with lid, chef's knife, cutting board, measuring cup, grater, wooden stirring spoon

Methods

Boiling, slow boil, chopping, dicing, mincing, peeling, slicing, grating, mixing (see Chapter 3)

Quantity

6 to 8 servings

Cooking/Preparation Directions

1. Place the potatoes in a large pot and cover with water. Set over high heat and bring to a boil.

2. Reduce the heat to medium-high and continue cooking the potatoes at a slow boil for about 20 minutes. Potatoes are done when still firm but allow a fork to pierce to the center with only slight resistance.

3. While the potatoes are boiling, peel the hard-boiled eggs. (See *How to Peel Hard Boiled Eggs* page 56.)

4. Wash the celery, trim ends, and finely chop, including leaves.

5. Peel and finely dice the onion.

6. Wash the parsley and pat dry. Pull the leaves from the stems, and mince.

7. Remove the potatoes from the heat, drain, and set aside until the potatoes are cool enough to handle, about 30 minutes.

8. Peel the cooled potatoes and cut into 1/2-inch thick slices.

9. Layer the potatoes in a large serving bowl, sprinkling with vinegar and salt and pepper between the layers.

10. Allow the potatoes to set for 5 minutes.

11. On the large-holed side of a grater, not the slicing side, grate the eggs and add to the potatoes.

12. Add the celery, onion, parsley, mayonnaise, mustard, and celery seed and mix gently to combine. Some potato slices will crumble, which is fine because the crumbled potatoes will add texture.

13. Adjust the seasoning with salt and pepper.

Variations

- Add more or less mayonnaise.
- Omit the eggs.
- Add 1/4 cup of any of the following: sliced green olives, pickle relish, fresh radishes, roasted garlic, chopped sundried tomatoes packed in olive oil, 1 tablespoon Hungarian paprika, ground cumin, curry powder, red chili powder. You can also add 3 tablespoons of minced fresh tarragon or other fresh herbs.

Pantry/Refrigerator Check

Eggs

Red wine vinegar

Mayonnaise

Dijon mustard

Salt

Black pepper

Celery seed

Shopping List

1 head of celery

1 small red onion

1 bunch fresh parsley

2 1/2 pounds russet potatoes, about 8 smallish potatoes

Quick Pasta Primavera Salad

Sometimes a pasta salad stored in the refrigerator dries slightly. To compensate, add a small amount of dressing just prior to serving.

Ingredients

8 oz. dried farfalle or shaped pasta

1 medium zucchini

1 medium red bell pepper

6 green onions

3 tablespoons fresh basil

1/2 cup pine nuts

1 6 oz. can pitted black olives

1 cup grated Parmesan or Romano cheese

1 cup *Balsamic Vinaigrette* (page 166)

tip

Fast Track by purchasing fresh pasta, which takes only minutes to cook. Save time by also purchasing bagged sliced vegetables, and a good quality bottled Italian or Balsamic dressing.

Equipment

Skillet, large pot with lid, large bowl, chef's knife, cutting board, measuring cup, grater, colander, wooden stirring spoon, timer

Methods

Boiling, slow boil, slicing, chiffonade, chopping, toasting nuts, mixing (see Chapter 3)

Quantity

10 servings

Cooking/Preparation directions

1. Place a large pot of water, covered, over high heat and bring to a boil.

2. Add the pasta to the boiling water and submerge the pasta completely.

3. Set the timer and cook pasta at a slow boil, according to package directions, stirring occasionally.

4. While the pasta is cooking, wash the zucchini, halve lengthwise, and slice into 1/4 inch-thick slices.

5. Wash the red pepper, halve lengthwise, remove the stem, core, and seed, and slice into 1/4-inch thick strips.

6. Wash the green onions, trim the root and tough upper greens, and slice.

7. Wash the basil and pat dry. Pull the leaves from the stems. Stack the leaves, roll into a tube and chiffonade (see Chapter 3).

8. Heat the skillet over medium heat and toast the pine nuts for 2 to 3 minutes until browned. Slide the nuts on to a plate to cool.

9. Drain the liquid from the canned olives.

10. Grate the cheese on the small holes of a box grater.

11. Check the pasta for doneness just before the timer rings. If still too firm, continue cooking and checking for a few more minutes.

12. Drain the pasta through a colander over the sink. Rinse the pasta under cold water to cool it and stop the cooking process.

13. Gently jiggle the colander to shake off excess water and transfer the pasta to a large bowl.

14. Add all the ingredients and stir to combine. Add more dressing if the salad is too dry.

Variations

■ Use yellow crookneck squash, halved cherry tomatoes, baby corn, blanched snow peas, asparagus, or broccoli.

Shopping List

1 medium zucchini

1 medium red bell pepper

1 bunch green onions

1 bunch fresh basil

4 oz. pine nuts

8 oz. dried farfalle or shaped pasta (see *About Pastas* page 237)

1 6 oz. can pitted black olives

1 bottle Italian or Balsamic salad dressing (unless making your own)

3 oz. Parmesan or Romano cheese

Oscar's Waldorf Salad

In 1893, Oscar Tschirky, a maître d' at the Waldorf Hotel in New York City invented this famous salad of celery, apples, and mayonnaise, and named it after the hotel. The walnuts were added to the recipe some time later. Start with Oscar's version, then throw caution to the wind—invent your own and name it yourself!

Ingredients

1/2 cup walnuts

1 cup diced celery

1 cup diced apple

3/4 cup mayonnaise

Equipment

Medium bowl, chef's knife, cutting board, measuring cup

Methods

Chopping, dicing, mixing (see Chapter 3)

Quantity

4 servings

tip

Once peeled or cut, apples will turn brown soon after being exposed to air. Mixing with the mayonnaise coats the apple and prevents browning. If for some reason, you cut an apple and are not able to use it immediately, lemon juice will prevent it from browning.

Preparation

1. Coarsely chop the walnuts.
2. Wash the celery, trim the ends, cut the ribs lengthwise, and dice into 1/2-inch thick pieces.
3. Wash the apple, cut in half and core. Dice into 1/2-inch thick pieces.

Assembly Directions

4. Combine the walnuts, celery, and apple with the mayonnaise in a medium bowl, mixing thoroughly.
5. Serve immediately or cover tightly and refrigerate. This does not keep well, so use as soon as possible.

Variations

- Substitute Asian pears for apples, pecans for walnuts, and add a dash of nutmeg or apple brandy.

Pantry/Refrigerator Check

Mayonnaise

Shopping List

1 head celery (need about 2 ribs)

1 medium apple

4 oz. walnuts

Fresh Fruit Salad with Prosciutto

Quality is much more important than quantity, so choose a few perfectly ripe, fresh fruits from your grocery produce section. If you cannot find ripe fresh fruit, don't bother making this salad. Fresh fruit is greatly enhanced by a splash of aged balsamic vinegar and served with thinly sliced prosciutto.

Ingredients

1 orange

1 pear

4 strawberries

1/4 honeydew melon

1/4 cantaloupe

4 thin slices prosciutto

1 tablespoon aged balsamic vinegar

Equipment

Medium platter, chef's knife, paring knife, tablespoon

Methods

Cutting, coring, slicing (see Chapter 3)

Quantity

2 servings

Preparation

1. Peel the orange, separate sections, and cut into chunks. Remove any visible seeds.

2. Wash the pear and cut in half lengthwise; remove the core and cut each half into 4 to 6 slices.

3. Wash the strawberries, cut in half, and remove the stems.

4. Cut the rind away from the melon and cantaloupe. Discard the rind and cut the melon and cantaloupe into chunks.

Assembly Directions

5. Arrange fruit and prosciutto on 2 plates or a serving platter and drizzle with balsamic vinegar.

Variations

- Substitute any combination of ripe fruit: apples, peaches, plums, kiwi, grapes, cherries, grapefruit, blueberries, watermelon, or banana.
- Drizzle with Cointreau, or flavored yogurt thinned with fruit juice.

Pantry/Refrigerator Check

Balsamic vinegar

Shopping List

4 or 5 fresh fruits

3 oz. prosciutto

Basic Dressings

Whether a squeeze of fresh lemon with a drizzle of olive oil or a complex mixture of exotic vinegars, imported oils, spices, nuts, herbs, flavoring, and minced aromatics, some thought should go into matching a dressing with the foods it will top. A dressing should not overpower, but rather enhance and complement the flavors of the dish. Splashed on salads of all kinds, a dressing is also a delightful accompaniment to steamed vegetables, grain dishes, grilled meats, chicken, and fish.

Dressings are either vinegar-based or cream-based with many variations of both. The fundamental ratios remain the same and once familiar with the basic recipes, you can create just the right dressing for any salad, entrée, or dessert. The following recipes are the basics and a few variations.

Basic Oil and Vinegar Dressing

The base formula for a classic vinaigrette is 1 part vinegar to 3 parts oil. If using this to dress something heavier than a salad, such as potatoes or chilled vegetables, the traditional ratio is 1 part vinegar to 4 parts oil. To this formula you can add an emulsifier, such as mustard and seasoning, to taste.

Ingredients

1 tablespoon vinegar

3 tablespoons extra virgin olive oil

1/8 teaspoon salt

Dash fresh-ground black pepper

Equipment

Jar with a tightly fitting lid, measuring spoons

Method

Emulsifying (see Chapter 3)

Quantity

1/4 cup

Assembly Directions

1. Place all ingredients in a jar, seal tightly with the lid, and shake vigorously until completely blended.

2. If you don't have a jar, vigorously whisk ingredients in a small, deep bowl until blended.

Variations

Red Wine Vinaigrette

Substitute red wine vinegar.

Add:

1 clove garlic, peeled and smashed

1/2 teaspoon minced fresh basil, parsley, or chives

Honey-Mustard Vinaigrette

Substitute white wine or champagne vinegar.

Add:

1 teaspoon dijon mustard

1 teaspoon fresh lemon juice

1/4 teaspoon minced fresh tarragon

1 teaspoon honey

Balsamic Vinaigrette

Substitute balsamic vinegar.

Add:

1 teaspoon dijon mustard

1 teaspoon minced fresh basil, parsley, or chives

Variation: add 1 tablespoon crumbled Gorgonzola cheese

Orange-Pecan Vinaigrette

Substitute white wine or champagne vinegar.

Add:

1 tablespoon fresh orange juice

1 tablespoon chopped pecans, pistachios, or almonds

1 teaspoon minced fresh chives or parsley

Variations: add 1 teaspoon honey

Sherry-Lemon Vinaigrette

Substitute sherry vinegar.

Add:

1 teaspoon fresh lemon juice

1/2 teaspoon minced shallots

1/4 teaspoon minced fresh chervil

Red Chili Vinaigrette

Substitute white wine or champagne vinegar.

Add:

1 teaspoon fresh lime juice

1/2 clove garlic, peeled and smashed

1/8 teaspoon red chili powder

1/8 teaspoon ground cumin

1/4 teaspoon minced fresh cilantro

Sesame-Soy Vinaigrette

Substitute rice wine vinegar.

Add:

1 teaspoon soy sauce

1 1/2 teaspoon sesame oil

1/4 teaspoon grated fresh ginger

1/4 teaspoon white sugar

1/2 teaspoon minced fresh cilantro

Lemon-Mustard Vinaigrette

Substitute cider vinegar.

Add:

1 teaspoon fresh lemon juice

1 teaspoon dijon mustard

1/2 teaspoon minced fresh parsley

Creamy Vinaigrette

Substitute white wine or champagne vinegar.

Replace:

1 tablespoon of olive oil with 1 tablespoon sour cream

Creamy Herbed-Garlic Vinaigrette

Substitute white wine vinegar.

Replace:

1 tablespoon olive oil with 1 tablespoon sour cream

Add:

1 clove garlic, peeled and smashed

1 teaspoon minced fresh dill, chives, parsley, basil, marjoram, or a mixture

Pantry/Refrigerator Check

Red wine vinegar

Extra virgin olive oil

Salt

Black pepper

Creamy Ranch Dressing

There are many versions of this dressing, but this is the basic formula. Add or delete ingredients as your taste guides you. This dressing is great on a wedge of iceberg lettuce with quartered ripe tomatoes and seasoned with salt and fresh-ground black pepper.

Ingredients

2 tablespoons minced fresh parsley

1 teaspoon minced fresh chives

1 medium shallot

1/4 cup mayonnaise

1/3 cup sour cream

1/3 cup buttermilk

1 teaspoon garlic powder

1/4 teaspoon onion powder

1/4 teaspoon dry mustard

1/2 teaspoon salt

1/4 teaspoon fresh-ground black pepper

Equipment

Medium bowl, chef's knife, cutting board, measuring cup, measuring spoons, whisk

Methods

Mincing, whisking (see Chapter 3)

Quantity

About 1 cup

Preparation

1. Wash the parsley, pat dry. Pull leaves from stems, and mince.

2. Wash and mince the chives.

3. Peel and mince the shallot.

Assembly Directions

4. In a medium bowl, whisk together all ingredients. If a thinner dressing is desired, add a little more buttermilk.

Variations

■ For added flavor, include 1 teaspoon Worcestershire sauce, lemon juice, or red wine vinegar.

Pantry/Refrigerator Check

Mayonnaise

Garlic powder

Onion powder

Dry mustard

Salt

Black pepper

Shopping List

1 bunch fresh parsley

1 bunch fresh chives

1 medium shallot

1 4 oz. container sour cream

1/2 pint buttermilk

Russian Dressing

Essential on a *Reuben Sandwich* (page 93) this dressing adds a hearty flavor to salads or sandwiches. Store in a tightly covered glass or plastic container in the refrigerator for 1 week.

Ingredients

1 clove garlic

1/2 cup mayonnaise

2 tablespoons chili sauce

1 teaspoon prepared horseradish

1/2 teaspoon Worcestershire sauce

1/2 teaspoon dried onion flakes

Equipment

Medium bowl, chef's knife, cutting board, measuring cup, measuring spoons, wire whisk

Methods

Mincing, whisking (see Chapter 3)

Quantity

3/4 cup

Preparation

1. Peel and mince the garlic.

Assembly Directions

2. Place all the ingredients in a bowl and whisk until well combined.

Variations

- Use 2 teaspoons of minced fresh onion and add 1 teaspoon of minced fresh parsley.

Pantry/Refrigerator Check

Garlic

Mayonnaise

Chili sauce

Prepared horseradish

Worcestershire sauce

Dried onion flakes

Creamy Cilantro Dressing

A great dressing or topping for salad made with chili-spiced grilled meats. Add chopped avocado and blend by hand for a thicker dressing to use as a dip for tortilla chips or crudités.

Ingredients

3 tablespoons chopped fresh cilantro

1/4 cup mayonnaise

1/4 cup sour cream

2 tablespoons fresh lime juice from 1 lime

2 tablespoons cojita cheese (you may substitute queso blanco)

1/4 teaspoon ground cumin

1/4 teaspoon red chili powder

Equipment

Blender or food processor, chef's knife, cutting board, measuring cup, measuring spoons

Methods

Chopping, blending (see Chapter 3)

Quantity

About 3/4 cup

Preparation

1. Wash the cilantro and pat dry. Pull the leaves from the stems, and chop (or estimate 2 tablespoons because the blender will chop).

Assembly Directions

2. Combine all ingredients in a blender or food processor and process until blended.

Variations

■ Add 1 teaspoon of minced fresh pasilla chili.

Pantry/Refrigerator Check

Mayonnaise

Ground cumin

Red chili powder

Shopping List

1 bunch fresh cilantro

1 4 oz. container sour cream

1 lime

1 oz. cojita cheese (or substitute queso blanco)

9

Meat—Beef, Pork, and Lamb

A walk down the meat aisle at the grocery store can be very confusing. Names of cuts vary from region to region and sometimes the only way to determine if a cut of meat is superior is by the price. There are really just two types of meat: tender cuts and tough cuts. The section of the animal that receives the least exercise—the middle of the back, called the loin and the ribs—is the most tender. The muscles that are worked the hardest—the chuck (shoulder), and neck, shank and round (the rear leg and rump)—produce the toughest cuts. The cut determines how the meat is best prepared. Tender cuts are best cooked with a dry heat, either roasted, broiled, grilled, or panfried. Tough, fibrous cuts require the long, slow cooking benefits of braising or stewing in a liquid. This breaks down the connective tissue that causes the meat's toughness, tenderizing the meat, and imparting the flavor of the cooking liquid.

Meat Basics

Before we get to the recipes, let's discuss how to use meat thermometers to tell when you've cooked your meat to the proper level of doneness. We'll also discuss how to choose the best cuts for your needs, and the right temperatures for roasting, broiling, and grilling the type of meat you want to cook.

How to Use a Meat Thermometer

What thermometer you use depends on the thickness of the cut. For larger cuts such as roasts, use an oven-safe dial meat thermometer.

1. Before roasting begins, insert the thermometer at least 2 inches into the center of the thickest part of the meat. Do not touch the fat, bone, or the pan with the tip of the thermometer.
2. Leave the thermometer in the roast during the entire cooking time.
3. Check the thermometer at the first cooking time according to the *Meat Charts* (pages 177-179).
4. When the thermometer reaches the desired temperature, push it further into the meat. If the temperature drops, continue cooking.
5. If the temperature remains the same, remove the meat from the heat and let the meat rest for 15 minutes.

For thinner cuts such as burgers and chops, use an instant-read thermometer.

1. When the meat has cooked for the recommended time, insert the thermometer 2 inches into the side of meat. Internal temperature will register within 15–20 seconds.
2. If the meat is not done, remove the thermometer and continue cooking, and repeat the process following the time recommendations of the recipe or chart.

tip

After roasting, loosely cover the meat with aluminum foil and let rest for 20 minutes.

How to Choose the Best Cuts

The following lists and charts are a guideline to help you determine which cut to buy for tonight's dinner.

The best cuts of meat for roasting:

- Beef: standing rib (called rib eye or, when boned, Delmonico), tenderloin, sirloin tip, boneless rolled rump
- Pork: ham, also called picnic shoulder (cooked or uncooked), pork-loin roasts, crown roast
- Lamb: whole leg, boneless leg, shank half of leg, hind shanks, rib roast, loin roast

The best cuts of meat for broiling or pan frying:

- Beef: porterhouse, T-bone, top sirloin, tri-tip, tenderized flank steak (tender steaks)
- Pork: rib chops, loin chops, bacon, center-cut ham slice
- Lamb: loin chop, sirloin chop, rib chop, blade chop

The best cuts of meat for braising:

- Beef: chuck steak, skirt steak, brisket, boneless round-rump roast, short ribs
- Pork: loin-back ribs, country style ribs, blade roasts, blade steak
- Lamb: boneless-shoulder roast, blade chop, hind shanks

Meat Roasting, Grilling, and Broiling Charts

Use the charts in Tables 9.1 through 9.4 for beef, pork, and lamb, respectively, to determine what temperature and cooking time will produce the right level of doneness.

TABLE 9.1   Beef Roasting Chart

Beef Cuts	Oven Temperature	Weight	Meat Thermometer Reading/Cooking Time (per pound unless otherwise indicated)				
			Rare 140°F	Medium Rare 145°F	Medium 160°F	Medium-Well 165°F	Well-Done 170°F
Standing rib	300° to 325°F	6- to 8-lbs	23 to 25 min	24 to 28 min	26 to 30 min	28 to 34 min	32 to 35 min
Rib roast (chine bone	350°F	6- to 8-lbs	15 to 18 min	17 to 22 min	21 to 28 min	27 to 30 min	29 to 32 min removed)
Rib eye roast	350°F	4- to 6-lbs	18 to 20 min	19 to 22 min	21 to 24 min	23 to 25 min	24 to 26 min
Eye round roast	325°F	2- to 3-lbs	35 to 38 min	37 to 45 min	42 to 53 min	49 to 60 min	54 to 65 min
Round tip roast	325°F	3- to 4-lbs	28 to 30 min	30 to 35 min	35 to 45 min	45 to 48 min	48 to 50 min
		6- to 8-lbs	16 to 18 min	18 to 20 min	21 to 25 min	25 to 28 min	28 to 30 min
Sirloin tip	300° to 325°F	3 1/2- to 4-lbs	35 min	36 min	37 min	38 min	40 min
Rolled rib	300° to 325°F	5- to 7-lbs	32 min	35 min	38 min	40 min	45 min
Rolled rump	300° to 325°F	4- to 6-lbs	25 min	26 min	27 min	29 min	30 min
Tenderloin (whole)	425°F	4- to 5-lbs	45 to 60 min	48 to 60 min	58 to 65 min		
Meatloaf	350°F	1 1/2 lbs			60 to 75 min		

TABLE 9.2 Pork Roasting Chart

Pork Cuts	Oven Temperature	Weight	Meat Thermometer Reading	Cooking Time (per pound unless otherwise indicated)
Fresh Cuts:				
Crown roast	350°F	6- to 10-lbs	160°F	22 min
Center loin roast with bone	350°F	3- to 5-lbs	160°F	22 min
Boneless top loin roast	350°F	2- to 4-lbs	160°F	22 min
Rolled loin	350°F	3- to 5-lbs	170°F	35 to 40 min
Fresh whole ham leg with bone	350°F	12- to 16-lbs	170°F	25 min
Tenderloin	425° to 450°F	1/2- to 1 1/2-lbs	160°F	25 to 35 min
Fresh picnic shoulder	350°F	5- to 8-lbs	170°F	30 to 40 min
Spareribs	350°F	3-lbs	Well-done	120 to 150 min
Smoked, must cook before eating:				
Half ham (with bone)	350°F	5- to 7-lbs	160°F	25 to 30 min
Whole ham	350°F	10- to 14-lbs	160°F	18 to 20 min
Smoked, fully-cooked:				
Half ham (boneless)	325°F	3- to 4-lbs	140°F	25 to 30 min
Whole ham (boneless)	325°F	6- to 8-lbs	140°F	10 to 12 min

TABLE 9.3 Lamb Roasting Chart

Lamb Cuts	Oven Temperature	Weight	Meat Thermometer Reading/Cooking Time (per pound unless otherwise indicated)		
			Medium-Rare 145°F	Medium 160°F	Well-Done 170°F
Leg (whole)	325°F	5- to 7-lbs	15 to 20 min	20 to 25 min	19 to 25 min
		7- to 9-lbs	24 to 30 min	24 to 30 min	29 to 35 min
Leg shank (half)	325°F	3- to 4-lbs	25 to 30 min	29 to 40 min	38 to 45 min
Leg roast (boneless)	325°F	4- to 7-lbs	20 min	25 min	30 min
Rib roast or rack	375°F	1 1/2- to 2 1/2-lbs	30 min	35 min	40 min
Crown roast, (unstuffed)	375°F	2- to 3-lbs	25 min	30 min	35 min
Shoulder roast (boneless)	325°F	3 1/2- to 6-lbs	35 min	40 min	45 min

Follow the chart in Table 9.4 when grilling or broiling beef.

TABLE 9.4   Beef Grilling or Broiling Chart

Cut	Thickness/ Weight	Rare 140°F	Medium- Rare 145°F	Medium 160°F	Medium- Well 165°F	Well-Done 170°F
New York strip	1-inch	8 to 10 min	9 to 11 min	10 to 12 min	11 to 13 min	12 to 14 min
Flank steak	1- to 1 1/2- lbs	10 to 15 min	14 to 18 min	16 to 20 min		
Porterhouse steak, Rib eye, and Top sirloin	1-inch	6 to 7 min	6 to 8 min	7 to 9 min	8 to 10 min	9 to 11 min
	1 1/2-inch	10 to 12 min	11 to 13 min	12 to 15 min	14 to 18 min	16 to 19 min
T-bone tenderloin	2-inch	15 to 17 min	16 to 18 min	17 to 19 min	18 to 20 min	19 to 22 min
Tri-tip	1-inch	8 to 9 min	9 to 10 min	10 to 12 min	12 to 15 min	
Hamburger patty	1-inch/6–oz.	4 min	5 min	6 min	7 min	8 min

Savory Roast Beef

As with all roasts, it is recommended that the meat be allowed to warm to room temperature before roasting. This requires planning—not always something that is easy to pull off. You shouldn't ever allow uncooked meat to stand at room temperature for more than ten to fifteen minutes. If you forget to pull the roast out of the refrigerator, just cook the meat a little longer. Serve with *Horseradish Sauce* (page 297) or *Brown Pan Gravy for Roasted Meats* (page 300).

Ingredients

2 cloves garlic

1 4-pound roast

Fresh-ground black pepper

Kosher or coarse salt

3/4 cup water

Equipment

Roasting pan, rack, paring knife, cutting board, meat thermometer

Methods

Mincing, roasting (see Chapter 3, "Glossary of Terms and Techniques, Conversions and Equivalents")

Quantity

6 to 8 servings

Preparation

1. Preheat the oven to 400°F.
2. Peel and thinly slice the garlic.
3. Make shallow slits in the fat side of the roast, and insert the garlic slivers.
4. Sprinkle the roast with salt and pepper, and insert the meat thermometer into the thickest part of meat.

tip

Salting the meat before roasting under high temperatures helps the natural sugars caramelize, forming a crust, which seals in the moisture and flavor.

Cooking Directions

5. Place the meat on the rack in the roasting pan, fat side up. If you don't have a roasting rack, place the meat on the bottom of the pan. Place the pan in the oven and roast for 30 minutes. This will slightly brown the meat to help retain the juices.

6. Reduce the oven heat to 350°F and roast for 30 minutes.

7. Add 3/4 cup of water to the bottom of the pan and continue cooking for 30 to 45 minutes.

8. Check the thermometer 1 hour from the time the heat was reduced. See *Meat Roasting Charts* (pages 177-179) for desired doneness.

9. Remove from the oven, loosely cover with aluminum foil, and allow the roast to rest for 20 minutes before carving.

Variations

Herb-Crusted Roast Beef

Combine 1/2 cup minced fresh parsley, 2 minced shallots, 1/2 cup plain bread crumbs, and 4 tablespoons softened butter. Remove the roast from the oven at step 6, and pat the mixture over the roast. Return to the pan to the oven and roast as directed.

Pantry/Refrigerator Check

Garlic

Black pepper

Salt

Shopping List

1 4-pound beef roast (rib roast, rib eye roast, or sirloin tip roast)

Meatloaf

Turn this classic into a great one-pot meal by arranging quartered potatoes and carrots around the meatloaf. If you have leftovers, try making a sandwich with sliced meatloaf on thick potato bread with pesto and fresh tomato slices. See the suggestions below for easy variations of this basic recipe. Serve with *Roasted Greek Potatoes* (page 277) and *Green Beans with Bacon and Shallots* (page 281) for a complete meal.

Ingredients

1/2 small onion

2 tablespoons minced fresh parsley

1 egg

1/4 cup half-and-half

1/4 cup tomato sauce

1/2 teaspoon dried thyme

1/4 teaspoon salt

1/2 teaspoon fresh-ground black pepper

1-pound ground beef

1/2 pound ground pork

1/2 cup plain bread crumbs

1/4 cup ketchup

3 thick slices bacon

Equipment

13×9×2-inch baking dish, large bowl, chef's knife, cutting board, wooden stirring spoon, measuring cup, measuring spoons

Methods

Dicing, mincing, whisking, baking (see Chapter 3)

Quantity

6 servings

Preparation

1. Preheat the oven to 375°F.
2. Peel and dice the onion.

3. Wash the parsley and pat dry. Pull the leaves from the stems, and mince.

4. In a large bowl, whisk together the egg, half-and-half, tomato sauce, thyme, salt, and pepper.

5. To the egg mixture, add the onion, parsley, meats, and bread crumbs, mixing thoroughly with a wooden spoon or clean hands.

6. Form the mixture into a large oval and place in the baking dish.

7. Pour ketchup over the top of the meatloaf and arrange the bacon slices lengthways over the ketchup.

Cooking Directions

8. Place the dish on the middle rack of the oven and bake for 1 to 1 1/4 hours.

9. Remove from the oven, loosely cover and allow to rest for 10 minutes before slicing.

Variations

Mexican Meatloaf

At step 5 add 1/2 teaspoon ground cumin, 1/2 teaspoon red chili powder, and 1 4 oz. canned diced green chilies.

Italian Meatloaf

At step 5 add 2 tablespoons fresh chopped basil, 1/4 cup pine nuts, and 1/4 cup chopped, oil-packed sundried tomatoes.

Cajun Meatloaf

At step 5 add 1/4 cup chopped green bell peppers, 1/4 cup chopped celery, and 1 teaspoon of cajun spice.

Pantry/Refrigerator Check

Eggs

1 6 oz. can tomato sauce

Dried thyme

Salt

Black pepper

Ketchup

Plain bread crumbs

Shopping List

1 small onion

1 bunch fresh parsley

1/2 pint half-and-half

1-pound ground beef

1/2-pound ground pork

1/2-pound thick sliced bacon

Roast Leg of Lamb

To make carving a snap, ask the butcher to bone, or butterfly, the lamb. Many times the butcher will place the lamb in string netting, which holds the lamb together while cooking. If not, roll the lamb and tie with kitchen string before roasting. This sounds difficult but it is actually very easy. Just remember, it does not have to look pretty—it's just a method to keep the lamb from falling apart.

Ingredients

2 cloves garlic

2 teaspoons minced fresh rosemary leaves

2 teaspoons minced fresh thyme leaves

2 tablespoons unsalted butter

1/4 teaspoon fresh-ground black pepper

1 tablespoon salt

1 6-pound leg of lamb

Equipment

Roasting pan, rack, chef's knife, cutting board, small bowl, meat thermometer

Methods

Roasting (see Chapter 3)

Quantity

10 servings

Preparation

1. Peel and thinly slice the garlic.
2. Wash the rosemary and pat dry. Pull the leaves from the stem, and finely mince.
3. Wash the thyme and pat dry. Pull the leaves from the stem, and finely mince.
4. Place the butter in a small bowl and soften at room temperature. Add the rosemary, thyme, salt, and pepper, and mix well to blend.
5. Make shallow slits with the knife tip randomly around the lamb and insert the slivers of garlic.
6. Rub the butter mixture on all sides of the lamb, and place the lamb on a rack in the roasting pan, fat side up. If you don't have a rack, place the meat on the bottom of the pan.

7. Insert the meat thermometer (see *How to Use A Meat Thermometer*, page 176) if you have one, and allow the lamb to sit for 20 minutes.

8. After the lamb has marinated for 10 minutes, turn the oven on and preheat to 325°F.

Cooking Directions

9. Place the pan in oven and roast the lamb, uncovered, for 1 1/4 to 1 1/2 hours to desired doneness. (see *Meat Roasting Charts*, pages 177-179)

10. Remove the lamb to a platter, cover with aluminum foil, and allow to sit for 15 minutes before carving.

Variations:

■ At step 9 toss 6 small red potatoes and 2 carrots cut into 1 1/2-inch pieces with olive oil, and roast along with lamb in bottom of the pan.

■ At step 4 add 1 tablespoon of fresh oregano and 1 tablespoon of lemon juice or lemon zest to the herb mix.

Pantry/Refrigerator Check

Garlic

Black pepper

Salt

1 stick unsalted butter

Shopping List

1 6-pound leg of lamb

1 bunch or small package fresh rosemary leaves

1 bunch or small package fresh thyme leaves

Baked Ham with Maple-Mustard Glaze

Perfect for a springtime Sunday celebration, this recipe includes instructions for a quick sauce. Pour the sauce into a small pitcher and pass with the thinly carved ham. Serve with *Scalloped Potatoes* (page 271), steamed asparagus, and *Savory Herbed-Pepper Biscuits* (page 80) for a delicious meal.

Ingredients

1 6- to 7-pound half ham, fully cooked

3/4 cup dijon mustard

1/4 cup dark brown sugar

1 tablespoon maple syrup

For sauce:

1/2 cup orange juice

1 tablespoon dijon mustard

1 tablespoon maple syrup

Equipment

Large roasting pan, rack, small bowl, chef's knife, cutting board, meat thermometer, measuring cup, measuring spoons, pot holder, wooden stirring spoon, brush, large spoon

Methods

Trimming, scoring, roasting, deglazing (see Chapter 3)

Quantity

10 servings

Preparation

1. Preheat the oven to 325°F.

2. With a sharp knife cut off and discard the leathery rind of the ham and all but 1/4-inch of the fat.

3. Score the fat by making diagonal cuts at 1/2-inch intervals to create a diamond pattern through the fat. Do not cut into the meat.

4. Place the ham, fat side up, on a rack in a shallow roasting pan and insert the meat thermometer into the thickest part of the ham without touching the bone. If you don't have a rack, place the ham on the bottom of the pan.

5. Add 1/2 cup water to the roasting pan and place the pan in the oven.

Cooking Directions

6. While the ham is roasting, whisk together 3/4 cup mustard, 1/4 cup brown sugar, and 1 tablespoon of syrup in a small bowl.

7. Roast the ham for 1 1/2 hours. Remove from the oven and spread the mustard mixture over the scored fat.

8. Return the ham to the oven and continue roasting for 45 minutes or until the thermometer registers 140°F.

9. Remove the pan from the oven, transfer the ham to platter, and loosely cover with aluminum foil and let sit for 15 minutes.

10. With a pot holder, grasp one end of the roasting pan and tilt to allow all the juices to gather in one corner. With a spoon, skim off the fat that accumulates on the surface.

11. Place the roasting pan on a stove-top burner over medium-high heat.

12. Add the orange juice and deglaze the pan by stirring and scraping up browned bits stuck to the bottom of the pan, incorporating them into the liquid.

13. Stir in the mustard and maple syrup and continue cooking until the sauce begins to thicken.

14. Pour the sauce into a small gravy boat or bowl, and pass with the thinly carved ham.

Variations

- At step 3 place whole cloves in the diamonds created by scoring.
- Make glazes from any combination of marmalades or preserves with mustard and syrup or brown sugar.
- At step 6 add nutmeg, clove, or cumin.
- At step 6 add a splash of wine, Madeira, sherry, cider vinegar, or fruit juice.

Pantry/Refrigerator Check

Dijon mustard

Dark brown sugar

Shopping List

Maple syrup

Orange juice

6 to 7 pound fully cooked half ham (bone in shank or butt)

Horseradish Encrusted Pork Loin with Mushroom Stuffing

This rich but light dish is prefect to prepare for a dinner party. The mushrooms, sautéed in cognac, are stuffed into the roast. The outside of the meat is browned and then coated with a breadcrumb-horseradish crust. The mouthwatering aroma while baking gives the guests a hint of what is in store. Best of all, you will have 40 minutes of hands-free time to prepare the rest of the dinner.

Ingredients

1 1/2 cups sliced fresh cremini mushrooms

1 large shallot

1 clove garlic

1 tablespoon unsalted butter

3 tablespoons extra virgin olive oil, divided

3 teaspoons dried tarragon, divided

2 tablespoons cognac or brandy

2 pounds boneless pork loin roast

1/2 teaspoon fresh-ground black pepper

1/4 teaspoon salt

1 1/2 tablespoons mayonnaise

1 1/2 tablespoons dijon mustard

3/4 cup plain bread crumbs

1 tablespoon prepared cream-style horseradish

Equipment

Medium oven-proof skillet, chef's knife, cutting board, 2 small bowls

Methods

Searing, encrusting, roasting (see Chapter 3)

Quantity

4 servings

Preparation

1. Preheat the oven to 475°F.

2. Clean the mushrooms with a damp paper towel and thinly slice.

3. Peel and mince the shallot.

4. Peel and mince the garlic.

5. In a skillet, heat the butter and 1 tablespoon of oil over medium-high heat.

6. Add the mushrooms, shallot, garlic, and 2 teaspoons of tarragon and sauté, stirring often, for 3 minutes.

7. Add the cognac and sauté for an additional 3 minutes, or until the mushrooms are softened but browned.

8. Remove from the heat and set aside to cool.

9. Place the pork roast on a cutting board, fat side up. Place your hand on top of the roast and insert a thin knife into one end of the roast. Push the knife into the center of the roast to create a cavity for the stuffing. Do not push the knife through the opposite end.

10. When the mushroom mixture is cool enough to handle, gently open the incision with your fingers, or the back of a spoon, and stuff the mushrooms deep into the cavity.

11. Salt and pepper the outside of the roast.

Cooking Directions

12. Place the skillet back onto the stove over medium-high heat and heat 1 tablespoon of oil until very hot but just below smoking point. (See Chapter 3 for definition of smoke point.)

13. When hot, place the roast in the pan and brown for 5 minutes, turning to brown all sides.

14. While the roast is browning, combine the mayonnaise, mustard, and remaining tarragon in a small bowl and set aside.

15. Combine the bread crumbs, 1 tablespoon oil, and horseradish in a small bowl and set aside.

16. When the roast is browned, remove from the stove. Let cool slightly.

17. Coat the top and sides of the roast with mayonnaise-mustard mixture and press the bread crumbs evenly into the coating.

18. Place the pork, uncovered, into the preheated oven and roast for 35 to 40 minutes or until a meat thermometer in the meat (not the stuffing) registers 160°F for medium-done.

19. If the bread crumb crust browns too quickly, cover loosely with aluminum foil.

20. Transfer the pork roast to a cutting board and allow to stand for 5 to 10 minutes.

21. Slice crosswise and serve.

Variations

- At step 7 add 1/4 cup of bread crumbs to sautéing mushrooms.
- Substitute fresh tarragon for dried, using 3 teaspoons of fresh for each teaspoon of dried herb.

Pantry/Refrigerator Check

Garlic

Extra virgin olive oil

1 stick unsalted butter

Dried tarragon

Cognac (or brandy)

Black pepper

Salt

Mayonnaise

Dijon mustard

6 oz. plain bread crumbs

Prepared cream-style horseradish

Shopping List

1/4 pound fresh cremini mushrooms

1 large shallot

2-pound boneless pork loin

Mediterranean Lamb Kabobs

For an aromatic treat, thread kabobs on thick rosemary skewers, available at specialty grocery stores. Serve with *Moroccan Couscous* (page 239) and a simple salad for a healthy mid-summer dinner. Set the table outside and dine under the stars.

Ingredients

1-pound boneless lamb shoulder

2 tablespoons lemon juice from 1 lemon

2 cloves garlic

2 tablespoons minced fresh oregano

1 red bell pepper

1/4 teaspoon salt

1/2 teaspoon fresh-ground black pepper

6 tablespoons extra virgin olive oil

Nonstick cooking spray

Equipment

Gas or charcoal grill, chef's knife, chopping board, small strainer, measuring spoons, small bowl, shallow baking dish, small saucepan, 8 long metal or bamboo skewers

Methods

Chopping, mincing, marinating, skewering, grilling (see Chapter 3)

Quantity

4 servings

Preparation

1. Cut the lamb into 1 1/2-inch thick pieces and place in a 1 gallon resealable plastic bag.

2. Squeeze the lemon over the strainer, and discard the seeds.

3. Peel and mince the garlic.

4. Wash the oregano and pat dry. Pull the leaves from the stems, and mince.

5. Wash the red bell pepper, halve lengthwise, remove the stem and seeds, and cut into 16 pieces.

6. In a small bowl, combine the lemon juice, garlic, oregano, salt, pepper, and olive oil, whisking to combine. Pour over the lamb in the bag.

7. Seal the bag well and shake to coat the lamb with marinade. Set in a shallow baking dish and refrigerate for 1 to 6 hours.

Cooking Directions

8. Lightly coat a grill rack with cooking spray. Prepare the charcoal or gas grill to medium heat.

9. Remove the lamb from the bag and pour the marinade into a small saucepan. Bring the marinade to a boil over medium heat, then remove to cool slightly.

10. Assemble the skewers by alternately threading the lamb and the red pepper.

11. Place the kabobs on a grill rack, cover the grill, and cook for 6 minutes.

12. Remove the grill cover, brush the kabobs with reserved marinade, and turn. Cook 6 to 8 minutes longer for medium-done.

caution

The marinade has been in contact with raw meat and must be brought to a boil to kill bacteria.

note

Kabobs may also be cooked under the broiler in the oven. Check at 6 minutes, brush with marinade, and cook for an additional 6 minutes.

Variations

■ At step 6 add 2 tablespoons of minced rosemary and 1/4 cup yogurt to marinade.

Pantry/Refrigerator Check

Garlic

Salt

Black pepper

Extra virgin olive oil

Nonstick cooking spray

Shopping List

1 pound boneless lamb shoulder

1 lemon

1 bunch or package fresh oregano

1 red bell pepper

Beef Bourguignonne

This is an easy dish with an elegant name, and every cook should have at least one elegant dish in his or her repertoire. The list of ingredients may lead you to believe this dish is difficult to make, and that is not the case. It is time-consuming, however, so try this on a weekend when you have plenty of time. The results are worth the effort. This is a good example of how braising tenderizes a tough, less-expensive cut of meat to create a tender and flavorful dish. Serve garnished with chopped, fresh, flat-leaf parsley. Finish your menu with *Mashed Potatoes* (page 269) or buttered egg noodles, steamed green beans, and purchased dinner rolls.

Ingredients

2 cups pearl onions

4 thick slices bacon

1 cup chopped yellow onion

2 cloves garlic

4 medium carrots

3 cups whole fresh mushrooms

3-pound boneless beef chuck roast

1 tablespoon extra virgin olive oil

1/2 teaspoon salt

1/4 teaspoon fresh-ground black pepper

2 tablespoons all-purpose white flour

1 1/2 cups Burgundy wine

1 teaspoon dried thyme

3/4 teaspoon dried rosemary

2 bay leaves

3/4 cup beef broth

2 tablespoons tomato paste

2 tablespoons minced flat leaf parsley

Equipment

Large Dutch oven or deep heavy-bottomed skillet/saucepan with lid, medium saucepan, chef's knife, cutting board, measuring cup, measuring spoons, slotted spoon, wooden stirring spoon

Methods

Dicing, mincing, chopping, sautéing, boiling, simmering (see Chapter 3)

Quantity:

6 servings

Preparation

1. Pour 4 cups of water into a medium saucepan, cover, and place over high heat to bring to a boil. When the water is boiling, drop in the pearl onions and cook for 30 seconds. Drain and rinse with cold water.

2. When the onions are drained, cut off the root ends and squeeze the pearl onions out of their skins from the opposite ends. Set aside.

3. Dice the bacon into small pieces.

4. Peel and dice the yellow onion.

5. Peel and mince the garlic.

6. Peel the carrots and chop into 1 1/2-inch thick pieces.

7. Wipe the mushrooms with a damp paper towel and set aside.

8. Cut the beef into 1-inch thick cubes.

Cooking Directions

9. In a Dutch oven or skillet, sauté the bacon over medium-high heat until crisp, turning once or twice. With a slotted spoon, transfer the bacon to a paper towel and drain. Set aside.

10. Tilt the pan and remove all but 1 tablespoon of the bacon fat.

11. Place the pan over medium-high heat; add the olive oil to the bacon fat and sauté the beef in batches, until browned on all sides. Remove each batch of browned beef to a separate dish when done. Do not crowd the pan.

12. When all the beef is browned, return all the meat to the pan, add the diced yellow onions, garlic, salt, pepper, and flour, sautéing over high heat, stirring constantly, for about 5 minutes.

13. Add the wine and deglaze the pan by stirring and scraping up browned bits from the bottom of the pan with a wooden spoon.

14. Crush the thyme and rosemary with your fingertips and add to the pan along with the bay leaves, beef broth, tomato paste, and carrots. Bring to a boil.

15. Reduce the heat, cover the pan, and simmer for 20 minutes.

16. Add the mushrooms, pearl onions, and crumbled bacon to the pan and simmer for 15 to 20 minutes, uncovered, or until the beef and vegetables are tender.

17. Wash the parsley and pat dry. Pull the leaves from stems, and mince.

18. Remove from the heat and garnish with the chopped parsley.

Pantry/Refrigerator Check

Garlic

Extra virgin olive oil

All-purpose white flour

Burgundy wine

6 oz. beef broth

Dried thyme

Dried rosemary

Salt

Black pepper

Bay leaves

Tomato paste

Shopping List

1 10 oz. package fresh pearl onions

1/2-pound thick sliced bacon

2 medium yellow onions

4 medium carrots

16 whole fresh mushrooms (depending on size)

3-pound boneless beef chuck roast

1 bunch or package flat leaf parsley

Oven Barbecue Spareribs

These spareribs are oven-barbequed by braising, a long, slow method of cooking that enhances flavors and produces tender meats. The ribs are oven-browned in a very high heat then slow-cooked. Smothered with barbecue sauce, they fall off the bone when presented at the table. This is a great way to have a barbecue in the middle of a snowstorm. The ribs are especially good served over rice.

Ingredients

1 lemon

1 large white onion

4- to 5-pounds pork spareribs

1 teaspoon salt

1 teaspoon celery seed

1/2 cup brown sugar

1/4 cup cider vinegar

1/4 cup Worcestershire sauce

1 cup ketchup

2 cups water

Dash Tabasco sauce

Equipment

Medium saucepan, large roasting pan, chef's knife, cutting board, measuring cup, wooden stirring spoon, large metal spoon or bulb baster.

Methods

Slicing, simmering, braising (see Chapter 3)

Quantity

4 servings

Preparation

1. Preheat the oven to 400°F.
2. Cut the lemon into thin slices.
3. Peel and cut the onion into thin slices.
4. Place the meat on the cutting board and cut into individual ribs.

Cooking Directions

5. In a medium saucepan over medium heat, combine the sliced lemon, salt, celery seed, brown sugar, vinegar, Worcestershire sauce, ketchup, water, and Tabasco sauce. Stir to blend.

6. When the sauce begins to bubble, reduce the heat to low and simmer, uncovered, for 45 minutes, stirring occasionally.

7. While the sauce is cooking, place the onions and spareribs in a roasting pan large enough to hold the ribs in a single layer without touching.

8. Place the uncovered roasting pan in the middle rack of the preheated oven and cook until browned, about 45 minutes.

9. Remove the pan from the oven and reduce the temperature to 350°F.

10. With a large spoon or bulb baster, remove and discard all rendered fat.

11. Pour the cooked barbecue sauce over the meat and return the meat to the oven.

12. Braise the ribs for 1 hour, basting every 15 minutes.

13. Reduce the heat to 325°F and continue cooking for 30 to 60 minutes, depending on the thickness of your meat. Pierce the meat with a fork. If the meat is tender, the ribs are done.

14. Remove the ribs from the oven and serve immediately.

Variations

■ Fast Track this recipe by boiling ribs for 30 minutes. Transfer the ribs to a large roasting pan, add the onions and sauce, and follow the instructions from step 12. Reduce the cooking time to about 1 hour, depending on the thickness of meat.

Pantry/Refrigerator Check

Salt

Celery seed

Brown sugar

Cider vinegar

Worcestershire sauce

Ketchup

Tabasco sauce

Shopping List

1 lemon

1 large white onion

4- to 5-pounds pork spareribs—choose ribs with lots of meat and less fat

Beef Stroganoff

This is a creamy, savory, and flavorful comfort food that is easy to whip up after work, making it ideal for a mid-week supper. The mushrooms add a rich texture, and the sour cream mixes with the beef juices to create a sumptuous gravy—a real treat spooned over wide egg noodles and served with petite green peas! Makes great leftovers because the flavors are enhanced by a night in the refrigerator.

Ingredients

2 shallots

3 cups sliced mushrooms

3/4-pound boneless beef steak

1 tablespoon extra virgin olive oil

1 tablespoon unsalted butter

1/4 teaspoon fresh-ground black pepper

1/2 cup beef stock

1 tablespoon tomato paste

1 teaspoon Worcestershire sauce

1/4 cup sour cream

2 tablespoons minced fresh parsley

Equipment

Large deep skillet, chef's knife, cutting board, measuring cup, measuring spoon

Methods

Slicing, sautéing, boiling, simmering (see Chapter 3)

Quantity

6 servings

Preparation

1. Peel and thinly slice the shallots.
2. Clean the mushrooms with a damp paper towel and slice.
3. Cut the meat into even slices about 1/2-inch thick. If the slices are the same size they will cook more evenly.

Cooking Directions

4. In a large skillet, heat the oil and butter over medium-high heat.

5. Add the shallots and mushrooms, and sauté until softened for about 5 minutes while stirring frequently.

6. Add the beef and black pepper and continue sautéing and stirring for about 1 to 3 minutes, until meat has browned on all sides. Thicker meat slices will take longer to cook.

7. Add the beef stock, tomato paste, and Worcestershire sauce and bring to a boil, stirring to combine.

8. Add the sour cream and cook over high heat, stirring until slightly thickened for about 1 minute.

9. Remove from the heat, garnish with parsley, and serve.

Variations:

■ At step 1 substitute 1 small onion for the shallots.

■ At step 7 omit the Worcestershire sauce and add 1 teaspoon of dijon mustard.

Pantry/Refrigerator Check

1 stick unsalted butter

Extra virgin olive oil

Black pepper

1 can beef stock

1 6 oz. can tomato paste or reusable tube

Worcestershire sauce

Shopping List

2 shallots

1/2-pound fresh mushrooms

3/4-pound boneless beef steak (flank steak, chuck, skirt, or top round)

1 4 oz. container sour cream

1 bunch fresh parsley

10

POULTRY—CHICKEN AND TURKEY

Succulent and rich in flavor, high in protein and low in fat, poultry is always a versatile meal choice. Chicken, the most popular poultry, is consumed in huge quantities worldwide and eaten roasted, grilled, sautéed, fried, stuffed, broiled, braised, or stewed. Low in cost, chicken is also a great bargain. Roast a whole chicken for a Sunday supper, slice the leftovers for sandwiches, and make stock from the roasted carcass. Easily paired with global spices, poultry is used extensively in Latin, Middle-Eastern, Asian, and European recipes.

Chicken Basics

Purchase plump poultry with smooth, un-bruised skin in packages that contain little or no liquid. Buy whole chickens because they are less expensive, and ask the butcher to cut it up for you. Chicken breasts that are individually frozen are easily available, and make it possible to defrost a single breast. For bone-in poultry allow about a pound per serving. For boneless poultry, allow about one-half pound per serving.

Store poultry in the refrigerator. For best results it should be cooked within 2 to 3 days of purchase. Remove the giblets from the whole birds before refrigerating. Thaw frozen poultry in the refrigerator for safety and retention of juices.

When roasting chicken, use the chart shown in Table 10.1 to determine the correct temperature and roasting time.

caution

All surfaces that have contact with raw chicken, including knives, cutting boards, and hands, must be thoroughly washed with hot soapy water to prevent the spread of salmonella bacteria.

TABLE 10.1 Poultry Roasting Chart

Type of Poultry	Weight	Oven Temperature	Roasting Time
Cornish game hen	1- to 2-pounds	350°F	1 to 1 1/4 hours
Whole chicken	2 1/2- to 3-pounds	375°F	1 1/4 to 1 1/2 hours
Whole chicken	3- to 4-pounds	375°F	1 1/2 to 1 3/4 hours
Whole chicken	4- to 6-pounds	375°F	1 3/4 to 2 hours
Whole chicken	4 1/2- to 5-pounds	375°F	1 1/2 to 2 hours
Capon (large roasting chicken)	5- to 7-pounds	325°F	1 3/4 to 2 1/2 hours
Goose	7- to 8-pounds	350°F	2 to 2 1/2 hours
Turkey	8- to 12-pounds	325°F	2 3/4 to 3 hours
Turkey	12- to 14-pounds	325°F	3 to 3 3/4 hours
Turkey	14- to 18-pounds	325°F	3 3/4 to 4 1/4 hours
Turkey	18- to 20-pounds	325°F	4 1/4 to 4 1/2 hours
Turkey	20- to 24-pounds	325°F	4 3/4 to 5 1/2 hours

Grilled Tequila-Lime Chicken

This dish can be cooked on the grill or under the broiler. Serve with grilled vegetables and Mexican spiced couscous, or slice the chicken for tacos and serve with black beans, guacamole, and pico de gallo. Double the recipe and freeze the extra chicken breasts for later use in *Tequila Chicken Salad* (page 88) with *Creamy Cilantro Dressing* (page 173).

Ingredients

4 boneless, skinless chicken breasts

3/4 cup *Tequila-Lime Marinade* (page 310)

1 tablespoon extra virgin olive oil

Equipment

Chef's knife, cutting board, tongs, 1 gallon resealable plastic bag

Methods

Marinating, grilling (see Chapter 3, "Glossary of Terms and Techniques, Conversions and Equivalents")

Quantity

4 servings

Preparation

1. Trim all excess fat and any remaining tendons from each breast.
2. Place the chicken and marinade in a 1-gallon resealable plastic bag, close securely, and shake a few times to coat.
3. Place the bag in the refrigerator and marinate for 20 minutes, but no longer, as the citrus in the marinade will begin to cook the chicken.
4. Pour the oil on a paper towel, and lightly wipe the grill rack with cooking oil. Prepare a charcoal or gas grill to medium-high heat.

Cooking Directions

5. Remove the chicken from the marinade, and place the chicken on the heated grill. Reserve the marinade if making a sauce.
6. Grill the chicken over medium-high heat until well-browned, about 6 to 8 minutes.

7. Turn the chicken and cook for an additional 8 to 12 minutes to desired doneness. When the chicken is pierced with a fork, the juices should run clear.

8. Transfer the chicken to a platter. If you want to serve the marinade as a sauce, boil the marinade for at least 5 minutes to kill any bacteria that is present from the raw chicken.

Variations

■ The chicken can also be broiled 4 inches under the oven broiler source.

■ At step 6 make a sauce with the reserved marinade by melting 1 tablespoon of butter in a small skillet over medium heat. Add the reserved marinade and 1/4 cup orange juice, and bring to a boil. Cook at a high simmer for 5 minutes; stir constantly until the sauce begins to reduce and slightly thicken.

Pantry/Refrigerator Check

Extra virgin olive oil

Tequila-Lime Marinade (page 310)

Shopping List

4 boneless, skinless chicken breasts

Broiled Tarragon-Mustard Chicken

The marinade is simmered to create a sauce that is wonderful when spooned over chicken breasts and couscous. Serve with a tossed green salad and steamed vegetables for a healthy mid-week meal in no time.

Ingredients

4 boneless, skinless chicken breasts

1 cup *Tarragon Mustard Marinade* (page 312)

1 tablespoon unsalted butter

1/2 cup dry white wine

Equipment

Chef's knife, cutting board, measuring cup, measuring spoons

Methods

Marinating, broiling, sautéing (see Chapter 3)

Quantity

4 servings

Preparation

1. Fold a piece of aluminum foil to about the size of your broiler pan. Fold the outer edges up to about 1/4 inch, and place on top of the broiler pan.
2. Preheat the broiler.
3. Place the chicken on the cutting board, and trim all excess fat and any remaining tendons from each breast.
4. Place the chicken and marinade in a 1 gallon resealable plastic bag, close securely, and shake a few times to coat. Allow to sit for 20 minutes.
5. Remove the chicken from the bag, and place on the foil-covered broiler pan. Reserve the remaining marinade.

Cooking Directions

6. Broil the chicken 4 inches from the heat source for 8 to 10 minutes.
7. Turn the chicken, removing the pan from the oven if necessary. Cook for another 6 to 10 minutes until the meat is no longer pink, and the juices run clear when chicken is pierced with a fork.

8. Transfer the chicken to a platter, and cover loosely to keep warm.

9. In a medium sauté pan over medium-high heat, melt the butter.

10. Add the wine and reserved marinade and bring to a boil. Reduce heat to medium, and simmer for 5 minutes; stir constantly until slightly thickened.

11. Serve immediately.

Variations

■ At step 4 add 1 tablespoon of fresh minced chives.

Pantry/Refrigerator Check

1 stick unsalted butter

White wine

Tarragon Mustard Marinade (page 312)

Shopping List

4 boneless, skinless chicken breasts

Roasted Greek Chicken with Potatoes

A roasted chicken can be enjoyed and anticipated all day long, not just when you eat it. The house fills with a warm, comforting aroma that hints of the coming feast. In this recipe, you roast the potatoes right along with the chicken, a real time-saver. Use the leftover carcass to make *Stock* (page 102).

Ingredients

1/2 cup fresh lemon juice (about 4 lemons)

1 3 1/2- to 4-pound chicken

2 tablespoons dried oregano, divided

3/4 teaspoon salt, divided

3/4 teaspoon pepper, divided

4 medium russet or Idaho potatoes

1/2 cup extra virgin olive oil, divided

Water as needed

Equipment

Large roasting pan, medium bowl, chef's knife, cutting board, measuring cup, measuring spoons, vegetable peeler, wooden stirring spoon, strainer, small bowl

Methods

Cutting, straining, roasting (see Chapter 3)

Quantity

4 servings

Preparation

1. Preheat the oven to 375°F.
2. Squeeze the lemons into a small bowl over the strainer, and discard any seeds.
3. Remove and discard any giblets or packets from inside the chicken. Rinse the chicken inside and out, and pat dry with paper towels.
4. Place the chicken in a large roasting pan. Pour 1/2 of the lemon juice over the chicken, and sprinkle with 1 tablespoon of oregano and 1/2 teaspoon of salt and pepper.
5. Peel the potatoes, cut in quarters lengthwise, and place in a medium bowl.

6. Pour the remaining lemon juice over the potatoes, and sprinkle with remaining oregano, salt, and pepper. Toss with your fingers or spoon to make sure potatoes are coated. Add 1/4 cup of olive oil and toss again to coat.

7. Arrange the potatoes around the chicken, and drizzle chicken and potatoes with the remaining olive oil.

Cooking Directions

8. Place the pan in the oven and bake, uncovered, for 45 minutes.

9. Carefully remove the chicken from the oven. Turn the potatoes with a spatula and pour 1/4 to 1/2 cup of water into pan.

10. Return the pan to the oven, and cook for another 30 to 45 minutes.

11. Test for doneness by piercing the chicken thigh with a fork. Juices should flow clear, not pink. If the juices are pink, return the pan to the oven and cook for 15 minutes longer, then test again.

12. Carve the chicken while it is in the pan, and serve with the potatoes.

Variations

- At step 5 add 6 garlic cloves and 1 peeled and quartered carrot to the potatoes.
- At step 4 substitute thyme for oregano.

Pantry/Refrigerator Check

Salt

Black pepper

Dried oregano

Extra virgin olive oil

Shopping List

4 lemons

4 Idaho potatoes

1 3 1/2- to 4-pound chicken

Roasted Turkey

A roasted turkey dinner is inexpensive, flavorful, and should not be limited to once a year. Purchase a small bird and experiment with the seasonings. Try different spice mixes ,such as red chili powder and cumin, added to the butter rub. Use the leftovers to make enchiladas or even turkey tacos.

Ingredients

10 sprigs fresh thyme

10 sprigs fresh parsley

1 large onion

2 ribs celery with leaves attached

1 16-pound turkey

Salt

Freshly ground black pepper

1 tablespoon unsalted butter

Equipment

Large roasting pan, roasting rack, chef's knife, cutting board, kitchen twine

Methods

Chopping, roasting (see Chapter 3)

Quantity

12 servings

Preparation

1. Preheat the oven to 350°F.
2. Wash and dry the thyme.
3. Wash and dry the parsley.
4. Peel the onion and chop into large pieces.
5. Wash the celery, trim the ends, and chop into large pieces.
6. Remove and reserve the neck and giblets (sometimes they are in a packet) from inside the turkey. Rinse the turkey inside and out, and pat dry with paper towels.
7. Sprinkle the inside cavity with salt and pepper.
8. Place the onion, celery, thyme, and parsley inside the turkey cavity.
9. Rub the outside with butter, and sprinkle with salt and pepper.

10. Tie the legs together with kitchen twine.

11. Place the turkey breast side up, on a roasting rack in a large roasting pan. If you do not have a roasting rack, set the turkey directly on the bottom of the pan. Insert a meat thermometer, if desired, into the thickest part of the thigh. The thermometer should not touch the bone.

Cooking Directions

12. Place the pan in the oven.

13. When the turkey has cooked for 30 minutes, add 1 cup of water to the roasting pan.

14. If the top of the turkey turns dark brown within the first 2 hours of cooking, cover loosely with aluminum foil, and uncover for the last 15 minutes of cooking.

15. Roast the turkey for 3 1/2 to 4 hours, basting from time to time.

16. The turkey is done when the meat thermometer registers 180°F, or when the juices run clear when the turkey is pierced with a fork. The drumsticks will also move easily in their joints.

17. Remove the turkey from the oven, cover, and let stand for 15 to 20 minutes before carving.

Variations

■ At step 9 rub softened butter mixed with minced herbs under the turkey breast skin.

■ At step 13 substitute 1 cup of Gewürztraminer, a crisp, spicy white wine for the water, and use it to baste the turkey as well.

Pantry/Refrigerator Check

Salt

Black pepper

1 stick unsalted butter

Shopping List

1 16-pound turkey

1 large onion

1 bunch celery

1 bunch fresh thyme

1 bunch fresh parsley

Balsamic Chicken with Fresh Thyme Sprigs

The chicken bakes along with carrots, onions, and mushrooms, so there is little clean-up for this one-dish dinner. Add sliced potatoes to the mix, and you have an almost foolproof meal with tender chicken and vegetables guaranteed.

Ingredients

4 boneless, skinless chicken breasts

2 carrots

1/2 medium onion

1 1/2 cups sliced mushrooms

4 fresh thyme sprigs

1/4 cup dry white wine

1/4 cup balsamic vinegar

3 tablespoons extra virgin olive oil

1/2 teaspoon salt

1 teaspoon freshly ground black pepper

Equipment

9×13-inch baking dish, chef's knife, cutting board, vegetable peeler, measuring cup, measuring spoon

Methods

Peeling, chopping, slicing, baking (see Chapter 3)

Quantity

4 servings

Preparation

1. Halve each chicken breast crosswise.
2. Peel the carrots and cut into 1/2-inch pieces on the bias.
3. Peel the onion, cut in half, and slice into 1/2-inch slices.
4. Wipe the mushrooms clean with a paper towel, and slice into 1/4-inch slices.
5. Wash and dry the thyme.

Cooking Directions

6. Preheat the oven to 375°F.

7. Place the carrots, onion, thyme sprigs, and mushrooms in the baking dish.

8. Place the chicken pieces on top of the vegetables.

9. Pour the wine and balsamic vinegar over the chicken. Drizzle with olive oil, and sprinkle with salt and pepper.

10. Cover the baking dish with foil, place in the oven, and bake for 20 minutes.

11. Uncover and bake an additional 10 minutes.

12. Serve the chicken and vegetables with the roasting juices spooned over the top.

Variations

■ At step 7 add vegetables of your choice, such as sliced potatoes, cauliflower, cabbage, or Brussels sprouts.

Pantry/Refrigerator Check

Extra virgin olive oil

White wine

Balsamic vinegar

Black pepper

Salt

Shopping List

4 boneless, skinless chicken breasts

2 carrots

1 medium onion

3 oz. mushrooms

1 bunch fresh thyme

Chicken Cacciatore

Braising is a method of cooking usually used to tenderize tough cuts of meat. Chicken does not need to be tenderized, so the purpose of braising is to impart flavor. When braising chicken, do not crowd the pan during browning or the chicken will stew rather than sauté. Place the chicken breasts on top of each other because the breast meat will cook faster, and should be kept farther from the heat.

Ingredients

1/2 cup white onion

2 cloves garlic

1 cup sliced mushrooms

3-pound whole chicken (purchased cut-up)

1/2 cup all-purpose white flour

1/2 teaspoon salt

1/2 teaspoon freshly ground black pepper

1/4 cup extra virgin olive oil

6 tablespoons tomato paste

3/4 cup dry white wine

1/2 cup chicken stock

1 bay leaf

1/2 teaspoon dried thyme

1/4 teaspoon dried marjoram

tip

Fast Track with boneless, skinless chicken breasts cut into bite-sized pieces (this will cut the cooking time to 20 minutes). Save more time by using purchased sliced mushrooms. Cook the pasta while the cacciatore is simmering, and serve with a pre-packaged Caesar salad.

Equipment

Heavy-bottomed deep skillet with lid or Dutch oven, chef's knife, cutting board, wooden stirring spoon, measuring cup, measuring spoons

Methods

Chopping, mincing, sautéing, stirring, braising (see Chapter 3)

Quantity

4 servings

Preparation

1. Peel the onion and coarsely chop.
2. Peel the garlic and mince.
3. Wipe the mushrooms clean with a damp paper towel and slice.
4. Wash the chicken pieces. Pat dry to ensure even browning.
5. Place the flour, salt, and pepper in a resealable plastic bag and shake to combine.
6. Add the chicken pieces a few at a time, shaking to coat. Remove to a plate and repeat until all the chicken is coated.

Cooking Directions

7. Heat the oil in the skillet over medium heat. Add the chicken and sauté until golden brown. Depending on the pan size, you may have to do this in batches.
8. When all the chicken is sautéed, remove to a plate.
9. With the heat still at medium, add the onion and mushrooms to the skillet and sauté. Stir occasionally for 5 minutes.
10. Add the garlic and sauté, stirring once or twice, for 2 minutes more.
11. Add all of the remaining ingredients, and stir to blend in the tomato paste.
12. Return the chicken to the skillet and reduce the heat to medium-low.
13. Cover and braise at a low simmer, for 1 hour or until tender.

Variations

- At step 1 and step 2, substitute 2 minced shallots for the onion and garlic.
- At step 11 add 3 tablespoons of good brandy.
- When serving, garnish with chopped fresh parsley.

Pantry/Refrigerator Check

Garlic

All-purpose white flour

Salt

Black pepper

Extra virgin olive oil

1 6 oz. can tomato paste (or tube)

1 bottle dry white wine

4 oz. chicken stock

Bay leaf

Dried thyme

Dried marjoram

Shopping list

1 small white onion

3 oz. fresh mushrooms

3-pound cut-up chicken

Chicken Piccata

This elegant sounding entrée is almost a one-pot operation. To really dress it up, purchase fresh pasta, such as lemon-pepper fettuccine, for an easy but spectacular mid-week dinner party. Throw together a quick salad of packaged baby greens, sliced pears, and chopped walnuts dressed with a *Honey-Mustard Vinaigrette* (page 166). Serve with crusty French bread.

Ingredients

1/4 cup chopped fresh flat leaf parsley

1/4 cup lemon juice from 2 lemons

4 boneless, skinless chicken breasts

1/2 cup all-purpose white flour

1 teaspoon salt

1 teaspoon freshly ground black pepper

5 tablespoons unsalted butter, divided

2 tablespoons extra virgin olive oil, divided

1/3 cup dry white wine

1/4 cup chicken stock

1/4 cup capers

Equipment

Large skillet, chef's knife, cutting board, small strainer, meat mallet (or improvise with a beer bottle), pie pan, dinner plate, wooden stirring spoon

Method

Pounding, chopping, dredging, sautéing, deglazing (see Chapter 3)

Quantity

4 servings

Preparation

1. Wash the parsley and dry. Pull the leaves from the stems and mince.

2. Squeeze the lemons through a strainer, and discard any seeds.

3. Place 2 chicken breasts between 2 large sheets of plastic wrap. Lightly pound the chicken to an even 1/4-inch thickness to ensure even cooking.

4. In a shallow pie pan mix the flour, salt, and pepper and set aside.

Cooking Directions

5. In a large skillet, melt 2 tablespoons of butter and 1 tablespoon of olive oil over medium-high heat.

6. Dip 2 chicken breasts into the flour, shake off excess, and place in the skillet.

7. Sauté until lightly browned, about 3 to 4 minutes on each side. Transfer the cooked chicken to a platter, and cover loosely with foil.

8. Add 2 tablespoons of butter and 1 tablespoon of olive oil to the skillet.

9. Dip 2 remaining chicken breasts into flour, shake off excess, and place in skillet when the oil and butter begin to sizzle.

10. Sauté until lightly browned, about 3 to 4 minutes on each side. Transfer the cooked chicken to the platter.

11. Add the lemon juice, wine, and chicken stock to the skillet.

12. Bring the mixture to a boil and deglaze by scraping up the browned bits from the bottom of the skillet with a wooden spoon.

13. Return all the chicken and any juices collected in the platter to the skillet and simmer for 3 minutes, turning the chicken once.

14. Add the remaining tablespoon of butter and the capers to the sauce; stir to blend.

15. Taste and adjust seasoning with salt and pepper.

16. Spoon the sauce over the chicken, and garnish with parsley.

Variations

- At step 13 cut the chicken into bite-sized pieces before adding back to the skillet.
- At step 15 add 4 cups cooked linguine and toss well to coat with the sauce.
- Garnish with grated Parmesan cheese and chopped parsley at the table.

Pantry/Refrigerator Check

All-purpose white flour

Salt

Black pepper

1 stick unsalted butter

Extra virgin olive oil

Dry white wine

2 oz. chicken stock

2 oz. capers

Shopping List

1 bunch fresh flat leaf parsley

4 boneless, skinless chicken breasts

2 lemons

Fried Chicken

If possible, choose a small fryer (a very young chicken), for this recipe because it greatly improves the flavor of the dish. "Bigger is better" does not apply here. There is only one way to fry a chicken, and that is in about 1/2-inch of oil. However, there is a hen-house full of ways to get the chicken ready for the skillet. After you prepare this basic recipe, you may want to try some of the variations listed below. Fried chicken is great served hot, at room temperature, or cold.

Ingredients

1 2 1/2- to 3-pound cut-up fryer chicken

2 cups all-purpose white flour

1/2 teaspoon salt

1/2 teaspoon freshly ground black pepper

2 cups canola oil (approximately)

Equipment

Large heavy-bottomed or cast iron skillet with lid, tongs, measuring cup, measuring spoons, rack

Methods

Dredging or bag coating, frying (see Chapter 3)

Quantity

8 pieces

Preparation

1. If the chicken breast is whole, cut it down the center to separate. Wash the chicken and pat dry.

2. Place the flour, salt, and pepper in a paper bag or a 1 gallon resealable plastic bag.

3. Add the chicken in small batches and shake to coat. Transfer the coated chicken to a rack while completing batches.

Cooking Directions

4. Place the skillet over medium-high heat and add enough canola oil to reach about 1/2-inch up the side of the pan.

5. Heat the oil until it is very hot. A sprinkle of flour will sizzle and bubble when it is ready.

6. Use tongs to place the chicken pieces into the hot oil, skin side down, without crowding the pan. If necessary, cook the chicken in batches.

7. Cover the pan and cook for 5 minutes.

8. Uncover and shuffle the chicken pieces if some are cooking faster than others. Adjust the heat up or down if the chicken is browning too quickly or if the frothy bubbling oil begins to subside.

9. Continue cooking uncovered, turning the pieces with tongs once or twice to brown all sides evenly, approximately 15 to 20 minutes longer.

10. Remove the cooked chicken pieces to a rack or onto a paper bag to drain.

tip

Save money and a tree by using a brown paper shopping bag turned inside-out to drain the cooked chicken pieces.

Variations

- At step 2 add 1 teaspoon of any of the following: paprika, poultry seasoning, cayenne pepper, garlic powder, onion powder, or curry powder. Replace 1/2 cup of flour with cornmeal or bread crumbs.

- At step 2 add 2 teaspoons Tabasco sauce to 2 beaten eggs and 1/2 cup milk. You can also use 1 cup of buttermilk. Place the flour in the pie pan. Dip the chicken pieces in the liquid mixture before dredging in the flour. Proceed with cooking instructions at step 4.

Pantry/Refrigerator Check

All-purpose white flour

Salt

Black pepper

1 16 oz. bottle canola oil

Shopping List

1 2 1/2- to 3-pound cut-up fryer chicken

11

FISH AND SHELLFISH

Here is a hint about cooking fish—usually a fish recipe suggests cooking the fish until it flakes easily. What that means is that the fish meat will slide apart along its natural divisions when nudged with a fork. But if you cook fish to that point, then it will continue cooking from its own internal heat and will be overdone by the time it is served. A better method is to check the fish near the end of the recommended cooking time by cutting a small slit in the thickest part of the fish. If the flesh inside is slightly opaque, having lost its wet look, remove the fish from the heat. By the time you get the fish on the table, the inside flesh will be white opaque (or pink opaque for salmon) and perfectly done.

Baked Ginger-Sesame Flounder

Baking fish frees up your time to prepare the other dinner dishes. As the fish bakes in the oven, steep a pot of *Couscous* (page 238) and steam some broccoli (*Vegetable Steaming Chart* page 268). Dinner will be ready in a snap.

Ingredients

1 teaspoon minced fresh cilantro

1 teaspoon minced garlic

1 teaspoon grated fresh ginger from 1 small piece of ginger root

1/4 cup rice wine vinegar

1/4 cup soy sauce

2 teaspoons sesame oil

4 6-oz. flounder fillets

Equipment

Small bowl, 9×9×2-inch baking dish, chef's knife, cutting board, grater

Methods

Mincing, grating, baking, testing for doneness (see Chapter 3, "Glossary of Terms and Techniques, Conversions and Equivalents")

Quantity

4 servings

Preparation

1. Preheat the oven to 400°F.
2. Wash the cilantro and pat dry. Pull the leaves from the stems and mince.
3. Peel and mince the garlic.
4. Peel and finely grate 1/2-inch of the ginger root.
5. In a small bowl, whisk together all the ingredients except the fish.

Cooking Directions

6. Place the fish in the baking dish. Pour the sauce over the fish.
7. Place the fish in the oven and bake, uncovered, for 12 minutes.
8. Check the fish for doneness by making a small slit in the thickest part of the fish. If the flesh is slightly opaque, it is done.

Variations

■ At step 6 substitute cod, tilapia, sole, or orange roughy for flounder.

■ At step 5 substitute orange juice for vinegar.

■ At step 5 add 1 tablespoon of minced green onions or shallots.

Pantry/Refrigerator Check

Garlic

Rice wine vinegar

Soy sauce

Sesame oil

Shopping List

1 bunch fresh cilantro

Small piece ginger root

1 1/2-pounds flounder fillets

Seared Lemon-Tarragon Tuna

Because the tuna in this recipe is seared only on the outside while still rare on the inside, it is necessary to use fresh, good quality tuna. Purchase tuna from a fish market or a butcher whom you trust. Serve the tuna as an entrée, sliced for *Nicoise Salad* (page 140), or with *Lemon-Caper Salsa* (page 304) .

Ingredients

1 teaspoon minced fresh tarragon

1 teaspoon lemon juice from 1 lemon

3 tablespoons extra virgin olive oil

4 6-oz. ahi tuna steaks

Equipment

Large heavy-bottomed skillet (preferably cast-iron), chef's knife, cutting board, small bowl, whisk, shallow dish or pan for marinating, strainer

Methods

Mincing, whisking, marinating, searing (see Chapter 3)

Quantity

4 servings

Preparation

1. Wash the tarragon and pat dry. Pull the leaves from the stems and mince.

2. Squeeze the lemon through the strainer into a small bowl.

3. Add the oil and tarragon, whisking to combine.

4. Arrange the tuna steaks in a shallow dish large enough to accommodate them without overlapping. Pour the marinade over the fish, turning to coat. Cover and place in the refrigerator for 10 minutes.

caution

Do not marinate longer than 20 minutes because the lemon juice will begin to cook the fish through the chemical reaction.

Cooking Directions

5. Heat a large heavy-bottomed skillet (preferably cast-iron), over medium-high heat until skillet is very hot.

6. Add the tuna and cook to desired doneness: 2 minutes per side for very rare; 3 minutes per side for rare; 4 to 6 minutes per side for medium. Tuna should be just blackened on the outside and very pink in the center.

7. Remove from the skillet and serve immediately.

Variations

■ At step 4 substitute other firm-fleshed fish steaks such as swordfish or salmon, cooking for 4 to 6 minutes to medium doneness.

Pantry/Refrigerator Check

Extra virgin olive oil

Shopping List

1 bunch or package fresh tarragon

1 lemon

4 6-oz. ahi tuna steaks (about 1-inch thick)

Grilled Cilantro-Lime Swordfish

Grilled fish makes excellent fish tacos. Serve sliced in heated corn or flour tortillas, garnished with salsa and shredded cabbage. Grilled fish served as an entrée also tastes wonderful with a fresh salsa topping.

Ingredients

2 cloves garlic

2 teaspoons minced fresh cilantro

1 small jalapeño chili pepper

2 tablespoons lime juice

2 tablespoons extra virgin olive oil

1 teaspoon ground cumin

1/8 teaspoon ground black pepper

4 6-oz. swordfish steaks

Nonstick cooking spray

Equipment

Small bowl, chef's knife, cutting board, measuring spoon, wire whisk, basting brush, wide metal spatula, charcoal or gas grill

Methods

Mincing, marinating, grilling (see Chapter 3)

Quantity

4 servings

Preparation

1. Peel and mince the garlic.

2. Wash the cilantro and pat dry. Pull the leaves from the stems and mince.

3. Wash the jalapeño, cut in half lengthwise, remove the stem and seed, and mince.

4. In a small bowl, whisk to combine the garlic, cilantro, chili, lime juice, oil, cumin, and pepper.

caution

Chili oil is very hot and transfers easily to the skin. DO NOT touch your eyes or your fingers after handling the chili.

5. Place the swordfish on the baking sheet and brush both sides with the marinade. Let this sit while you are preparing the grill.

6. Lightly coat a grill rack with cooking spray. Prepare the charcoal or gas grill to medium heat.

Cooking Directions

7. Place the swordfish steaks on the rack and grill for 6 to 8 minutes on each side, turning once.

8. Check the fish for doneness by making a small slit in the thickest part of the fish. If the flesh is white opaque, it is done.

Variations

■ At step 5 substitute halibut, shark, or tuna for swordfish.

■ Instead of grilling, you may broil the steaks in the oven broiler 4 inches from the heat.

Pantry/Refrigerator Check

Garlic

Extra virgin olive oil

Ground cumin

Black pepper

Nonstick cooking spray

Shopping List

1 1/2-pounds swordfish steaks (about 1-inch thick)

1 bunch fresh cilantro

1 small jalapeño chili pepper

1 lime (to make fresh lime juice)

Shrimp Scampi

Scampi are actually a type of shrimp from the Adriatic Sea, not the garlic-butter shrimp dish that we associate with the name. A staple on many restaurant menus, the price defies the ease with which this dish is created.

Ingredients

1 pound medium-sized raw shrimp

2 tablespoons minced fresh parsley

4 cloves garlic

2 tablespoons lemon juice from 1 lemon

5 tablespoons unsalted butter

1 tablespoon extra virgin olive oil

1/4 teaspoon salt

Equipment

Large skillet, chef's knife, cutting board, small strainer, measuring spoons, wooden stirring spoon

Methods

Mincing, sautéing, stirring (see Chapter 3)

Quantity

4 servings

Preparation

1. Thaw shrimp if frozen. Peel and de-vein, leaving tails intact.
2. Wash the parsley and pat dry. Pull the leaves from the stems and mince.
3. Peel and mince the garlic.
4. Squeeze the lemon through the strainer, and discard any seeds.

tip

Fast Track by purchasing fresh, peeled, de-veined shrimp from the fish case at the supermarket. Serve the shrimp over rice or angel hair pasta.

note

Follow these steps to peel and de-vein shrimp:

1. Remove the legs from the underside of the shrimp.
2. Pull the shell open and remove the shrimp.
3. If necessary to remove the tail shell, grasp and gently tug free.
4. Make a shallow cut down the back of the shrimp meat to expose the sand vein. Rinse under cold running water. It may be necessary to use the tip of a knife to hook the vein, pulling it up and out of the cut. Flush with running water.
5. Pat the shrimp dry.

Cooking Directions

5. In a large skillet, melt the butter and oil over medium heat.

6. Add the garlic, parsley, lemon juice, and salt; stir frequently until bubbly.

7. Add the shrimp to the pan and cook, stirring occasionally until shrimp turn pink, about 3 to 5 minutes.

8. Stir in parsley.

9. Remove from the heat and serve immediately.

Variations

- At step 1 substitute 1 pound of fresh scallops instead of shrimp.
- At step 6 add 2 tablespoons of white wine.

Pantry/Refrigerator Check

Garlic

1 stick unsalted butter

Extra virgin olive oil

Salt

Shopping List

1 pound medium-sized raw shrimp

1 bunch fresh parsley

1 lemon

Poached Salmon with Dill Sauce

Poaching usually calls for food to be completely submerged in the poaching liquid. This recipe uses only a small amount of liquid, which is easily reduced, to create a quick sauce. Serve with rice, buttered egg noodles, or couscous.

Ingredients

1 clove garlic

2 shallots

4 sprigs fresh dill weed

5 tablespoons unsalted butter, divided

1/4 cup dry white wine

1/4 cup chicken broth

1/4 teaspoon salt

1/4 teaspoon fresh ground black pepper

4 6-oz. salmon fillets

Equipment

Large skillet with lid, chef's knife, cutting board, measuring cup, measuring spoon, spatula

Methods

Mincing, poaching (see Chapter 3)

Quantity

4 servings

Preparation

1. Peel and mince the garlic.
2. Peel and mince the shallots.
3. Wash the dill sprigs and shake off excess water.

Cooking Directions

4. Melt 3 tablespoons butter in a large skillet over medium heat.
5. Add the shallots and garlic, and sauté. Stir frequently until softened, about 3 minutes.

6. Stir in the wine, chicken broth, salt, and pepper. Bring to a boil.

7. Place the salmon in the skillet, in a single layer. Cover the pan, and reduce the heat to medium low.

8. Simmer the fish for 8 to 10 minutes, depending on the thickness of the fillets.

9. Check the fish for doneness by making a small slit in the thickest part of the meat. If the flesh is an opaque pink, it is done.

10. Using a wide spatula, transfer the fish to a platter. Cover to keep warm.

11. Remove the dill sprigs from the poaching liquid.

12. Turn the heat to high, add the remaining butter and bring the liquid to a boil; stir frequently for 2 to 3 minutes until the sauce is thickened.

13. Taste and adjust the seasoning with salt and black pepper.

14. Serve the salmon with the sauce spooned over the top.

Variations

■ At step 6 add 2 tablespoons of lemon juice or 1/2 cup chopped tomatoes to the poaching sauce.

Pantry/Refrigerator Check

Garlic

1 stick unsalted butter

Chicken stock

White wine

Salt

Black pepper

Shopping List

2 shallots

1 bunch fresh dill weed

4 6-oz. salmon fillets (about 1/2-inch thick)

Steamed Mussels

The gourmet name for this dish is Moules Marinere. A simple dish to prepare, the hardest part is cleaning the mussels. Serve this in bowls over linguine with crusty French bread.

ABOUT MUSSELS

Aqua-farmers are now cultivating mussels on rope ladders. This keeps the mussels away from the refuse on the bottom of the mussel beds and produces unpolluted, healthier mussels. If purchasing mussels, check to see if they are alive by tapping on the shell. Any mussels that do not close up are goners and should be discarded. Look for cleaned mussels in mesh bags at the grocery store or fish market. Bags often carry a location tag and it is interesting to note the how the flavors and sizes vary with the locations where the mussels are grown.

Mussels should be cooked the same day they are purchased. However, mussels will keep in the refrigerator for one or two days spread out in a single layer and covered with a damp towel. Do not de-beard mussels until just before cooking or they will die.

Ingredients

2 dozen mussels

2 shallots

2 cloves garlic

1/4 cup chopped fresh basil

1 tablespoon extra virgin olive oil

1 cup dry white wine

1/4 cup water

4 tablespoons unsalted butter

1/2 teaspoon ground black pepper

Equipment

Large saucepan with lid, chef's knife, cutting board, measuring cup, measuring spoons

Methods

Mincing, chopping, sautéing, simmering (see Chapter 3); cleaning and de-bearding mussels

note

To clean and de-beard a mussel, follow these steps:

1. Hold the mussel under running water, and scrub the outside of the shell with a stiff brush.

2. You cannot miss the beard: It is the scraggly looking thing that sticks out from the crack. Using the side of a knife for leverage, position the beard between your thumb and the knife, and pull the beard away from the mussel.

Quantity

4 servings

Preparation

1. Scrub and de-beard the mussels.
2. Peel and mince the shallots.
3. Peel and mince the garlic.
4. Wash the basil and dry. Pull the leaves from the stems and coarsely chop.

Cooking Directions

5. In a large saucepan, heat the oil over medium heat.
6. Add the shallots and sauté for 2 minutes stirring frequently.
7. Add the garlic, basil, wine, water, butter, and pepper, and bring back up to a simmer.
8. Add the mussels, cover the pot, and steam until the shells open, about 4 to 6 minutes.
9. Discard any mussels that do not open.
10. Add the butter to the pan and continue cooking, gently stirring, until the butter is melted.
11. Serve immediately in bowls with sauce ladled over the top.

Variations

Thai-Ginger Mussels

Thai-Ginger Mussels are a quick and easy taste treat that only requires a few extra ingredients and one different step than the recipe for steamed mussels.

■ At step 7 replace the wine with coconut milk, and add 1 teaspoon minced ginger, 1/2 teaspoon Asian hot chili paste, and 1/4 cup minced fresh cilantro. Squeeze the juice of 1 lime over the mussels just before serving.

Pantry/Refrigerator Check

Garlic

Extra virgin olive oil

Black pepper

White wine

1 stick unsalted butter

Shopping List

2 dozen mussels

2 shallots

1 bunch fresh basil

12

GRAINS, BEANS, AND PASTA DISHES

Pasta, grains, and beans play multiple roles when planning a menu. They can act as a contrasting accompaniment or as a neutral background, providing a delicious base to soak up flavors and sauces. They can also act as the central point of the meal itself when combined with vegetables and delicate sauces. Low in cost, widely available, and easy to prepare, they are a standard that should grace the shelves of your pantry. Experiment with the many varieties of grains, beans, and pasta to discover which you like best. The charts, instructions, and recipes below will help you get started.

Beans

To prepare beans, follow these steps:

1. Pour beans onto a large plate, and find and discard any small pebbles and extremely shriveled beans.

2. Rinse the remaining beans.

3. Unless otherwise instructed by the recipe, place the beans in a medium saucepan and cover with cold water. Discard any beans that float. Soak the beans for 8 hours.

4. Discard the soaking water, and add fresh cold water according to the *Bean Cooking Chart* which follows. The rule-of-thumb ratio is 3 parts water to 1 part beans unless otherwise instructed.

5. Bring the water to a boil. Reduce the heat to medium-low, or low. Simmer and cover according to the chart below.

tip

Fast Track this process by boiling beans for 5 minutes, removing from the heat, and letting them sit for 2 hours.

The following are some variations:

- Add a few tablespoons of fresh or dried herbs, garlic cloves, a few chunks of celery, onion, bell pepper, fennel, a teaspoon of grated ginger, or sliced hot pepper.

- Replace all or some of the water with vegetable, chicken, or beef stock.

When cooking beans, follow the chart shown in Table 12.1 to know how much water or broth to use and how long to cook.

TABLE 12.1 Bean Cooking Chart

Beans—1 cup dry	Water or Broth	Cooking Time	Yields
Adzuki (soaked)	3 cups	45-60 minutes	2 cups
Black beans (soaked)	3 1/2 cups	60-90 minutes	2 cups
Black-eyed peas (soaked)	3 cups	30-45 minutes	2 cups
Fava beans (soaked)	2 cups	90 minutes	1 1/2 cups
Garbanzo beans (soaked)	4 cups	90-120 minutes	2 cups
Kidney beans (soaked)	3 cups	60-120 minutes	2 cups
Lentils; green or brown (do not soak)	3 cups	15-20 minutes	2 1/4 cups
Navy beans (soaked)	3 to 4 cups	60-90 minutes	2 cups
Split peas (do not soak)	3 1/2 cups	30 minutes	2 1/4 cups
Pinto beans (soaked)	3 cups	75-90 minutes	2 cups
Small red beans	3 cups	120-150 minutes	2 cups

Pasta

There are so many types, sizes, and shapes of pasta that it is no wonder that pasta has become a staple in everyone's pantry! Pastas range from those simply made from wheat flour and water to more complex types flavored with everything from eggs to squid ink. Pasta can be purchased dried or fresh in dozens of shapes and sizes.

Fresh pasta is more expensive than dried, but some feel the flavor is worth the extra cost. Others claim the difference in flavor is minimal and the extra money is better spent splurging on expensive ingredients for the sauce. Fresh pasta cooks in 2 to 3 minutes while dried takes anywhere from 8 to 15 minutes. Fresh pasta can be kept frozen until needed, while dried is kept in the pantry. It really is a matter of personal taste, so try both types and decide for yourself.

Serving sizes also vary with personal taste and needs, but plan on 4 oz. of dried pasta to make about 2 to 2 1/2 cups of cooked pasta. That should be enough pasta for 4 side servings or a hearty entrée for one. Dried pasta usually comes in 16 oz. packages, enough for 4 entrée -sized servings.

Here are a few guidelines to assist you in choosing the best pasta for your sauce and occasion:

- Thin and light sauces, such as marinara or a wine sauce, pair well with fine delicate pasta such as vermicelli (thin spaghetti) or capellini(angel hair).
- Chunky vegetable or meat sauces pair well with ridged or tubular pastas that catch and hold the sauce, such as penne, rigatoni, ziti, farfalle, fusilli, rotini, or radiatore.
- Heavy creamy sauces pair well with long flat strands such as linguine, fettuccine, or tagliatelle.

How to Cook Pasta

Pasta cooking times vary with size and shape, but the test for doneness is universal—boil until al dente. Al dente is an Italian term for "to the tooth," and means to cook pasta until tender, but firm to the bite, for the absolute best flavor.

Fill a large stockpot 1/2 to 3/4 full of water and add 1/2 teaspoon salt. Cover and bring the water to a boil. When the water is at a full boil, add up to 1 pound of pasta, a handful at a time, stirring to submerge. For spaghetti that is too long for the pot, hold a handful by one end and gently push the other end into the boiling water until the strands soften and submerge. Set the timer according to the package directions. Cook, uncovered, and stir every few minutes to prevent pasta from sticking. When the timer rings, test a piece by tasting. If the pasta is not al dente, continue to cook for a few minutes longer. Remove the pan from the heat and drain the pasta in a colander or strainer over the sink. Rinse with cold water only if you plan to use the pasta in a salad or need to cool noodles for handling. Transfer to a serving bowl and toss with sauce.

Couscous

Couscous is a fine-grained pasta made with durum flour. Its mild but nutty flavor makes it a delicate side dish to be served with meat, poultry, or fish. Couscous is also good cold when mixed with chopped tomatoes, green onions, fresh herbs, and a splash of olive oil.

Ingredients

1 1/2 cups chicken broth, vegetable broth, or water

2 tablespoons unsalted butter

1 cup dried couscous

1/4 teaspoon salt

1/4 teaspoon fresh-ground black pepper

Equipment

Medium saucepan, measuring cup

Methods

Steeping (see Chapter 3, "Glossary of Terms and Techniques, Conversions and Equivalents")

Quantity

4 servings

Cooking Directions

1. Bring the broth or water to a boil in a medium saucepan over high heat.

2. Add the butter and let it melt in the broth. Add the salt and pepper.

3. Add the couscous, and stir once or twice.

4. Cover the pan, remove from the heat, and allow to set (steep) for 10 minutes.

5. Fluff with a fork and serve.

Variations

Moroccan Couscous

At step 3 add 1/8 teaspoon each of cinnamon, turmeric, and ground ginger. Also add 2 sliced green onions, 2 tablespoons of minced fresh parsley, 2 tablespoons of raisins, and 2 tablespoons of chopped nuts. At step 5 add 1 cup of chopped cooked lamb.

Pantry/Refrigerator Check

1 stick unsalted butter

Black pepper

Salt

Shopping List

8 oz. couscous

12 oz. chicken stock or vegetable broth

Risotto

Risotto is simple to make, but requires constant attention. Serve as a special side dish, or double this recipe for an elegant entrée. Risotto is accepting of variations, so use your imagination and add ingredients that are a complement to the other dishes in your meal. See the variations that follow for a few suggestions.

Ingredients

1/2 small white onion

3 tablespoons minced fresh parsley

1 cup grated Parmesan cheese

5 cups chicken stock

3 tablespoons extra virgin olive oil

1 cup arborio rice

1/2 cup white wine

Salt and pepper to taste

Equipment

Medium saucepan, large saucepan, chef's knife, cutting board, measuring cup, measuring spoons, ladle, wooden stirring spoon, grater

Methods

Dicing, mincing, grating, sautéing, simmering, stirring (see Chapter 3)

Quantity

4 servings

Preparation

1. Peel and dice the onion.
2. Wash the parsley and pat dry. Pull the leaves from the stems, and mince.
3. Finely grate the cheese on the small holes of the grater.

Cooking Directions

4. In a medium saucepan, heat the chicken stock over low heat and keep at a simmer.
5. In a large saucepan, heat the oil over medium heat, add the onion, and sauté for 5 minutes or until softened. Stir frequently.

6. Add the rice. Sauté for an additional minute.

7. Add the wine and stir constantly, until the wine is absorbed. Adjust the heat to medium-low to keep the mixture at a simmer.

8. Stir in 1 cup of chicken broth and simmer, stirring constantly until the broth is absorbed. Continue adding the broth in 1/2-cup increments, stirring constantly and cooking at a simmer. Let each addition of broth become almost completely absorbed before adding more. The rice will become tender and creamy, but still firm in the center, after about 20 minutes. It is not necessary to use all of the broth.

9. Stir in the parsley, cheese, and black pepper.

Variations

■ At step 9 add 1/2 cup of petite peas, sautéed mushrooms, steamed asparagus, cooked chicken, or seafood.

Pantry/Refrigerator Check

40 oz. chicken stock

Extra virgin olive oil

Salt

Black pepper

Shopping List

1 small white onion

1 bunch fresh parsley

4 oz. Parmesan cheese

8 oz. arborio rice

White wine

Basic White Rice

One of the most important things to remember is to not lift the lid too often while simmering the rice. The steam will escape and this slows the cooking process. Stirring the rice while cooking is also a huge no-no and will completely undermine the cooking process. 1 cup of uncooked rice makes 3 cups of cooked rice. Serve rice as a side dish with meats, poultry, fish, or vegetables.

Ingredients

1 teaspoon extra virgin olive oil

1 cup white rice

2 cups water

Equipment

Medium saucepan, measuring cup, measuring spoons

Methods

Boiling, simmering (see Chapter 3)

Quantity

4 servings

Cooking Directions

1. In a medium saucepan heat the oil over medium heat.
2. Add the rice and sauté for 1 minute to coat the rice with oil.
3. Add the water, increase the heat, and bring to a boil.
4. Reduce the heat to low, cover the pan, and cook on a slow simmer for 25 to 30 minutes—or until rice is al dente—and all the liquid is absorbed
5. Remove from the heat and let sit for 5 minutes.
6. Fluff with a fork and serve hot.

Variations

■ Substitute chicken broth for water.

■ At step 3 add 2 tablespoons fresh herbs, or salt and pepper.

Pantry/Refrigerator Check

Extra virgin olive oil

8 oz. white rice

Basic Brown Rice

Brown rice is a healthy choice with more nutrients than white rice because the hulls are still intact. Brown rice is a great addition to a stir-fry, or served on its own with grilled chicken or fish, topped with a little butter.

Ingredients

1 teaspoon extra virgin olive oil

1 cup brown rice

2 1/2 cups water

Equipment

Medium saucepan, measuring cup, measuring spoons

Methods

Boiling, simmering (see Chapter 3)

Quantity

4 servings

Cooking Directions

1. Follow the steps for *Basic White Rice* (page 242), increasing the cooking time to 40 minutes.

Variations

■ At step 1 substitute sesame oil for olive oil, and add 1 teaspoon of soy sauce and 1/2 teaspoon of grated fresh ginger.

Pantry/Refrigerator Check

Extra virgin olive oil

8 oz. brown rice

Basic Wild Rice

Traditionally grown lakeside in the northern Midwest, wild rice is actually not rice, but a seed from a shallow water grass. Wild rice is a bit more expensive than white or brown rice and it provides a rich yet light accompaniment to roasted or sautéed meats, chicken, or fish.

Ingredients

1 cup wild rice

4 cups water

Equipment

Medium saucepan, measuring cup

Methods

Boiling, simmering, strainer (see Chapter 3)

Quantity

4 servings

Preparation

1. Rinse the rice by placing it in a medium saucepan and adding water. Stir with your hand. Drain through a strainer, add more water, and repeat until the drained water is clear.

Cooking Directions

2. Return the rice to the saucepan and add 4 cups of water.

3. Place the pan over high heat and bring to a boil.

4. Reduce the heat to low, cover the pan, and cook on a slow simmer (see Chapter 3) for 50 to 55 minutes, or until the rice is al dente and all the liquid is absorbed.

5. Remove from the heat and pour the rice into a strainer to let any remaining water drain.

6. Let the rice sit in the strainer for 5 minutes.

7. Fluff the rice with a fork and serve hot.

Variations

- At step 6 sauté 1/2 cup diced apples, 2 tablespoons each of raisins and chopped nuts, and 2 sliced green onions sautéed in butter, and add to the cooked rice.

- At step 2 replace 1/2 cup water with orange juice. Add cumin and finely chopped red bell pepper to rice before cooking.

Pantry/Refrigerator Check

8 oz. wild rice

Basic Rice Pilaf

Pilaf is simply rice cooked with whatever the chef feels like throwing into the pot. It is the prefect way to use leftovers or vegetables wilting in the refrigerator. Adding cooked meats creates a hearty dish that can be served as an entrée. Experiment with seasonings and flavors by adding 1/4 teaspoon of curry or red chili powder, or drop in a tablespoon of pesto. A splash of sherry, soy sauce, or flavored oil adds extra zip.

Ingredients

1 small onion

2 tablespoons minced fresh parsley

1 tablespoon extra virgin olive oil

2 tablespoons unsalted butter

1 cup long-grain white rice

2 cups chicken stock

Salt and pepper to taste

Equipment

Medium saucepan, measuring cup, measuring spoons, wooden stirring spoon, chef's knife, cutting board

Methods

Chopping, mincing, sautéing, boiling, simmering (see Chapter 3)

Quantity

4 servings

Preparation

1. Peel and chop the onion.
2. Wash the parsley and pat dry. Pull the leaves from the stems and mince.

Cooking Directions

3. In a medium saucepan, heat the oil and melt the butter over medium heat.
4. Add the onion and sauté until softened, stirring to prevent sticking, for about 5 minutes.

5. Add the rice and sauté for 5 minutes, stirring occasionally, until the rice is golden brown.

6. Add the broth, increase the heat, and bring to a boil.

7. When the rice water boils, immediately reduce the heat to low, cover the pan, and cook on a slow simmer (see Chapter 3) for 25 to 30 minutes. The rice should be al dente and all the liquid absorbed.

8. Remove from the heat; add parsley, salt, and pepper, and fluff with a fork.

Variations

■ At step 4 add 2 cloves minced garlic, 1/2 cup sliced mushrooms, or chopped red bell pepper.

■ At step 7 add 2 tablespoons minced fresh herbs 5 minutes before cooking is done.

■ At step 5 substitute brown rice or kasha for the white rice.

Pantry/Refrigerator Check

Extra virgin olive oil

1 stick unsalted butter

8 oz. long-grain white rice

16 oz. chicken stock

Salt

Black pepper

Shopping List

1 small onion

1 bunch fresh parsley

Baked Beans

These beans are great with hot dogs and hamburgers at a summer barbecue, but are in a completely different class from canned baked beans. With maple syrup, onion, and bacon, these beans offer outstanding flavors for any occasion.

Ingredients

2 1/2 cups dry navy beans

1 medium onion

2 cloves garlic

5 strips bacon

1/2 cup brown sugar

1/4 cup maple syrup

1/4 cup molasses

2 cups ketchup

3 tablespoons Worcestershire sauce

1 teaspoon dry mustard

1/2 teaspoon salt

1/4 teaspoon fresh-ground black pepper

tip

Fast Track this recipe by using 5 cups of canned navy or kidney beans.

Equipment

Large stockpot, Dutch oven, or large oven-proof saucepan with lid, chef's knife, cutting board, measuring cup, measuring spoons, wooden stirring spoon

Methods

Chopping, mincing, sautéing, boiling, simmering, baking (see Chapter 3)

Quantity

10 to 12 servings

Preparation

1. Prepare and cook beans according to the *Bean Cooking Chart* (page 236).

2. Drain the beans, reserving 1 cup of cooking liquid.

3. Preheat the oven to 300°F.

4. Peel and chop the onion.

5. Peel and mince the garlic.

6. Cut the bacon into 1-inch pieces.

Cooking Directions

7. In a Dutch oven or ovenproof large saucepan, over medium heat, sauté the bacon until slightly crisp, about 5 minutes.

8. Add the onion and garlic and sauté until softened, about 5 minutes. Stir occasionally.

9. Add the brown sugar, maple syrup, molasses, ketchup, Worcestershire sauce, mustard, salt, pepper, and drained beans, stirring to combine.

10. Cover and place the pan on the middle rack in the preheated oven.

11. Bake for 2 1/2 to 3 hours, stirring occasionally. If the beans are getting too dry toward the end of cooking, stir in some of the reserved bean liquid.

Variations

■ At step 9 omit the maple syrup and increase the molasses to 1/2 cup.

■ At step 9 add an additional 1/2 cup of brown sugar for a sweeter flavor.

■ At step 7 add 1 or 2 chopped jalapeño chili peppers to the sauté for spicy beans.

Pantry/Refrigerator Check

Garlic

Brown sugar

Maple syrup

Molasses

Ketchup

Worcestershire sauce

Dry mustard

Salt

Black pepper

Shopping List

1 pound of dry navy or Great Northern beans

1/2 pound of bacon

1 medium onion

Linguine with Clams

If fresh clams are readily available, by all means use them, along with a bottle of clam juice. If not, use canned clams and the results will still be excellent. To clean clams, follow the instructions for cleaning mussels (see the note on cleaning and de-bearding a mussel in Chapter 11, "Fish and Shellfish," page 221), disregarding the beard removal. Serve this dish hot, right from the skillet. Top with grated Parmesan cheese, and serve with crusty French bread and a tossed green salad for a simple and light summer meal.

Ingredients

1/2 medium onion

4 cloves garlic

10 large basil leaves

1 15 oz. can whole tomatoes with juice

1/2 cup grated Parmesan cheese

4 tablespoons extra virgin olive oil

1 tablespoon unsalted butter

1/4 cup dry white wine

1/4 teaspoon red pepper flakes

1/4 teaspoon salt

1/8 teaspoon fresh-ground black pepper

2 6 1/2 oz cans clams

10 oz. dried linguine

Equipment

Large saucepan or stock pot with lid, large skillet, chef's knife, cutting board, measuring cup, measuring spoons, colander, wooden stirring spoon

Methods

Dicing, mincing, crushing, boiling, sautéing (see Chapter 3)

Quantity

4 servings

Preparation

1. Peel and dice the onion.

2. Peel and mince the garlic.

3. Wash the basil and pat dry. Pull the leaves from the stems and mince.

4. Pour the tomatoes into a bowl and crush with hands.

5. Finely grate the cheese using the small holes of the grater.

Cooking Directions

6. Fill a large pot 1/2 to 3/4 full of water, cover, and place over medium-low heat.

7. Heat the oil and melt the butter over medium heat in a large skillet

8. Add the onion and garlic to the skillet and sauté for 5 minutes until the onion begins to soften.

9. Add the tomatoes and juices to skillet.

10. Reduce the heat under the skillet to medium-low, and add the white wine, red pepper flakes, salt, pepper, and juice from the canned clams, reserving the clams until later. Sauté and stir occasionally for about 15 minutes.

11. When the water in the large pot is boiling, add the pasta, and stir to submerge it completely.

12. Cook the pasta, uncovered, stirring occasionally, until tender but still al dente. Drain the pasta through the colander over the sink.

13. Add the clams and basil to the skillet, increase the heat to medium-high, and cook. Stir for 2 to 3 minutes until the clams are heated through.

14. Turn off the heat, add the drained pasta to the skillet, and stir to combine.

15. Garnish with grated cheese.

Variations

- At step 10 add raw, peeled shrimp to the sauce after the mixture has cooked for about 10 minutes.

Pantry/Refrigerator Check

Garlic

1 stick unsalted butter

Extra virgin olive oil

Red pepper flakes

Salt

Pepper

1 15 oz. can whole tomatoes with juice

Dry white wine

Shopping List

1 medium onion

1 bunch fresh basil

1 16 oz. package dried linguine

2 6 1/2 oz. cans clams

2 oz. Parmesan cheese

Chicken in Wine Sauce with Farfalle

This sumptuous meal holds its own at a dinner party. The preparation is quick and simple, so it is also a good candidate for a mid-week supper. If you put a pot of water on to boil when you walk in the door from work, the water will be ready to cook the pasta when you need it. If the water boils before you are ready, simply turn the heat to low and let the water simmer, turning it back to high when you are ready to cook the pasta. Pass grated Parmesan cheese at the table for a garnish, and add a Caesar salad.

Ingredients

2 chicken breasts

2 cloves garlic

1/4 cup chopped fresh parsley

1/4 cup toasted pine nuts

1/2 cup grated Parmesan cheese

8 oz. dried farfalle

2 tablespoons extra virgin olive oil

1/2 cup dry white wine

2 tablespoons lemon juice from 1 lemon

4 tablespoons unsalted butter

2 tablespoons capers

Salt and freshly ground black pepper to taste

Equipment

Large stockpot with lid, large skillet, chef's knife, cutting board, measuring cup, measuring spoons, grater, wooden stirring spoon, colander

Methods

Chopping, mincing, toasting nuts, grating, boiling, simmering, sautéing (see Chapter 3)

Quantity

4 servings

Preparation

1. Wash the chicken breasts, pat dry, and cut into 1/2 inch-thick strips.
2. Peel and mince the garlic.
3. Wash the parsley and pat dry. Pull the leaves from the stems and coarsely chop.
4. Toast the pine nuts in the skillet over medium heat for 2 to 3 minutes, until golden but not browned. Slide on to a plate to cool.
5. Finely grate the cheese using the small holes of the grater.

Cooking Directions

6. Fill a large pot 1/2 to 3/4 full of water, cover, and bring to a boil over high heat.
7. Add the pasta to the boiling water, and stir to submerge completely.
8. Reduce the heat slightly and cook the pasta, uncovered, at a low boil, stir occasionally for 10 minutes.
9. While the pasta is cooking, heat the olive oil in a large skillet over medium-high heat.
10. Add the chicken and sauté until cooked golden, about 5 minutes, stir occasionally to brown all sides.
11. Push the chicken to the sides of the skillet; add the garlic and sauté for 1 minute.
12. Add the wine and lemon juice, stirring and scraping any browned bits from the bottom of pan.
13. Add the butter, capers, parsley, and pine nuts.
14. Turn the heat to low, cover and simmer for 5 minutes, stir occasionally.
15. While the sauce is cooking, taste the pasta. If it is still too firm, continue cooking for a few more minutes.
16. Place the colander in the sink and pour the pasta into the colander.
17. When the sauce is done, taste and adjust the seasoning with salt and pepper.
18. Transfer the pasta to the skillet, and toss with the sauce to combine.
19. Serve topped with Parmesan cheese.

Variations

- At step 11 add 1 cup thin asparagus cut into 1-inch pieces and increase the sauté time to 3 minutes.
- At step 13 add 10 to 12 peeled shrimp and 1/2 teaspoon red pepper flakes.

Pantry/Refrigerator Check

White wine

Garlic

Extra virgin olive oil

1 stick unsalted butter

Capers

Black pepper

Salt

Shopping List

2 chicken breasts

1 bunch fresh parsley

2 oz. pine nuts

2 oz. Parmesan cheese

8 oz. dried farfalle

1 lemon

Traditional Italian Lasagna

Lasagna can be prepared and cooked in advance, refrigerated, and then reheated before serving. The flavors expand and the dish benefits from the time spent in the refrigerator. Make a double batch and freeze for up to 1 month. Thaw the frozen lasagna in the refrigerator and reheat at dinnertime for a quick meal when time is short.

Ingredients

1 medium onion

2 cloves garlic

1 cup finely grated Parmesan cheese

1 1/2 cups shredded mozzarella cheese

1 egg

1 15 oz. container ricotta cheese

1 tablespoon extra virgin olive oil

6 oz. ground beef

6 oz. ground pork

1 15 oz. can chopped tomatoes with juice

1 8 oz. can tomato sauce

2 tablespoons tomato paste

1 teaspoon dried oregano

1 teaspoon dried basil

1 teaspoon dried parsley

1/2 teaspoon fresh-ground black pepper

6 dried lasagna noodles

Equipment

Large deep skillet with lid, large stock pot with lid, 9×13×2-inch baking dish, medium bowl, chef's knife, cutting board, measuring cup, measuring spoons, grater, wooden stirring spoon, colander

Methods

Dicing, mincing, sautéing, grating, layering, baking (see Chapter 3)

Quantity

6 to 8 servings

Preparation

1. Peel and dice the onion.
2. Peel and mince the garlic.
3. Grate the cheeses.
4. In a medium bowl, beat the egg until slightly scrambled. Add the ricotta, 1 cup mozzarella, and 1/2 cup Parmesan cheese, and mix to combine.

note

You are reserving 1/2 cup mozzarella and 1/2 cup Parmesan cheese.

Cooking Directions

5. In a large skillet, heat the oil over medium heat, add the onion, and sauté for 5 minutes.
6. Add the garlic, and sauté for 1 minute.
7. Add the meat and sauté for 10 minutes, breaking up large pieces with the back of a wooden spoon. When the meat is done, remove the pan from the heat. Tilt the pan to one side, push the meat away from the bottom edge, and scoop out the fat with a large spoon. Discard the fat into a used can or metal container.
8. To the skillet add the chopped tomatoes, tomato sauce, tomato paste, oregano, basil, parsley, and pepper.
9. Bring to a boil; reduce the heat and cook, covered, at a slow simmer for 15 minutes, stirring occasionally.
10. While the sauce is cooking, fill a large pot of water 1/2 to 3/4 full, cover, and bring to a boil over high heat.
11. Add the lasagna noodles to the boiling water and stir to submerge completely.
12. Reduce the heat slightly and cook the pasta at a low boil, stir occasionally for 10 to 12 minutes. When the pasta is tender, remove from the heat, and drain through the colander placed over the sink.
13. Preheat the oven to 350°F.
14. Thinly cover the bottom of the baking dish with about 1/2 cup of sauce to keep the noodles from sticking.
15. Arrange 3 noodles on top of the sauce.
16. Spread 1/2 of the cheese mixture over the noodles using a spatula or the back of a large spoon.
17. Top with 1/2 of the remaining meat sauce.

caution

Never pour fat down the drain or directly into the garbage.

18. Arrange the remaining noodles over the meat sauce.

19. Spread the remaining cheese mixture over the noodles.

20. Top with the remaining meat sauce.

21. Sprinkle the top with the reserved Parmesan and mozzarella cheeses.

22. Place in the preheated oven and bake for 35 to 40 minutes.

23. Remove the lasagna from the oven and let stand for at least 10 minutes before cutting.

Variations

■ At step 4 add 1 teaspoon nutmeg to ricotta cheese mixture.

■ At step 8 add 1/2 teaspoon red pepper flakes to the meat sauce.

Pantry/Refrigerator Check

Garlic

Extra virgin olive oil

Dried oregano

Dried basil

Dried parsley

Black pepper

1 15 oz. can chopped tomatoes with juice

1 8 oz. can tomato sauce

1 6 oz. tomato paste or 1 re-sealable tube

Egg

Shopping List

1 medium onion

6 oz. ground beef

6 oz. ground pork

1 16 oz. package dried lasagna noodles

1 15 oz. container ricotta cheese

4 oz. Parmesan cheese

6 oz. mozzarella cheese

Fettuccini Alfredo

A classic recipe that was popular in the '70s, this is super easy to make. Serve on a platter, or dinner plates, garnished with fresh-ground black pepper and minced fresh parsley. *Fresh Fruit Salad with Prosciutto* (page 163) is a side dish that goes well with this entrée.

Ingredients

1 cup heavy cream

6 tablespoons unsalted butter

1 clove garlic

2 tablespoons chopped flat-leaf parsley

1 cup Parmesan cheese

8 oz. dried fettuccini

1/4 teaspoon fresh-ground black pepper

Equipment

Large saucepan with lid, chef's knife, cutting board, colander, wooden stirring spoon

Methods

Mincing, grating, boiling (see Chapter 3)

Quantity

2 servings

Preparation

1. Remove the cream and butter from the refrigerator and allow each to come to room temperature. This will take about 40 minutes.

2. Peel the garlic and finely mince.

3. Wash the parsley and dry. Pull the leaves from the stems and mince.

4. Finely grate the cheese on the small holes of the grater.

Cooking Directions

5. Fill the saucepan 1/2 to 3/4 full of water, cover, and bring to a boil over high heat.

6. When the water is boiling add the pasta, reduce the heat slightly and cook at a low boil for 8 to 10 minutes. Taste the pasta; if it is still too firm, continue cooking for a few more minutes.

7. Drain the pasta through the colander over the sink.

8. While still hot return the pasta to the saucepan and immediately add the cream, butter, garlic, and cheese.

9. Gently toss until the pasta is well coated.

10. Season with pepper, garnish with parsley, and serve immediately.

Variations

■ At step 6 substitute a fettuccine flavored with spinach, tomato, or herbs

■ At step 6 use fresh pasta and cook according to the package directions. This will reduce your prep time by several minutes.

■ At step 8 add 1 cup sautéed sliced green onion or asparagus

Pantry/Refrigerator Check

1 stick unsalted butter

Garlic

Black pepper

Shopping List

8 oz. fettuccini

1/2 pint heavy cream

4 oz. Parmesan cheese

1 bunch fresh flat-leaf parsley

Spaghetti Bolognese

Spaghetti with meat sauce is Italian comfort food and always a crowd pleaser. If you are short on time and plan on using a purchased bolognese, you are better off buying marinara sauce and adding your own meat to ensure quality and quantity. Serve with garlic bread and a tossed green salad with *Creamy Herbed Garlic Vinaigrette* (page 167).

Ingredients

1 small onion

3 cloves garlic

1 28 oz. can whole plum tomatoes with juice

1 cup finely grated Parmesan cheese

1 tablespoon extra virgin olive oil

12 oz. ground beef

4 tablespoons tomato paste

1/2 cup dry red wine

2 teaspoons dried oregano

1 teaspoon dried basil

1/2 teaspoon white sugar

Fresh-ground black pepper

12 oz. dried spaghetti

Equipment

Large skillet with lid, large stockpot with lid, medium bowl, chef's knife, cutting board, measuring cup, measuring spoon, grater, wooden stirring spoon, colander

Methods

Dicing, mincing, sautéing, grating (see Chapter 3)

Quantity

6 servings

Preparation

1. Peel the onion and dice.

2. Peel the garlic and mince.

3. Pour the plum tomatoes into a medium bowl and crush with clean hands.

4. Finely grate the cheese on the small holes of the grater.

Cooking Directions

5. In a large skillet, heat the oil over medium heat, add the onion, and sauté for 5 minutes, stirring occasionally.

6. Add the garlic and sauté for 1 minute.

7. Add the meat and sauté for 10 minutes, breaking up large pieces with the back of a wooden spoon. When the meat is done, remove the pan from the heat. Tilt the pan to one side, push the meat away from the bottom edge, and scoop out the fat with a large spoon. Place the fat into a can or metal container and discard.

8. Add to the skillet the chopped tomatoes with juice, tomato paste, wine, oregano, basil, sugar, and pepper and bring to a boil over high heat.

9. When the mixture is boiling, reduce the heat to medium, and cover and simmer for 30 minutes, stirring occasionally. Water, wine, or broth may be added to the sauce if you desire a thinner consistency.

10. While the sauce is cooking, fill a large pot 1/2 to 3/4 full with water, cover, and bring to a boil over high heat.

11. Add the spaghetti to the boiling water and stir to submerge completely.

12. Reduce the heat slightly and cook the pasta at a low boil, stirring occasionally, for 8 to 10 minutes. Taste the pasta; if it is still too firm, continue cooking for a few more minutes.

13. Remove the pasta from the heat and drain in a colander placed in the sink.

14. Return the pasta to the pot or transfer to a serving platter. Top the hot pasta with sauce and garnish with Parmesan cheese.

Variations

- At step 5 sauté 1/2-cup carrots, celery, or mushrooms along with the onion.
- Substitute 1 tablespoon fresh herbs for each teaspoon of dried herbs.

Pantry/Refrigerator Check

Garlic

Extra virgin olive oil

1 28 oz. can whole plum tomatoes with juice

1 6 oz. can tomato paste or 1 re-closeable tube

Dry red wine

Dried oregano

Dried basil

Sugar

Black pepper

Shopping List

1 small onion

12 oz. ground beef

16 oz. spaghetti

4 oz. Parmesan cheese

Angel Hair with Broccoli

A super quick and easy pasta dish with ingredients you most likely have on hand. When unexpected company shows up for dinner, whip this up and serve with crusty French bread.

Ingredients

1 head of broccoli

2 cloves garlic

1 cup grated Parmesan or Romano cheese

1/2 teaspoon red pepper flakes

3 tablespoons extra virgin olive oil

8 oz. dried angel hair pasta

Salt and freshly ground black pepper to taste

Equipment

Large stockpot with lid, medium skillet, chef's knife, cutting board, measuring spoons, grater, wooden stirring spoon, colander

Methods

Chopping, mincing, grating, boiling, simmering, sautéing (see Chapter 3)

Quantity

4 servings

Preparation

1. Wash the broccoli and trim the small florets from the stalk.
2. Peel the garlic and mince.
3. Finely grate the cheese on the small holes of the grater.

Cooking Directions

4. Fill a large pot 1/2 to 3/4 full of water, cover, and bring to a boil on high heat.
5. Add the pasta to the boiling water and stir to submerge and separate the pasta.

6. Reduce the heat slightly and cook pasta, uncovered, at a low boil, stirring occasionally, for 6 to 8 minutes.

7. When the pasta has cooked for 2 or 3 minutes, add the broccoli florets to the pot.

8. While the pasta cooks, heat the olive oil in a large skillet over medium heat.

9. Add the garlic and red pepper flakes to the skillet and sauté for 1 minute.

10. When the pasta is cooked al dente, remove the pot from the heat and drain the pasta in a colander over the sink.

11. Transfer the pasta to the skillet and toss with olive oil and garlic to combine.

12. Add the cheese and toss again

13. Taste and adjust seasoning with salt and pepper.

Variations

- At step 11 add 2 tablespoons fresh minced basil or oregano to the skillet
- At step 11 add chopped and warmed leftover chicken breast, shrimp, or steak cut into strips

Pantry/Refrigerator Check

Garlic

Extra virgin olive oil

Red pepper flakes

Black pepper

Salt

Shopping List

1 head of broccoli

16 oz. package dried angel hair pasta

4 oz. Parmesan or Romano cheese

13

SIDE DISHES—VEGETABLES AND POTATOES

If you aren't particularly fond of vegetables, you probably have never had them cooked properly. Overcooked vegetables are mushy, faded in color, and devoid of flavor. Precisely cooked vegetables are crisp with a bright taste and an appealing hue. Vegetables round out the plate—the ideal balance between rich meats, heavy sauces, and starchy grains. While vegetables are absolutely wonderful grilled, roasted, sautéed, or paired with a sauce, they shine when they are perfectly steamed. The chart shown in Table 13.1 is a guide to the correct timing. When the water boils, toss the vegetables in the steamer, and set a timer. Vegetables are not uniform in size, so check on them 1 or 2 minutes before the timer goes off.

TABLE 13.1   Vegetable Steaming Chart

Vegetable	Preparation	Steaming Time
Artichoke	See *Steamed Artichokes* (page 279)	40 minutes
Asparagus	Wash and snap off tough ends	3 to 5 minutes (depending on thickness)
Beans, green	Wash and trim tips; leave whole or cut into 2-inch pieces	10 to 15 minutes
Beets	Remove tops and wash; leave whole	Boil in a covered pot for 20 to 45 minutes (depending on size); chill and remove skins
Broccoli	Rinse well, remove leaves, and cut small florets from tough stalk	3 to 5 minutes
Brussels sprouts	Wash and trim stem end; remove any discolored leaves	6 to 8 minutes
Carrots	Remove tops and scrub or peel; cut into 1-inch pieces	6 to 10 minutes
Cauliflower	Remove outer leaves, cut out core, and wash well; cut florets from the stalk	4 to 5 minutes
Corn on the cob	Remove husk and silk; wash well	6 to 8 minutes (small ears) 9 to 11 minutes (large ears)
Peas, green	Wash and shell peas	5 minutes
Peas, snow	Wash and trim tips	3 to 4 minutes
Potatoes	Wash and cut into 2-inch pieces	20 to 25 minutes
Yellow squash	Wash and cut into 1/4-inch slices	3 to 4 minutes
Zucchini	Wash and cut into 1/4-inch slices	3 to 4 minutes

Mashed Potatoes

The ultimate comfort food, mashed potatoes are great served with roasted meats, meatloaf, grilled steaks, or even on their own topped with lots of butter. Overcooked potatoes can become soggy and sticky while mashing. Stirring in a circular motion can also create the same result, so try to mash in an up-and-down motion. For best results, warm the milk before adding it to the potatoes to avoid a starchy, offensive flavor.

Ingredients

4 large russet or Idaho potatoes

1/4 teaspoon salt

1/2 cup half-and-half

4 tablespoons unsalted butter

Salt

Fresh-ground pepper to taste

Equipment

Medium saucepan with lid, chef's knife, cutting board, vegetable peeler, potato masher, measuring cup, measuring spoons

Methods

Peeling, cutting, mashing (see Chapter 3, "Glossary of Terms and Techniques, Conversions and Equivalents")

Quantity

4 servings

Preparation

1. Peel the potatoes and cut into quarters.

Cooking Directions

2. Place the potatoes in the saucepan, cover with water, and add 1/4 teaspoon of salt. Cover the pan and bring the water to a boil over high heat.

3. Reduce the heat to medium and cook, covered, for 25 minutes, or until tender. Potatoes are done when still slightly firm, but can be pierced with a fork in the center without any resistance.

4. Just before draining the potatoes, heat the half-and-half in a microwave or on the stove top in a small pan.

5. Drain the potatoes and return the potatoes to pan.

6. Add the butter and mash the potatoes, using a potato masher in an up-and-down motion, until the largest lumps are gone.

7. Slowly add the warmed half-and-half and mash again to desired consistency.

8. Taste and adjust the seasoning with salt and pepper.

Variations

■ At step 4 substitute chicken broth for the half-and-half.

■ At step 6 add 1/4 cup sour cream, Gorgonzola, or 6 cloves of peeled *Herb Roasted Garlic* (page 323).

Pantry/Refrigerator Check

1 stick unsalted butter

Salt

Black pepper

Shopping List

4 large russet or Idaho potatoes

1/2 pint half-and-half

Scalloped Potatoes

If potatoes are not stored in a dark place, they can develop a greenish tint from exposure to light. Cut or peel away the affected area as it will impart a bitter taste. Serve scalloped potatoes with baked ham, roasted meats, fried chicken, or pork chops, and a side of green beans.

Ingredients

3 medium potatoes

1/2 small white onion

3 tablespoons unsalted butter

2 tablespoons all-purpose white flour

1/2 teaspoon salt

1/4 teaspoon fresh-ground black pepper

1/2 teaspoon ground nutmeg

1 1/4 cups milk

Nonstick cooking spray

Equipment

8×8×2-inch baking dish, chef's knife, cutting board, measuring cup, small pan, measuring spoons, wooden stirring spoon

Methods

Peeling, slicing, sautéing, baking (see Chapter 3)

Quantity

4 servings

Preparation

1. Preheat the oven to 350°F.
2. Peel and slice the potatoes into 1/4-inch thick slices.
3. Peel and thinly slice the onion.

Cooking Directions

4. Melt the butter in a small saucepan over medium heat.

5. Stir constantly while adding the flour, salt, pepper, and nutmeg to the melted butter.

6. When well-combined add the milk and cook, stirring constantly until the sauce is thickened. Remove from the heat.

7. Coat the inside and bottom of the baking dish with cooking spray.

8. Layer 1/2 of the potato slices, then layer all of the onion slices, and cover with 1/2 of the sauce.

9. Add the layer of remaining potato slices, and cover with remaining sauce.

10. Cover with aluminum foil and bake for 30 minutes.

11. Uncover and bake for an additional 20 minutes or until the potatoes are tender.

Variations

■ At step 6 add 1/2 cup of grated Swiss cheese to the sauce.

■ At step 8 layer 8 oz. of sliced ham after the onion and before the sauce.

■ At step 9 sprinkle the top layer of sauce with 3/4 cup of bread crumbs mixed with 1/4 cup of grated Parmesan cheese.

Pantry/Refrigerator Check

1 stick unsalted butter

All-purpose white flour

Salt

Black pepper

Ground nutmeg

Milk

Shopping List

3 medium potatoes

1 small white onion

Baked Potatoes

As a holder for a myriad of toppings, a baked potato can be a meal in itself. Top with chili or leftover beef stew, curry, or steamed vegetables and shredded cheese. Be sure to eat the skin because it holds most of the nutrients of the potato. Wrapping a baked potato in foil will not cook it faster, but will produce a potato with a soft skin. The fastest way to bake a potato is to put an aluminum nail or skewer through the center lengthwise. You can also speed the cooking time by rubbing the skin with vegetable oil.

Ingredients

2 medium russet or Idaho potatoes

Salt and fresh-ground black pepper to taste

Butter

Sour cream

Chives

Bacon, crumbled

Equipment

Paring knife

Methods

Baking (see Chapter 3)

Quantity

2 servings

Preparation

1. Preheat the oven to 375°F.
2. Scrub the potatoes to clean the skins.
3. Pierce each potato with a knife or fork through the skin in 6 or 8 places.
4. Wrap each potato in foil. Oil the skin if desired.

Cooking Directions

5. Place the potatoes directly on the middle rack in the oven and bake for 1 to 1 1/4 hours. The potato is done when it feels soft when gently squeezed.

6. Cut through the potato center lengthwise, mash gently with a fork, and add the remaining ingredients or any filling you desire.

Variations

■ Yams or sweet potatoes can be baked in the same manner, but be sure to place them on a piece of aluminum foil. They will drip during cooking because they have a high sugar content. Reduce the cooking time by about 10 minutes.

Pantry/Refrigerator Check

Salt

Black pepper

1 stick unsalted butter

Shopping List

2 medium russet or Idaho potatoes

1 4 oz sour cream

1 bunch fresh chives

1/2 pound bacon

Twice-baked Potatoes

High in flavor and calories, these are not an everyday meal. Serve with a bowl of chili or a Caesar salad for a quick meal. As a variation, use 6 small red potatoes instead of russet or Idaho potatoes. You can cut the oven time to 10 minutes, and serve as a half-time appetizer on football Sunday.

Ingredients

2 *Baked Potatoes* (page 273)

1/4 cup sharp cheddar cheese

1/2 cup sour cream

1/4 teaspoon garlic salt

1/4 teaspoon fresh-ground black pepper

1 teaspoon dried chives

Equipment

Mixing bowl, baking sheet, chef's knife, cutting board, measuring cup, measuring spoons, grater

Methods

Grating, baking (see Chapter 3)

Quantity

2 servings

Preparation

1. Preheat the oven to 400°F.
2. Grate the cheese using the large holes of the grater.

Cooking Directions

3. Combine the sour cream, cheese, garlic salt, black pepper, and dried chives in a small mixing bowl. Stir to blend.
4. When the baked potatoes are cool enough to handle, cut each in half lengthwise.
5. Carefully scoop out the potato, taking care to keep the skin intact, and place the potato shells on the baking sheet.

6. Add the potato meat to the sour cream mixture, mashing with a fork to remove most of the lumps. Mix well to blend.

7. Divide the potato/sour cream mixture between the 4 potato shells, mounding the excess about the brim.

8. Place the baking sheet in the oven and bake for 15 minutes, or until hot and lightly browned on top.

Variations

- At step 6 add 1 tablespoon of minced fresh chives.
- At step 6 add 4 cloves of *Herb Roasted Garlic* (page 323) with 2 tablespoons of sliced oil-packed sundried tomatoes.
- At step 6 add 2 tablespoons of diced green chilies and substitute Monterey Jack cheese for cheddar.
- At step 6 add 2 tablespoons of diced ham or crisp-cooked chopped bacon, and top each half with 1 teaspoon crumbled Gorgonzola cheese.

Pantry/Refrigerator Check

Garlic salt

Black pepper

Dried chives

Shopping List

2 medium russet or Idaho potatoes

4 oz. sour cream

1 oz. sharp cheddar cheese

Roasted Greek Potatoes

These tender, lemon-flavored potatoes are crisp-roasted on the outside, which make these the perfect accompaniment for roasted lamb or chicken. Serve with green beans or asparagus drizzled with a squeeze of lemon juice to tie the flavors together.

Ingredients

4 medium russet or Idaho potatoes

2 tablespoons fresh lemon juice from 1 lemon

1 tablespoon dried oregano

1/4 teaspoon salt

1/4 teaspoon fresh-ground black pepper

3 tablespoons extra virgin olive oil

Equipment

Large roasting pan, chef's knife, cutting board, measuring spoons, vegetable peeler, strainer

Methods

Peeling, cutting, straining, roasting (see Chapter 3)

Quantity

4 servings

Preparation

1. Preheat the oven to 375°F.
2. Peel and cut the potatoes in quarters lengthwise and place in the roasting pan.
3. Squeeze the lemon through a wire strainer, and pour the juice over the potatoes.
4. Crumble the oregano with your fingertips over the potatoes, and sprinkle with salt and pepper. Toss with your fingers until the potatoes are well-coated.
5. Pour the olive oil over the potatoes. Toss again.

Cooking Directions

6. Place the pan in the oven and bake, uncovered for 40 minutes, turning the potatoes with a spatula after cooking 20 minutes.

Variations

- At step 5 add 2 tablespoons of minced garlic with the olive oil.

Pantry/Refrigerator Check

Salt

Black pepper

Dried oregano

Extra virgin olive oil

Shopping List

4 medium russet or Idaho potatoes

1 lemon

Steamed Artichokes

Yes, you can burn a pan, especially when cooking artichokes. With only an inch of water in the bottom of the pan, it is necessary to check the water level periodically to ensure it does not evaporate completely. Artichokes are full of vitamins and add a touch of elegance to any dinner. These are easy to prepare and fun to eat. Dipping preferences vary from melted butter to mayonnaise with lemon juice.

Ingredients

2 large artichokes

Equipment

Large stockpot, chef's knife, cutting board, kitchen shears (optional)

Methods

Steaming (see Chapter 3)

Quantity

2 servings

Preparation

1. Wash the artichokes.
2. Cut off the artichoke stem at the base.
3. Peel back and break off the small tough leaves around the base.
4. Grasp the artichoke at the stem end with one hand and, with a sharp knife, carefully slice off 1-inch of the artichoke's top, using a straight cut.
5. If desired, snip off the tips of the remaining leaves with kitchen shears.

caution

Artichoke leaves are tough; keep an even pressure on the knife as you slice through the leaves, taking care not to let the knife slip.

Cooking Directions

6. In a pot large enough to hold the artichokes, pour about 1 inch of water. Place the artichokes in the pot with the stems end up. If you have a collapsible steamer, place it in the pot and place the artichokes on the steamer.
7. Bring the water to a simmer and steam the artichokes for about 40 minutes. Less time is required for smaller artichokes. Check the water level, and add more water if it is evaporating too quickly.

8. To check for doneness, pierce the stem end with a knife. If the stem end is tender, the artichoke is done.

Variations

- Add 2 cloves of peeled, smashed garlic to the water in the pan.

Shopping List

2 large artichokes

note

The stem is edible if the tough outer layer is cut away. Cook the stem with the artichoke.

Green Beans with Bacon and Shallots

A fresh twist on an old country classic, orange juice adds a refreshing hint of sweetness.

Ingredients

1 pound fresh green beans

1 shallot

2 teaspoons fresh orange juice from 1 orange

1 bay leaf

4 slices bacon

1 teaspoon extra virgin olive oil

1/2 teaspoon fresh-ground black pepper

tip

Fast Track by using frozen green beans and purchased orange juice. Serve this dish with *Meatloaf* (page 182 or roasted leg of lamb and *Mashed Potatoes* (page 269 with *Lemon Bars* (page 361) for dessert.

Equipment

Large skillet, large saucepan with lid, chef's knife, cutting board, wire-mesh strainer, measuring spoons

Methods

Mincing, straining, steaming, sautéing (see Chapter 3)

Quantity

4 servings

Preparation

1. Wash the beans and snap off the stem end. Any tough string from the edge of the bean will come along with the stem.

2. Peel and mince the shallot.

3. Cut the orange and squeeze through the strainer to catch the seeds.

Cooking Directions

4. Fill a saucepan with 2 inches of water, add the bay leaf, and insert a collapsible steamer basket. Bring the water to a boil, place the beans in the basket, and steam for 10 to 15 minutes until tender-crisp. If you do not have a collapsible steamer basket, cook the beans and bay leaf covered with water in a pan.

5. While the beans are cooking, place the bacon in a cold skillet, turn the heat to medium-high, and sauté, turning as needed, until crisp. Transfer the bacon to paper towels to drain. Crumble when cooled.

6. When the skillet is cool, tilt the skillet and spoon out all but 1 teaspoon of bacon fat into a can.

7. Add the olive oil to the same skillet and heat over medium-low heat. Add the shallots and sauté for 5 minutes, stirring frequently.

> **caution**
>
> Do not pour the bacon fat down the sink drain or directly into the garbage.

8. When the beans are done, drain them in the colander and shake off any excess water.

9. Add the beans, pepper, and orange juice to the skillet and toss to combine.

10. Top with crumbled bacon.

Variations

- At step 9 add 1/4 cup toasted walnuts, omit orange juice, and add 3 tablespoons of crumbled blue cheese.

Pantry/Refrigerator Check

Bay leaf

Extra virgin olive oil

Black pepper

Shopping List

1 pound fresh green beans

1 orange

1 shallot

1/2 pound bacon

Sautéed Mushrooms in Butter and Wine

When mushrooms are fresh, use them in a salad; when they are past their prime, they are ideal sautéed in butter and a good quality red or white wine. Serve as a topping for grilled meats, sautéed chicken, *Baked Potatoes* (page 273), or over pasta.

Ingredients

1/2 pound fresh mushrooms

1 tablespoon minced fresh parsley

3 tablespoons unsalted butter

1 tablespoon extra virgin olive oil

2 tablespoons red wine

1/8 teaspoon salt

1/8 teaspoon fresh-ground black pepper

Equipment

Medium skillet, chef's knife, cutting board, measuring spoons

Methods

Slicing, mincing, sautéing (see Chapter 3)

Quantity

2 servings

Preparation

1. Wipe the mushrooms clean with a damp paper towel and thinly slice.

2. Wash the parsley and pat dry. Pull the leaves from the stems, and mince.

Cooking Directions

3. Melt the butter and oil in a small skillet over medium-high heat. When sizzling, add the mushrooms and sauté. Stir frequently until the mushrooms soften and begin to brown, about 8 minutes.

4. Add the wine, parsley, salt, and pepper and continue sautéing for an additional 2 to 3 minutes.

5. Remove from the heat and serve immediately.

Variations

■ Add 2 tablespoons brandy, or substitute white wine for red, and use fresh minced tarragon.

Pantry/Refrigerator Check

1 stick unsalted butter

Extra virgin olive oil

Salt

Black pepper

Shopping List

1/2 pound fresh mushrooms

1 bottle good red wine

1 bunch fresh parsley

Balsamic Roasted Root Vegetables

Roasting root vegetables brings out natural sugars that caramelize and brown the outside of the vegetables while cooking. If you are roasting meat, toss these vegetables in the same pan. Serve with a side of fresh steamed green vegetables for a balanced plate.

Ingredients

4 red potatoes

2 carrots

1 turnip

1 garnet yam

1 large white onion

2 tablespoons minced fresh thyme

4 tablespoons extra virgin olive oil

1 tablespoon balsamic vinegar

Salt and fresh-ground black pepper to taste

Equipment

Large roasting pan, chef's knife, paring knife, cutting board, measuring spoons, vegetable peeler

Methods

Cutting, peeling, mincing, roasting (see Chapter 3)

Quantity

4 servings

Preparation

1. Preheat the oven to 425°F.
2. Wash the potatoes, carrots, and turnip, and cut into 1 1/2-inch pieces.
3. Peel the yam with a paring knife and cut into 1 1/2-inch pieces.
4. Peel and cut the onion into quarters.
5. Wash the thyme and pat dry. Pull the leaves from the stems, and mince.
6. Place all the vegetables in a roasting pan large enough to hold the vegetables in a single layer.

7. Toss with olive oil, balsamic vinegar, and thyme to coat.

8. Cover the pan tightly with aluminum foil.

Cooking Directions

9. Place the pan in the oven and bake for 25 minutes.

10. Remove the pan from the oven, remove the foil, and toss the vegetables with a spatula.

11. Return the pan to the oven and bake, uncovered, for an additional 20 minutes. Check the vegetables after 10 minutes and toss again if necessary to brown evenly.

12. The vegetables are done when browned and crisp on the outside and tender inside.

13. Taste and adjust seasoning with salt and pepper.

Variations

■ At step 2 add 1 beet or parsnip, peeled and cut into quarters.

■ At step 11 add 6 cloves of garlic when returning the pan to oven.

Pantry/Refrigerator Check

Extra virgin olive oil

Salt

Black pepper

Balsamic vinegar

Shopping List

4 red potatoes

2 carrots

1 turnip

1 garnet yam

1 large white onion

1 bunch fresh thyme

Stir-fried Vegetables

Timing is everything, especially with stir-fry! You must plan your cooking time carefully because different vegetables require different cooking times—carrots and cauliflower take longer to cook then green onions or mushrooms. To make stir-frying a snap, just divide the prepared vegetables into batches according to the length of time they need to cook. Add them to the skillet when it is their turn. Stir-frying is a good way to use up those veggies that you couldn't pass up at the store, but somehow never got around to cooking. Serve these over rice for a main dish for two.

Ingredients

First batch (longest cooking time):

1 medium carrot

1 small onion

1 large stalk broccoli

1/2 red bell pepper

Second batch (less cooking time):

6 mushrooms

Third batch (shortest cooking time):

1/2 cup bean sprouts

Other Ingredients

1/2-inch piece fresh ginger

1 tablespoon soy sauce

1 teaspoon sesame oil

1/4 teaspoon fresh-ground black pepper

1/2 teaspoon red pepper flakes

3 teaspoons canola oil

Equipment

Large nonstick skillet, small bowl, chef's knife, cutting board, measuring spoons, whisk, wooden stirring spoon

Methods

Slicing, grating, whisking, heating to smoking point, stir-frying (see Chapter 3)

Quantity

4 servings

Preparation

1. Wash the carrot, halve lengthwise, and cut into thin slices.
2. Cut the onion in half lengthwise, trim off the ends, peel, and cut into thin wedges.
3. Wash the broccoli, trim the florets from the stalk, and cut into 1/2-inch pieces. Peel the stalk and slice into thin rounds.
4. Wash the pepper, cut in half lengthwise, remove the stem and seeds, and slice into 1/2-inch strips.
5. Wipe the mushrooms clean with a damp paper towel and thinly slice.
6. Wash the bean sprouts and drain well.
7. Peel and grate the ginger using the smallest holes of the grater.
8. Whisk to combine the ginger, soy sauce, sesame oil, black pepper, and red pepper flakes in a small bowl.

Cooking Directions

9. Pour the canola oil into a large nonstick skillet and heat over medium-high heat until hot, but not smoking. Grasp the pan by the handle and tilt it in all directions so the oil coats the entire bottom of the pan.
10. Add the first batch of vegetables: carrots, onion, broccoli, and red pepper. Stir-fry for about 4 minutes.
11. Move the vegetables to the sides, add 1 teaspoon of oil, and let it heat for 30 seconds.
12. Add the mushrooms and stir-fry for 2 minutes.
13. Add the bean sprouts and stir-fry for 1 minute.
14. Whisk ginger-soy mixture once or twice to blend, pour over vegetables, and stir-fry for 1 minute.
15. Remove from the heat and serve immediately.

Variations

- At step 8 add 1 tablespoon of orange or lemon juice and 1/2 teaspoon Asian hot chili paste (omitting red pepper flakes) to the soy sauce mixture.
- At step 13 add 1 cup of cooked meat, chicken, shrimp, or tofu with the last batch of vegetables.

■ Substitute vegetables from the following list

First batch substitutes (longest cooking time):

Cauliflower

Bell peppe

Green beans

Second batch substitutes (less cooking time):

Asparagus

Celery

Cabbage

Zucchini

Chard

Snow peas

Third batch substitutes (shortest cooking time):

Green onions

Spinach

Fresh herbs

Water chestnuts

Bamboo shoots

Pantry/Refrigerator Check

Soy sauce

Sesame oil

Fresh-ground black pepper

Red pepper flakes

Canola oil

Shopping List

1 medium carrot

1 small onion

1 large stalk broccoli

1/2 red bell pepper

6 mushrooms

1/2 cup bean sprouts

1/2-inch piece fresh ginger

Grilled Vegetables

Great hot, warm, or chilled, grilled vegetables make a delicious side dish, salad platter, or addition to your sandwich the next day. If you are grilling meat as well, grill the vegetables first and keep them warm in the oven until they are served. They tend to stick to the grill unless the grill is very clean. See Chapter 3 for grilling tips.

Ingredients

1 tablespoon extra virgin olive oil

1 large portobello mushroom

1 zucchini

1 yellow crookneck squash

1 medium red onion

2 yukon gold potatoes

Salt and fresh-ground black pepper to taste

Equipment

Chef's knife, cutting board, measuring spoon, spatula or tongs, gas or charcoal grill

Methods

Slicing, grilling (see Chapter 3)

Quantity

2 servings

Preparation

1. Place the oil on a paper towel and wipe over the grill rack; light or prepare the coals.

2. Remove the mushroom stem and wipe the mushroom cap clean with a damp paper towel.

3. Wash the zucchini and slice lengthwise into 1/2-inch wide slices.

4. Wash the yellow squash, and slice lengthwise into 1/2-inch wide slices.

5. Carefully cut the ends off the onion, and peel and cut crosswise into 1-inch slices, taking care to keep the rings together.

6. Wash the potatoes, pierce with a fork, and microwave for 5 minutes. Remove, cool, and slice into 1-inch slices.

7. Place the vegetables on the baking sheet and lightly drizzle with oil. Use your fingers to distribute the oil and coat the vegetable slices. Lightly salt and pepper.

8. Turn the vegetables over and repeat, doing this in batches if necessary.

9. Carry the vegetables to the grill on the baking sheet.

Cooking Directions

10. Arrange the vegetables on top of the hot grill and cook over high heat for 3 to 5 minutes, depending on the vegetables and your grill. For example, zucchini takes less time than potatoes.

11. Use the tongs or spatula to lift the vegetables and check for browning; flip and cook until the vegetables are fork tender.

Variations

- Use garlic-flavored oil, and sprinkle vegetables with 2 tablespoons of minced fresh parsley, rosemary, tarragon, basil, oregano, or thyme.
- Use sweet or red potatoes, eggplant, asparagus, corn, or fennel. Splash with balsamic vinegar.

Pantry/Refrigerator Check

Extra virgin olive oil

Salt

Black pepper

Shopping List

1 large portobello mushroom

1 yellow crookneck squash

1 zucchini

1 medium red onion

2 yukon gold potatoes

14

SAUCES, TOPPINGS, AND MARINADES

Sauces, toppings, and marinades add to or enhance the flavor of a dish. Sauces and toppings give dishes a bit of moisture, add an interesting texture, and increase the overall visual appeal. Some dishes require a sauce as an essential part of the dish, such as *Eggs Benedict* (page 61) or *Barbequed Spare Ribs* (page 197), while other dishes are simply enhanced by the sauce's flavor. Chicken or fish, which are lean meats with little fat, can become quite dry while grilling. The moisture and flavor of a sauce or salsa adds both flavorful and visual interest, as well as much needed moisture. Marinades, used to add flavor and tenderize meat or poultry, also make wonderful sauces.

Sauces and toppings need not be complicated. Chopped herbs or vegetables with a splash of oil and vinegar make a great topping for everything from lamb chops to crostini. Sour cream mixed with spices creates a tangy counterpoint with complementary flavors. Yogurt mixed with fruit and honey gives a boost to pound cake or granola. Try some of the sauces in this chapter and then use your imagination to create your own.

Hollandaise Sauce

Hollandaise has a "bad rap" as a temperamental sauce that is easy to ruin. However, it's not as tricky as you might think. The success or failure of this sauce is in the quality and freshness of the ingredients.

Ingredients

1/2 cup unsalted butter

3 egg yolks (see *Separating Eggs,* page 55)

2 tablespoons lemon juice from 1 lemon

1 tablespoon water

Dash of cayenne pepper

Dash of salt

Dash of white pepper

Equipment

Double boiler or substitute a saucepan with a stainless steel bowl

Methods

Whisking, boiling, simmering (see Chapter 3, "Glossary of Terms and Techniques, Conversions and Equivalents")

Quantity

1 cup

Preparation

1. Place the butter in a small saucepan and melt over low heat. Set aside to cool to room temperature.

Cooking Directions

2. Fill the bottom of the pan of the double boiler with water, place over high heat, and bring it almost to a boil.

3. Reduce the heat so that the water is at a rapid simmer.

4. In the top insert part of the double boiler, whisk the egg yolks, lemon juice, and water.

5. Place the pan insert into the pan over the simmering water and continue whisking until smooth.

6. In a slow steady stream, pour the cooled, melted butter into the egg mixture for about 1 minute while whisking to incorporate fully.

7. Whisk in the cayenne, salt, and pepper.

8. If the mixture becomes too thick, immediately whisk in 1 to 2 tablespoons hot water.

9. Use and serve immediately.

note

Improvise a double boiler by placing a stainless steel mixing bowl over a saucepan. The mixing bowl should not touch the water.

Variations

Béarnaise Sauce

Place 1 tablespoon of minced shallots, 1 tablespoon of minced fresh tarragon, and 1/4 cup of white wine in a small saucepan and simmer over medium heat until the liquid is reduced to 3 tablespoons. At step 4, whisk the sautéed mixture with the egg yolks, omitting the lemon juice and water. Continue steps 5 through 8, omitting the cayenne.

Pantry/Refrigerator Check

1 stick unsalted butter

Eggs

Cayenne pepper

Salt

White pepper

Shopping List

1 lemon

Basic White Sauce

Setting the stage for a multitude of savory sauces, this is a great recipe to have on hand. Sautéed butter and flour create a roux, a classic French thickening agent, and act as the base for many sauces and gravies. Add this white sauce to peas with pearl onions, make creamed spinach, or create the variations suggested below and serve the sauce over steamed vegetables and poached meats or fish.

Ingredients

3 tablespoons unsalted butter

3 tablespoons all-purpose white flour

1 1/2 cups whole milk

Salt and fresh-ground white pepper, to taste

Equipment

Medium saucepan, wire whisk, measuring cup, measuring spoons

Methods

Whisking, simmering (see Chapter 3)

Quantity

1 1/4 cups

Cooking Directions

1. Melt the butter over low heat, until just melted but not brown. If the butter browns, you can kiss your white sauce goodbye because you now have light brown sauce.

2. Gradually add the flour while constantly whisking.

3. Continue to cook, constantly whisking, for about 3 to 4 minutes as the roux thickens into a paste and the flour loses its raw taste.

4. Slowly add the milk while constantly whisking.

5. Simmer and stir over low heat for about 5 minutes until the sauce is smooth and has thickened.

6. Taste and adjust seasoning with salt and pepper.

Variations

■ At step 6 add 1 teaspoon of any of the following: nutmeg, curry powder, Worcestershire sauce, lemon juice, dry sherry, or chopped fresh herbs.

Béchamel Sauce

Follow the above instructions for Basic White Sauce. At step 6 add a pinch of nutmeg, a pinch of paprika, and salt and pepper to taste. Stir well to blend, remove from the heat and serve. This is good in soufflés, classic lasagna, and moussaka. It is also good with vegetables and grilled or poached meats.

Mornay Sauce

Follow the above instructions for Basic White Sauce. At step 6 add 1/4 cup grated Gruyére and 1/4 cup grated Parmesan cheeses, a pinch of nutmeg, a pinch of paprika, and salt and pepper to taste. Stir well to blend and continue cooking until the cheese melts and the sauce is smooth. Remove from the heat and serve. Good with broccoli, cauliflower, potatoes, crab, oysters, scallops, pasta, eggs, and crepes.

Cheddar Sauce

Follow the above instructions for Basic White Sauce. At step 6 add 1/3 cup grated sharp cheddar cheese, a pinch of paprika, and salt and pepper to taste. Stir well to blend and continue cooking until the cheese melts and the sauce is smooth. Remove from the heat and serve. Good with broccoli, cauliflower, potatoes, other vegetables, omelets, and crepes.

Cream Sauce

Follow the above instructions for Basic White Sauce. At the end of step 6 add 1/3 cup of heavy cream, a pinch of paprika, and salt and pepper to taste. Stir well to blend. Remove from the heat and serve. Good with vegetables, potatoes, crab, poached fish, crepes, and in casseroles.

Volute Sauce

Follow the above instructions for Basic White Sauce, substituting 1 1/2 cups of light stock such as chicken, fish, or vegetable stock for the 1 1/2 cups of milk. Use fish stock for fish sauce, chicken stock for chicken sauce, and vegetable stock for vegetable sauce.

Horseradish Sauce

Follow the above instructions for Basic White Sauce. At step 6 add 3 tablespoons of prepared creamed horseradish, 3 tablespoons of heavy cream, and 1 tablespoon of dijon mustard. Stir well to blend. Remove from the heat and serve. Good with any cut of beef, corned beef, smoked or braised fish, and Brussels sprouts.

Pantry/Refrigerator Check

1 stick unsalted butter

All-purpose white flour

Whole milk

Salt

White pepper

Country Skillet Gravy

Beginning cooks seem to have an aversion to gravy because of all the horror stories told by their moms and aunts. When Roosevelt said, "The only thing we have to fear, is fear itself," he was definitely talking about gravy. Try making gravy while no one is looking. It is amazing how much easier it goes without the loving guidance of your mother-in-law. You will wonder what all the fuss was about. Pan drippings from fried chicken or pork chops add flavor to this gravy. It can also be made using pork sausage patties or bacon drippings, a Southern classic served over biscuits. In a pinch, use butter instead of the drippings.

Ingredients

2 tablespoons pan drippings from cooked chicken, meat, or bacon, or use butter

2 tablespoons all-purpose white flour

1/4 teaspoon freshly ground black pepper

1 3/4 cups milk

Salt to taste

Equipment

The skillet that was used to cook the chicken or meat, measuring cup, measuring spoons, wire whisk

Methods

Whisking (see Chapter 3)

Quantity

1 1/2 cups

Preparation

1. Remove the cooked chicken or meat from the skillet and pour off all but 2 tablespoons of the drippings.

Cooking Directions

2. Return the pan to the stove and heat the drippings over medium heat.

3. Add the flour, pepper, and salt to the drippings while stirring constantly with a wire whisk. A thin smooth paste will begin to form.

4. Whisk the mixture for 1 minute or until bubbly and smooth.

5. Add the milk in a steady stream while constantly whisking. Continue cooking and whisking until the gravy is smooth.

6. Cook for about 1 minute until the mixture has thickened and is bubbly.

7. If the gravy becomes too thick, add milk, a little at a time.

8. Taste and adjust the seasoning with salt and pepper.

9. Remove from the heat and serve.

Variations

■ If making country gravy from sausage drippings, crumble the sausage into the gravy and serve over biscuits.

Pantry/Refrigerator Check

Chicken, pork chop, or bacon drippings

All-purpose white flour

Black pepper

Salt

Milk

Brown Pan Gravy For Roasted Meats

Make this gravy in the same pan used for roasting the meat. If you have roasted the meat without a rack, you will have tasty little browned bits in the bottom of the roasting pan that go a long way towards the flavor of your gravy. Serve the gravy in a small pitcher to accompany the sliced roasted meat.

Ingredients

Drippings from roasted meat

2 1/2 cups beef stock

3 tablespoons all-purpose white flour

Salt and fresh-ground black pepper to taste

Equipment

Roasting pan, measuring cup, measuring spoons, wire whisk, small pan

Methods

Whisking, simmering (see Chapter 3)

Quantity

2 cups

Preparation

1. Transfer the meat from the roasting pan to the platter and loosely cover with aluminum foil.
2. In a small pan, heat the beef stock on the stovetop or in the microwave.
3. Measure the flour into a small cup for easier handling later in recipe.
4. Tilt the roasting pan to allow all the juices to collect in one corner.
5. Spoon off and discard all but 3 tablespoons of the fat that accumulates on the surface, leaving the juices, the darker liquid at the bottom of the pool. If there is not enough fat, add melted butter or oil to equal 3 tablespoons.

Cooking Directions

6. Place the roasting pan on the stovetop burner over medium heat.
7. When the drippings are hot, gradually add flour, a tablespoon at a time, while stirring constantly and scraping up the browned bits with a wire whisk. Do this until the mixture becomes a smooth, thin paste.

8. Continue whisking and cooking for about 3 minutes or until the mixture is lightly browned.

9. While constantly whisking, gradually add 2 cups beef stock and cook until thickened and bubbly.

10. If the gravy is too thick, then add a little more beef stock.

11. Taste and adjust seasoning with salt and pepper.

Variations

■ At step 9 substitute 1/4 cup Madeira or red wine for 1/4 cup stock.

Pantry/Refrigerator Check

Drippings from roasted meat

All-purpose white flour

20 oz. beef stock

Salt

Black pepper

Basil Pesto

Pesto can be made from a variety of combinations of herbs, vegetables, or beans with oil, nuts and sometimes cheese. When basil is plentiful, make a double batch of Basil Pesto and freeze the extra in oiled ice cube trays. When the pesto cubes are frozen solid, remove and store in re-sealable plastic freezer bags. Add thawed cubes to soups, sauces, pastas, quiches, omelets, and casseroles or on pizza.

Ingredients

1/4 cup pine nuts

3 large cloves garlic

2 cups fresh basil leaves, tightly packed

1/2 cup freshly grated Parmesan cheese

1/2 teaspoon salt

1/2 teaspoon freshly ground black pepper

1/2 cup extra virgin olive oil

Equipment

Chef's knife, cutting board, measuring cup, grater, food processor

Methods

Toasting, crushing, grating, processing (see Chapter 3)

Quantity

1 cup

Preparation

1. Toast the pine nuts.
2. Peel the garlic and crush with the side of the knife.
3. Wash and pat dry the basil. Pull the leaves from the stem.
4. Grate the cheese using the large holes of the grater.

Assembly Directions

5. Place the pine nuts, garlic, basil, cheese, salt, and pepper in the bowl of the food processor and process until combined, but still very rough.
6. With the food processor motor running, drizzle in the oil, and process until smooth.

Variations

■ Substitute spinach and walnuts for pine nuts and basil.

■ At step 3 substitute cilantro for basil and add 1 tablespoon of lime juice.

Pantry/Refrigerator Check

Extra virgin olive oil

Salt

Pepper

Garlic

Shopping List

7 oz. pine nuts

1 bunch or package of fresh basil

2 oz. Parmesan cheese

Lemon Caper Salsa

The fresh flavors of this pungent salsa are the perfect complement to grilled or seared meats, fish, or chicken. It also makes a great appetizer topping for pita chips or crostini.

Ingredients

1 teaspoon minced flat leaf parsley

1/4 medium yellow bell pepper

5 kalamata or black olives

2 tablespoons extra virgin olive oil

1 teaspoon lemon juice

1/8 teaspoon salt

1/4 teaspoon fresh-ground black pepper

1 tablespoon capers, drained

Equipment

Small bowl, chef's knife, cutting board, measuring spoons

Methods

Mincing, chopping, whisking, stirring (see Chapter 3)

Quantity

1/2 cup

Preparation

1. Wash the parsley and pat dry. Pull the leaves from the stems, and mince.
2. Wash the pepper, cut in half lengthwise, remove the stem and seeds, and coarsely chop.
3. Pit the olives and coarsely chop.

Assembly Directions

4. In a small bowl, whisk together the oil, lemon juice, salt, and pepper.
5. Add the capers, yellow pepper, olives and parsley. Stir to mix.

Variations

- Substitute curly parsley, and red or green bell pepper.
- At step 5 add 1 teaspoon of minced garlic and 1 chopped ripe tomato.

Pantry/Refrigerator Check

Extra virgin olive oil

Salt

Black pepper

Capers

Shopping List

1 bunch fresh flat leaf parsley

1 yellow bell pepper

1 14-oz. can kalamata olives

1 lemon

Mango Lime Salsa

This tangy salsa with a hint of sweetness is versatile and easy to make. Serve as a dipping salsa with blue or white corn chips, or as a topping for quesadillas, grilled chicken, or fish. Store covered in the refrigerator for 2 to 3 days.

Ingredients

2 ripe mangos

2 ripe tomatoes

1/2 cup white onion

1/4 cup minced fresh cilantro

1 small serrano chili pepper

2 tablespoons fresh lime juice from 1 lime

1/2 teaspoon cumin

1/2 teaspoon fresh-ground black pepper

1/2 teaspoon salt

1 tablespoon extra virgin olive oil

1 tablespoon red wine vinegar

Equipment

Medium bowl, chef's knife, paring knife, cutting board, measuring spoons, wooden stirring spoon

Methods

Peeling, chopping, mincing (see Chapter 3)

Quantity

4 cups

Preparation

1. Peel the mango with a paring knife. Place the mango on its side on a cutting board. The seed is long and narrow and in the center, so cut lengthwise down both sides. Discard the center sliver of fruit, cut the remaining fruit into strips, and chop.

2. Wash the tomatoes, cut in half, remove the seeds if desired, and chop.

3. Peel the onion and coarsely chop.

4. Wash the cilantro and pat dry. Pull the leaves from the stems, and mince.

5. Wash the serrano chili pepper, cut off the stem top, and halve lengthwise. Remove the seeds and finely mince.

Assembly

6. In a medium bowl combine all ingredients, stirring to blend.

caution

Chili oil is hot and transfers easily to the skin. DO NOT touch your eyes with your fingers after cutting the chili.

Variations

- Add 1 cup of chopped nectarine or melon.
- At step 3 substitute red onion for white.
- Add 1 chopped avocado.
- At step 5 substitute canned green chilies for the fresh serrano.
- Add 1 15 oz. can of drained black beans.

Pantry/Refrigerator Check

Ground cumin

Black pepper

Salt

Extra virgin olive oil

Red wine vinegar

Shopping List

2 ripe mangos

2 ripe tomatoes

1 small white onion

1 bunch fresh cilantro

1 small serrano chili pepper

1 lime

El Greco Salsa

Super quick and easy to make, this topping is wonderful on eggs, grilled meats, vegetables, baked potatoes, crostini, feta and olive quesadillas, or as a dip with pita chips. Store the salsa covered in the refrigerator for 2 to 3 days.

Ingredients

1/2 medium red onion

2 cloves garlic

2 ripe Roma tomatoes

1/2 green bell pepper

3 tablespoons minced fresh oregano

2 tablespoons extra virgin olive oil

2 tablespoons red wine vinegar

1/4 teaspoon salt

1/4 teaspoon fresh-ground black pepper

Equipment

Large bowl, chef's knife, cutting board, measuring cups, measuring spoons, wooden stirring spoon

Methods

Chopping, mincing (see Chapter 3)

Quantity

2 cups

Preparation

1. Peel and chop the onion.
2. Peel and mince the garlic.
3. Wash the tomatoes, cut in half, remove the seeds, and coarsely chop.
4. Wash the bell pepper. Cut in half lengthwise, remove the stem and seeds, and chop.
5. Wash the oregano and pat dry. Pull the leaves from the stems, and mince.

Assembly Directions

6. Place all ingredients in a large bowl and stir to combine.

7. Set aside for 10 to 15 minutes to blend flavors.

Variations

■ At step 6 pulse the ingredients in a blender or food processor for a smoother salsa.

Pantry/Refrigerator Check

Salt

Ground black pepper

Garlic

Extra virgin olive oil

Red wine vinegar

Shopping List

1 medium red onion

2 ripe Roma tomatoes

1 green bell pepper

1 bunch fresh oregano

Tequila Lime Marinade

Use this marinade to give a flavorful boost to chicken, fish, shrimp, or pork. Citrus juice begins to cook food so this is not an overnight marinade—one hour in the refrigerator is sufficient. Serve marinated and grilled meat, chicken, or fish with warmed flour tortillas, black beans topped with crumbly queso blanco (a white Mexican cheese), and a green salad with *Creamy Cilantro Dressing* (page 173).

Ingredients

3 tablespoons fresh cilantro

2 cloves garlic

1 green onion

1 small serrano chili pepper

1/4 cup lime juice from 2 limes

2 tablespoons orange juice

2 tablespoons tequila

1/4 cup extra virgin olive oil

1/2 teaspoon ground cumin

1/2 teaspoon salt

1/4 teaspoon fresh-ground black pepper

Equipment

Medium bowl, chef's knife, cutting board, wire whisk

Methods

Mincing, slicing (see Chapter 3)

Quantity

3/4 cups, enough for 2 1/2 pounds meat

Preparation

1. Wash the cilantro and dry. Pull the leaves from the stems, and mince.
2. Peel and mince the garlic.
3. Wash the green onion, trim the root end and tough upper greens, and slice.
4. Wash the chili, cut in half lengthwise, remove the stem and seeds, and mince.

Assembly Directions

5. Place all the ingredients in a medium bowl and whisk until well blended.

Variations

■ Add 1 teaspoon of orange or lime zest.

Pantry/Refrigerator Check

Garlic

Tequila

Extra virgin olive oil

Ground cumin

Salt

Black pepper

Shopping List

2 sprigs fresh cilantro

1 bunch green onions

1 small serrano chili pepper

2 limes

1 orange

Tarragon Mustard Marinade

After removing the chicken or fish from this marinade, use it to create a sauce that enhances the flavor of the dish. This is easiest to prepare if the meat has been sautéed. Simply deglaze (see Chapter 3) the pan with the remaining marinade, and add 1 to 2 tablespoons of butter. Bring to a boil to kill any bacteria remaining from the raw meat. Reduce the heat to medium, and simmer until the sauce is thickened and reduced by half. Serve this sauce spooned over the sautéed meat or chicken.

Ingredients

1/4 cup extra virgin olive oil

2 tablespoons dry sherry

2 tablespoons white wine vinegar

2 tablespoons dijon mustard

1 tablespoon dried tarragon

1/2 teaspoon salt

1/2 teaspoon fresh-ground black pepper

Equipment

A glass jar with air-tight lid, measuring spoons

Methods

Mixing (see Chapter 3)

Quantity

3/4 cup, enough to marinate 2 1/2 pounds meat, chicken or fish

Assembly Directions

1. Place all the ingredients in a glass jar, tighten the lid, and shake well to blend.

Variations

- Use 3 tablespoons of fresh tarragon, and add 1 teaspoon of minced garlic.

Pantry/Refrigerator Check

Extra virgin olive oil

Dry sherry

White wine vinegar

Dijon mustard

Dried tarragon

Salt

Black pepper

Safi Spice Rub

A spice rub adds flavor to meats or chicken. While the meat cooks, the rub locks in juices that keep the meat moist inside and the searing creates a pleasing crusty, browned outside. Rub the spice mix on pork tenderloin, lamb chops or lamb kabobs, chicken breasts, or steaks. A tablespoon of this rub added to 1 cup of plain yogurt creates a quick complementary sauce for your meat.

Ingredients

4 tablespoons Hungarian paprika

2 tablespoons ground coriander

2 tablespoons ground cumin

2 tablespoons ground turmeric

2 tablespoons ground cardamom

3 teaspoons ground ginger

3 teaspoons ground allspice

1 teaspoon fresh-ground black pepper

1 teaspoon salt

Equipment

Measuring spoons, glass jar with air-tight lid

Methods

Mixing (see Chapter 3)

Quantity

About 3/4 cup, enough for 5 pounds of meat or chicken

Assembly Directions

1. Place all the ingredients in a glass jar and shake well to blend.

2. Store in an air-tight jar in the pantry for up to 3 months.

Variations

■ Add or delete spices to your taste; add cinnamon and nutmeg, garlic and onion salt, or red chili powder

Pantry/Refrigerator Check

Hungarian paprika

Ground coriander

Ground cumin

Ground turmeric

Ground cardamom

Ground ginger

Ground allspice

Black pepper

Salt

15

APPETIZERS AND DIPS

A menu of *Beef Bourguignonne* (page 194) with *Gorgonzola Mashed Potatoes* (page 270) is nice for guests, but the addition of an appetizer elevates the event from dinner to a dinner party. In this instance, an appetizer need not be fussy, expensive, or excessive. This is more about "pre-dinner time" set aside to relax and socialize, than about the platter of food sitting on the coffee table. However, some thought should be taken to ensure the appetizer does not conflict with, but rather reflects, the flavors of the dinner to come. This meal would benefit from a simple appetizer dish of olives, a small platter of thinly-sliced prosciutto, and some pungent cheese.

When the appetizers are the stars of the show, spend some time creating a menu balanced in color, texture, and type of food. A table entirely filled with crackers, breads, and chips is too much of the same thing. Add a platter of sliced provolone, salami, black olives, artichoke hearts, cherry tomatoes, and Italian peppers. Include an olive pesto spread and an avocado cilantro dip, and suddenly the bread, crackers, and chips are a meaningful part of a balanced offering. For a more substantial spread, add a couple of cooked items like warm *Nor'Eastern Crab Cakes* (page 335), and *New Potato Bites* (page 331) with caviar.

Use baskets or large bowls lined with colorful kitchen towels or cloth napkins to hold breads, chips, and crackers. Assemble an array of meats and cheeses on a cutting board, and arrange bite-sized hors d'oeuvres and crudités (a fancy word for cut up vegetables) on leaf-lined platters or large plates. In a pinch, cover a baking sheet or a piece of cardboard with aluminum foil, arrange leafy greens, such as kale, over the foil, add cut flowers or snips from a backyard shrub, and your foil-covered cardboard begins to look like an party platter.

Suggested Appetizers to Purchase

When time is short, consider purchasing quality packaged foods at the local market or ordering take-out from a favorite restaurant. You can cut the entrées into small serving sizes and use as appetizers. Remove the foods from the take-out cartons to serve them on your own platters, baskets, or bowls. Quality breads, rolls, and desserts can be purchased at the corner bakery.

Local Market Purchases

These are some great appetizers you can purchase from your local market:

- Assorted olives: kalamata, Spanish, black, and Greek
- Hearts of palm, marinated artichoke hearts, asparagus spears, marinated mushrooms, and marinated garlic
- Blue, white, or spicy-bean corn chips with roasted garlic salsa and guacamole
- Assorted kettle potato chips with sour cream-based dips
- Packaged crostini with a container of pesto or sun-dried tomato spread
- Hummus with pita chips
- Assorted nuts, spiced nuts, and popcorn

Favorite Restaurant Purchases

Buy these appetizers from your favorite restaurants:

- Italian ravioli or tortellini served on toothpicks with the sauce on the side for dipping
- Manicotti, gourmet pizza, calzone, or garlic bread cut into small pieces
- Mexican tamales or quesadillas cut into small pieces, and served with purchased chips, salsa, and guacamole
- Middle Eastern baba ghanoush with pita chips, and chicken or lamb kabobs with garlic sauce
- Chinese- or Thai-chicken satay, egg rolls with dipping sauce, wontons, and paper-wrapped spicy chicken
- Japanese sushi platters with edamame and pickled ginger
- Barbequed sausages, brisket, ribs, or chicken cut into small pieces with dipping sauces

Crudités Platter from the Market

For a crudités platter from the market, use the following ingredients:

- Vegetables: Use a variety of precut bagged or packaged vegetables for a pleasing presentation

  Examples: Green broccoli, orange baby carrots, red bell pepper strips, white cauliflower, long green beans, asparagus, tiny round cherry tomatoes or yellow baby pear tomatoes, zucchini, yellow squash, pale green patty pan, or tiny, yellow summer squash

- Bottled dressings: Use your favorite good quality dressing

  Examples: Ranch, blue cheese, green goddess, Caesar, sesame shitake, creamy avocado, French, creamy Italian, creamy garlic

To assemble, follow these steps:

1. Take red or yellow bell peppers, cut off the tops, and remove their seeds. Fill the peppers with the purchased salad dressing.
2. Place the dressing-filled pepper on a platter lined with leafy greens and surround with the other cut vegetables.

Cheese Board from the Market

When putting together a cheese board, think quality not quantity. A nice selection should include cheeses with different flavors, textures, and styles. Create a balanced cheese board with a firm cheese, a crumbly cheese, a semi-soft cheese, and a soft cheese. Add a goat cheese and a blue cheese to expand the variety. It is very important to serve cheese at room temperature to bring out the maximum flavor.

Choose 4 or 5 cheeses from the list below, and serve with sliced dark or nut bread, sliced baguette, biscotti, plain gourmet crackers, sliced fresh pears, apples, figs, grapes, or dried fruits and assorted nuts. Keep it simple. To find out more about the characteristics of a particular cheese, see the *Basic Cheese Chart* in Chapter 2, "Food Essentials for Your Pantry" (page 17).

- Firm or crumbly cheeses: Double Gloucester, Edam, Emmentaler, Gruyère, jarlsberg, Parmesan, provolone, Romano, cheddar
- Semi-soft cheeses: Gouda, Monterey Jack, fontina
- Soft cheeses: Brie, Camembert, feta, fresh mozzarella
- Blue cheeses: Gorgonzola, Roquefort, Stilton

Crostini

Crostini, Italian for "little crusts," were traditionally grilled over an open fire, brushed with extra virgin olive oil, and topped with savory treats as a way to of using the last bits of yesterday's bread. Quick and easy to prepare, crostini is one of the most versatile staples in your appetizer arsenal. Stored in an airtight container, crostini freezes well for up to 1 month. Top with roasted garlic or chopped ripe tomato, basil, and fresh buffalo mozzarella.

Ingredients

1 large sourdough or seeded baguette

Equipment

Serrated knife, cutting board, baking sheet

Methods

Slicing (see Chapter 3, "Glossary of Terms and Techniques, Conversions and Equivalents")

Quantity

40 crostini

Preparation

1. Preheat the oven to 350°F.
2. Slice the baguette crosswise into 40 little rounds.

Cooking Directions

3. Arrange the rounds on the baking sheet in batches and place in the oven.
4. Bake for 10 to 12 minutes until crisp and golden. Check frequently because the time will vary with individual ovens.
5. Remove from the oven and cool.
6. Store in an airtight container.

Variations

- Brush each crostini with extra virgin olive oil or garlic butter, and top with red chili powder or minced fresh herbs before toasting.

Pantry/Refrigerator Check

Extra virgin olive oil

Shopping List

1 large sourdough or seeded baguette

Herb Roasted Garlic

Serve whole heads of garlic on a platter surrounded by fresh thyme and toasted crostini. Let guests scoop the soft, nutty-flavored roasted garlic right from the head to spread on crackers or the crostini. The garlic slips easily out of its little papery skin when squeezed from the bottom, and is great when added to sauces, soups, or stews.

Ingredients

8 large firm heads of garlic

8 tablespoons extra virgin olive oil

2 tablespoons dried thyme

2 tablespoons dried basil

1 teaspoon fresh-ground black pepper

1 teaspoon salt

Equipment

Chef's knife, cutting board, measuring spoons, heavy aluminum foil

Methods

Slicing (see Chapter 3)

Quantity

8 roasted garlic heads

Preparation

1. Preheat the oven to 350°F.

2. Cut the foil into eight 10-inch squares.

3. Peel and discard the loose papery outer skins from each head of garlic. On the cutting board, turn each head on its side, and cut off and discard about 3/4- to 1-inch of the top pointed end. This will expose the inside cloves. Looking down at the cut surface you will see a cluster of little circles.

Cooking Directions

4. Place each garlic head with the cut side up in the center of a foil square.

5. Drizzle each with 1 tablespoon of oil and sprinkle with 3/4 teaspoon each of thyme and basil, and a dash of salt and pepper.

6. For each head, fold all four corners of the foil to the center. Leave an air pocket around the garlic, and twist and crimp the edges of foil to seal.

7. Place all the garlic packets on a baking sheet and place in the oven.

8. Roast for 45 minutes to 1 hour.

9. Remove the packets from the oven and let cool slightly. Remove the garlic heads from the packets. The garlic skins should be slightly golden and the garlic should be soft.

Variations

■ Vary each packet with different herbs such as rosemary, marjoram, tarragon, sage, and parsley.

Pantry/Refrigerator Check

Extra virgin olive oil

Dried thyme

Dried basil

Black pepper

Salt

Shopping List

8 large heads garlic

White Bean Spread

This simple but elegant spread with an earthy, satisfying flavor is whipped up quickly because of the canned beans. The fresh sage and extra virgin olive oil that grace the top add flavor and a touch of color. Place a bowl filled with the spread on a platter surrounded with crostini or purchased crackers. If you would like to use home cooked beans, consult the *Bean Cooking Chart* (page 236).

Ingredients

1 19 oz.can cannellini (white kidney beans)

1 green onion

2 cloves garlic

2 tablespoons fresh sage leaves, divided

2 tablespoons fresh lemon juice from 1 lemon

4 tablespoons extra virgin olive oil, divided

1/2 teaspoon fresh-ground black pepper

1/2 teaspoon salt

Equipment

Food processor, chef's knife, cutting board, large wire- mesh strainer, measuring spoons, wooden stirring spoon

Methods

Chopping, sautéing, boiling, simmering (see Chapter 3)

Quantity

6 to 8 servings

Preparation

1. Drain and rinse the beans in the wire-mesh strainer.
2. Peel the tough outer leaves from the green onion, trim the end, and the tough top. Slice lengthwise and mince.
3. Peel and mince the garlic.
4. Wash, pat dry, and mince the sage leaves.
5. Squeeze the lemon through the strainer, and discard the seeds.

Assembly Directions

6. Place all the ingredients except 1 tablespoon of the olive oil and 1/2 tablespoon of sage in the work bowl of a food processor.

7. Process, pulsing on and off, until coarsely chopped and slightly chunky. This can also be done with a masher or fork.

8. Transfer to a small serving bowl, and drizzle with the reserved olive oil and sage.

Variations

- At step 2 substitute 1 small minced shallot for the green onion, and fresh rosemary or flat leaf parsley for sage.
- At step 7 pulse until smooth.

Pantry/Refrigerator Check

1 19 oz.can cannellini (white kidney beans)

Extra virgin olive oil

Garlic

Black pepper

Salt

Shopping List

1 bunch green onions

1 lemon

1 bunch or package fresh sage

New Mexican Quesadilla

Quesadilla fillings can be elaborate, gourmet concoctions of savory or sweet ingredients, or simply grated cheese. Use your imagination to create combinations to your liking. Cook quesadillas in a skillet or in the oven. If pan-grilling, try folding a large tortilla in half rather than stacking 2 tortillas. It is much easier to flip. Serve quesadillas warm with *Mango Lime Salsa* (page 306) or *Guacamole* (page 329).

Ingredients

1 cup grated Monterey Jack jalapeño cheese

1 cup grated cheddar cheese

1/4 cup toasted pine nuts

8 large flour tortillas

1 4 oz. can chopped green chilies

1 tablespoon canola oil

Equipment

Large skillet, medium bowl, chef's knife, cutting board, measuring cup, measuring spoons, grater, wooden stirring spoon, spatula

Methods

Grating, toasting nuts, mincing, pan-grilling (see Chapter 3)

Quantity

8 quesadillas

Preparation

1. Grate cheeses and mix together in a medium bowl.
2. Toast the pine nuts in the skillet over medium heat for 2 to 3 minutes, until golden but not browned. Slide the nuts onto a plate to cool.

Cooking Directions

3. Spread 1/4 cup of the cheese mix on one half of each tortilla. Try to keep the cheese 1/4-inch away from the edge of the tortilla to prevent the cheese from melting over the edges.
4. Top the cheese with 1/2 of the tablespoon green chilies and 1 1/2 teaspoons of the pine nuts.

5. Fold the empty half of tortilla over the cheese and lightly press.

6. Heat the oil in the skillet over medium heat.

7. Place 1 or 2 quesadillas in the skillet and cook for 2 to 3 minutes per side, turning carefully with a spatula until the cheese melts and the tortilla is golden brown.

8. Remove the quesadilla to the cutting board and cut into wedges.

Variations

- At step 4 add chopped leftover vegetables, meats, or fish.

- Substitute favorite nuts and spices like cumin, fresh cilantro, basil, or red chili flakes.

- Try chunks of brie cheese and sliced fruit, such as strawberries with walnuts, and top with fruit-flavored yogurt or fruit salsa.

Pantry/Refrigerator Check

1 4 oz. can chopped green chilies

2 oz. pine nuts

Canola oil

Shopping List

8 large flour tortillas

4 oz. Monterey jack jalapeño cheese

4 oz. cheddar cheese

The Best Guacamole

Guacamole is always a favorite and usually the first dip to disappear at a party. This recipe is very simple and widely used in the Southwest. Choose avocados that are purple-black, slightly firm and heavy for their size. Avoid those with soft spots. Use ripe avocados and tomatoes for best results and remember that fresh lime juice is essential to authentic guacamole, so make no substitutions.

tip

Fast Track this recipe by replacing the tomatoes and the serrano chili with a good quality jarred salsa. Guacamole is best when served immediately, but if storing, cover the bowl tightly and store in the refrigerator to avoid discoloration.

Ingredients

3 ripe Haas avocados

2 ripe tomatoes

1 small serrano chili

3 tablespoons fresh lime juice from 1 lime

Salt and fresh-ground black pepper to taste

Equipment

Small bowl, chef's knife, serrated knife, cutting board, measuring spoons, large fork, wooden stirring spoon

Methods

Chopping, mincing, peeling and pitting an avocado, mashing, stirring (see Chapter 3)

Quantity

2 cups

Preparation

1. Peel and pit the avocados and scoop the flesh into a small bowl.

2. Wash the tomatoes, cut in half, and coarsely chop.

3. Wash the serrano chili, cut off the top with stem, and half lengthwise. Remove the seeds and finely mince.

caution

Chili oil is hot and transfers easily to the skin. DO NOT touch your eyes with your fingers after cutting chili.

Assembly Directions

4. Add the lime juice to the avocados. Roughly mash them with the back of a large fork, leaving the mixture a bit chunky.

5. Stir in the remaining ingredients to slightly blend.

6. Taste and adjust the seasoning with salt and pepper.

Variations

- At step 5 add 1/4 cup minced red onion and 1/4 cup chopped fresh cilantro.

Pantry/Refrigerator Check

Salt

Black pepper

Shopping List

3 ripe Haas avocados

1 large lime

2 ripe tomatoes

1 small serrano chili pepper

New Potato Bites

Inexpensive and easy to assemble, these bite-sized hors d'oeuvres add substance to an appetizer table. Splurge for a special occasion and replace the chopped olives with caviar.

Ingredients

10 small red potatoes

2 cloves garlic

3 tablespoons minced fresh parsley

3 tablespoons minced fresh basil

3 tablespoons minced fresh chives

2 tablespoons extra virgin olive oil

1/2 teaspoon salt

1 tablespoon freshly ground pepper

1/2 cup sour cream

1 4 oz. can chopped black olives, drained

Nonstick cooking spray

Equipment

Baking sheet, chef's knife, cutting board, measuring spoons, spatula

Methods

Mincing, roasting (see Chapter 3)

Quantity

60 slices

Preparation

1. Preheat the oven to 350°F.
2. Wash the potatoes and cut each into 6 slices crosswise.
3. Peel and mince the garlic.
4. Wash the parsley and pat dry. Pull the leaves from the stems, and finely mince.
5. Wash the basil and pat dry. Pull the leaves from the stems, and finely mince.
6. Wash the chives, pat dry, and finely mince.

7. In a medium bowl, combine the potato slices, olive oil, garlic, parsley, basil, chives, salt, and pepper. Mix well to coat.

8. Spray the bottom of a baking sheet with cooking spray.

Cooking Directions

9. Place the potatoes on the sheet and roast for 40 to 60 minutes until golden brown.

10. Check occasionally and if the potatoes are sticking, gently loosen them from the baking sheet with a spatula.

11. Remove the pan from the oven and allow to cool.

12. Top each potato round with a teaspoon of sour cream and 1/2 teaspoon of chopped black olives.

Variations

- At step 12 add 1 teaspoon paprika to sour cream.
- At step 12 substitute caviar for black olives.
- For a fresher presentation, boil the potatoes whole, cool slightly, and cut in half lengthwise. Scoop out half of the flesh and combine with the sour cream, salt, pepper, and minced herbs. Fill the potato skins with the potato/sour cream mix, top with black olives, and refrigerate for 1 hour.

Pantry/Refrigerator Check

10 small red potatoes

Extra virgin olive oil

Garlic

Black pepper

Salt

1 4 oz. can chopped black olives

Nonstick cooking spray

Shopping List

1 bunch or package fresh parsley

1 bunch or package fresh basil

1 bunch or package fresh chives

Sour cream (you will need at least 4 oz.)

Baked Pita Triangles

Crunchy and flavorful, yet low in fat, homemade chips are so much better and less expensive than purchased ones. Store the triangles in a tightly sealed container on the countertop for 1 week, or in the freezer for up to one month. Use for dipping with hummus, or top each triangle with cream cheese and sliced salmon.

Ingredients

1/4 cup grated Parmesan cheese

1/2 teaspoon dried basil

1/2 teaspoon dried parsley

2 pita bread rounds

Nonstick cooking spray

Equipment

Baking sheet, small bowl, chef's knife, cutting board, grater

Methods

Cutting, baking (see Chapter 3)

Quantity

16 triangles

Preparation

1. Preheat the oven to 350°F.
2. Finely grate the cheese, and place it in a small bowl.
3. Crush the herbs with your fingertips, add to the cheese, and mix to combine.
4. Cut the pita bread in half, split apart, and cut each half into 4 wedges.
5. Place 4 pita triangles on a baking sheet. Lightly spray the triangles with non-stick cooking oil, and sprinkle with the herb-cheese mix.
6. Repeat the process until all the pita triangles are coated. Divide any remaining herb-cheese mix evenly among pita triangles.

Cooking Directions

7. Place the baking sheet in the preheated oven, and bake for 10 to 12 minutes or until the triangles are crisp.

8. Let the triangles cool slightly before serving. The triangles will crisp as they cool.

Variations

■ At step 3 add 1/8 teaspoon garlic powder to the bowl.

Pantry/Refrigerator Check

Dried basil

Dried parsley

Nonstick cooking spray

Shopping List

2 pita bread rounds

1 oz. Parmesan cheese

Nor'Eastern Crab Cakes

The classic Eastern seaboard recipe calls for blue crabs—expensive, seasonal crabs that come from the Atlantic Ocean. Use the canned crab for your first stab at this recipe. If it becomes a favorite, switch to fresh crab, using the less expensive and more plentiful Dungeness Crabs from the Pacific. Canned crab may taste metallic. If it does, soak the crab in ice water for 6 to 8 minutes, drain, and dry with paper towels. Old Bay seasoning is a popular East Coast spice that goes well with all types of seafood. Serve the crab cakes with lemon wedges or *Tartar Sauce* (page 338).

Ingredients

Two 6 oz. cans lump crabmeat OR one 12 oz. fresh lump crabmeat

1/2 cup diced celery

1/2 cup diced white onion

1/4 cup minced parsley

1 tablespoon fresh lemon juice

1/2 cup mayonnaise

1 egg

1 1/2 tablespoon Old Bay or seafood seasoning

1/2 teaspoon Worcestershire sauce

1/2 teaspoon salt

1/2 teaspoon freshly ground black pepper

1/2 cup unseasoned bread crumbs

1 1/2 cups cornmeal

1 lemon for garnish, cut into wedges

Canola oil

Equipment

Large nonstick or cast iron skillet, baking sheet, medium bowl, large plate, chef's knife, cutting board, measuring cup, measuring spoons, wire-mesh strainer, rubber spatula, metal spatula

Methods

Mincing, dredging, folding in, sautéing (see Chapter 3)

Quantity

16 small crab cakes

Preparation

1. If using fresh crabmeat, pick through the meat to remove cartilage or shell fragments.
2. Wash the celery, cut in half lengthwise, and finely mince.
3. Peel the onion, cut in half, and finely mince.
4. Wash the parsley and pat dry. Pull the leaves from the stem, and finely mince.
5. Squeeze the lemon juice through the strainer, and discard the seeds.
6. In a medium bowl, use a rubber spatula to stir together the mayonnaise, egg, Old Bay seasoning, Worcestershire sauce, lemon juice, salt, and pepper.
7. Add the celery, onion, and parsley. Mix to combine.
8. Fold in the crabmeat and the bread crumbs, gently mixing to combine.
9. Using a 1/4-cup measure, form the mixture into 16 1/2-inch thick patties.
10. Pour the cornmeal onto a plate.
11. As the crab cakes are formed, place each into the cornmeal, carefully turning to coat all sides. Transfer to a baking sheet.
12. When all the crab cakes are formed, coated, and placed on baking sheet, cover with plastic wrap, and refrigerate for 1 hour or up to overnight.

Cooking Directions

13. Preheat the oven to 200°F.
14. Place the skillet over medium-high heat, and add enough oil to thickly coat the bottom of the pan. Heat the oil to very hot without allowing smoke to come off of the pan.
15. Use a spatula to carefully add the crab cakes to the pan without crowding. It will be necessary to work in batches.
16. Cook the crab cakes for 3 to 4 minutes on each side, until golden brown.
17. When done, transfer the crab cakes to a paper towel-lined plate, and place in the oven to keep warm.
18. Remove the skillet from the heat, wipe the skillet clean with a few folded paper towels, and remove any browned cornmeal.
19. Add enough oil to thinly coat the bottom of the skillet. Repeat steps 15 through 17 until all of the crab cakes are cooked.
20. Cut the lemon into wedges for garnish.

Variations

- At step 3 substitute red onion for white onion
- At step 6 add a dash of Tabasco sauce and 1 teaspoon of lemon zest
- For a lighter version, preheat the broiler and cook the crab cakes on a greased baking sheet 4 inches under the broiler for about 3 minutes per side. Turn once and cook until lightly browned.

Pantry/Refrigerator Check

Mayonnaise

Egg

Old Bay or other seafood seasoning

Worcestershire sauce

Salt

Black pepper

Unseasoned bread crumbs

Cornmeal

Canola oil

Shopping List

Two 6 oz. cans lump crabmeat OR one 12 oz. fresh lump crabmeat

1 head celery

1 white onion

1 bunch or package fresh parsley

2 lemons

Tartar Sauce

Homemade tartar sauce is easy to make and far superior to purchased sauce. It is a moist and tangy accompaniment to fried fish and seafood. Try it with catfish or with fried calamari as a change of pace from marinara.

Ingredients

3 tablespoons minced shallot

1/4 cup chopped dill pickle

2 tablespoons minced fresh flat leaf parsley

1 cup mayonnaise

1 tablespoon cider vinegar

Dash of Tabasco sauce

2 tablespoons drained tiny capers

Salt and fresh-ground black pepper to taste

Equipment

Small bowl, chef's knife, cutting board, measuring cup, measuring spoons, wire whisk, rubber spatula

Methods

Mincing, mixing (see Chapter 3)

Quantity

1 1/2 cups

Preparation

1. Peel and mince the shallot.

2. Finely mince the pickle.

3. Wash the parsley and pat dry. Pull the leaves from the stems, and mince.

Assembly Directions

4. Whisk together the mayonnaise, vinegar, and Tabasco sauce in a small bowl.

5. Use the rubber spatula to fold in the shallots, pickles, parsley, and capers. Gently mix until the tartar sauce is well combined.

6. Taste and adjust the seasoning with salt and fresh-ground black pepper.

7. For best flavor, chill for at least 1 hour before serving. You may also chill the sauce overnight.

Variations

■ At step 2 substitute cornichons (French sour gherkins) for the dill pickles. Cornichons are available at specialty foods shops and some supermarkets.

Pantry/Refrigerator Check

Dill pickles

Tiny capers

Mayonnaise

Cider vinegar

Tabasco sauce

Salt

Black pepper

Shopping List

1 shallot

1 bunch flat leaf parsley

Deviled Eggs

This is a basic recipe and begs for variations. Some suggestions are listed below, but let your imagination, and what you have in your pantry, be your guide. These are great low-carb snacks for at work or at home. Pop them in a cooler as a great addition to a picnic but remember, they contain mayonnaise, and must be kept refrigerated.

Ingredients

6 *eggs, hard boiled* (page 57)

2 tablespoons mayonnaise

2 1/2 teaspoon dijon mustard

1 teaspoon red wine vinegar

Salt and freshly ground black pepper to taste

Dash Hungarian paprika

Equipment

Medium bowl, chef's knife, cutting board, spoon, fork

Methods

Mashing (see Chapter 3)

Quantity

12 egg halves

Preparation

1. Peel the eggs (see *How to Peel Hard Boiled Eggs,* page 56).

2. Cut the eggs in half lengthwise.

3. Taking care not to damage the whites, gently scoop out the yolks, and place them in the medium bowl. Set the whites aside.

4. Add the remaining ingredients to the yolks, and gently mash with a fork to combine.

5. Spoon the egg mix into each of the reserved whites.

6. Garnish each with a dash of paprika.

Variations

- Add or garnish with 1 tablespoon minced fresh chives, chervil, parsley, or cayenne pepper.

- Substitute tarragon vinegar for red wine vinegar, and garnish with 1 tablespoon minced fresh tarragon.

- Add 3 tablespoons chopped ham or crumbled bacon.

- Omit the vinegar and mustard and substitute any of the following combinations:

  - 1 teaspoon curry powder and 1 tablespoon chutney, garnished with 1 tablespoon of minced fresh mint

  - 1 teaspoon soy sauce and 1/2 teaspoon Asian hot chili paste, garnished with 1 tablespoon minced fresh chives

  - 2 tablespoons softened cream cheese and 1 tablespoon capers, garnished with small pieces of smoked salmon

Pantry/Refrigerator Check

Eggs

Mayonnaise

Dijon mustard

Red wine vinegar

Salt

Black pepper

Hungarian paprika

16

DESSERTS

A dessert is the sparkling punctuation that completes a meal, the icing on the cake. A special meal is made spectacular with the addition of dessert. We anticipate its enjoyment, delight in each indulging bite, and savor the sweet memory. A simple pairing of sliced fresh fruit with a good piece of cheese, or a scoop of vanilla bean ice cream, drizzled with *Raspberry Sauce* (page 373), and a fresh-baked cookie, are more than just the sum of their parts; they are dessert.

Most desserts are created from the same basic pantry ingredients and follow simple, but specific, steps. While most entrées accept personal interpretation—a little more wine, a little less oil, with only flavor variances as the result—many desserts require precise measurements. A little more milk can cause a lot less rising in a baked dessert. For best results, follow the recipe to the letter, at least the first time you make it, substituting and modifying only after you are familiar with the characteristics of the ingredients.

Pie Crust

The quality of frozen pie dough has come a long way, but this recipe is so easy to make with basic ingredients that it's a must try. Use ice cold water, adding it in small amounts, and do not over-handle the dough or it will become tough. This is the classic pie dough recipe, producing a flaky, slightly crisp crust.

Ingredients

1/2 cup + 2 tablespoons shortening

2 1/2 cups all-purpose white flour

1/4 teaspoon salt

5 to 6 tablespoons ice-cold water

Equipment

Large bowl, fork, 2 table knives

Methods

Mixing, cutting-in (see Chapter 3, "Glossary of Terms and Techniques, Conversions and Equivalents")

Quantity

2 9-inch single pie crusts

Assembly Directions

1. Place the shortening in the refrigerator to chill.

2. Combine the flour and salt in a large bowl.

3. Add the chilled shortening in small pieces. Using 2 table knives, or clean fingertips, cut the shortening into the flour mixture until coarse crumbs, about the size of small peas, begin to form.

4. Add 5 tablespoons of cold water and mix lightly with a fork, or clean hands, until the dough holds together. The dough should not be wet or sticky, but if the mixture seems dry and crumbly, add more water, a few drops at a time. The dough will begin to form a ball. Grab any dough bits from the sides of the bowl.

5. Gather the dough with your hands, form into 2 equal-sized balls, and flatten each into a disk.

6. Wrap each disk individually in plastic wrap and chill for 1 hour before using. This allows the dough to rest and makes it easier to handle.

Variations

■ At step 2 add 1 tablespoon of sugar for a sweet crust.

Pantry/Refrigerator Check

All-purpose white flour

Salt

Shortening

tip

To freeze dough for later use, lightly cover the dough disk with shortening before wrapping at step 6. Place the dough in a resealable plastic freezer bag and freeze for up to 3 months. When needed, remove the dough from the freezer, and thaw until softened. Follow your favorite recipe instructions.

Blackberry Pie

When blackberries are plentiful, double this recipe and freeze the extra pie. Thaw the frozen pie in the refrigerator and pop it in the oven when it's time to chase away the winter blues. Serve warm, or at room temperature, with vanilla ice cream or whipped cream.

Ingredients

2 9-inch pie crust disks (*Pie Crust,* page 344)

6 cups whole blackberries

1 1/2 cup sugar

4 tablespoons cornstarch

3 tablespoons unsalted butter

3 tablespoons milk

1 tablespoon white sugar

Equipment

9-inch pie pan, large bowl, wooden stirring spoon, rolling pin (or wine bottle), measuring cup, measuring spoons, wire rack

Methods

Rolling, crimping, baking (see Chapter 3)

Quantity

8 servings

Preparation

1. Preheat the oven to 425°F.
2. Prepare the pie pastry according to the recipe (page 344), or defrost 2 frozen pastry disks. Remember, freshly made pastry must rest in the refrigerator for 1 hour before using.
3. Combine the berries, sugar, and cornstarch in a large bowl. Stir gently to combine. Set aside.
4. Remove the pastry from the refrigerator, and allow it to warm to a workable softness.

5. Scatter a dusting (see Chapter 3) of flour over a work surface, such as a clean kitchen counter, and rub flour over the surface of the rolling pin.

6. Place 1 pastry disk on the lightly floured work surface.

7. Place the rolling pin in the center of the pastry disk and begin rolling, from the center to the edge, with an even light stroke.

8. Change the position of the rolling pin after each few rolls, rolling crosswise, then diagonally, so the pastry is rolled evenly out to a 12-inch round.

9. Test the size by setting the pie pan facedown on the pastry. The pastry must be about 2 inches wider, all around, than the pan to allow for the pan's depth.

10. Gently fold the pastry in half over itself.

11. Carefully transfer the folded pastry to one-half of the pie pan, with the fold along the center line of the pan. Open the folded pastry over the other half of the pan. Using your fingers, ease the pastry into the pan and trim off any excess.

12. Place the berries with their juices in the pastry shell and dot with pieces of butter.

13. Roll out the remaining pastry disk, following steps 6 through 8.

14. Gently fold the pastry in half, and place over half of the berries in the bottom crust. Open the folded pastry over the other half of berries.

15. Crimp the edges with your fingers or fork tines to seal the top and bottom crusts together. (See Chapter 3.)

16. Brush the top crust with milk and sprinkle with sugar.

17. To prevent the edge of the crust from browning too quickly, cut 2-inch strips of aluminum foil, and loosely wrap them over edges of the pastry.

Cooking Directions

18. Place the pie on a rimmed baking sheet and place on lowest rack in oven.

19. Bake for 30 to 45 minutes. Remove the foil and continue to bake for an additional 25 to 30 minutes until crust is golden brown.

20. Remove the pie to a rack to cool.

Variations

■ At step 3 substitute blueberries, adding 1 tablespoon of lemon juice.

Pantry/Refrigerator Check

    White sugar

    Cornstarch

    Unsalted butter

    Milk

Shopping List

    6 cups whole blackberries

note

Be sure to include ingredients needed for two 9-inch pie crusts (*Pie Crust,* page 344) when making your shopping list.

Old-Fashioned Peach Cobbler

Select peaches that are colorful and free of bruises. Unripened peaches will soften if left at room temperature for a few days.

Ingredients

tip

Fast Track this recipe by using thawed, frozen sliced peaches. Serve warm with *Whipped Cream* (page 367), or vanilla ice cream.

2 cups peaches

1/2 cup chopped pecans

1 cup white sugar

1/2 cup brown sugar

1/2 teaspoon vanilla extract

1/2 cup unsalted butter

3/4 cup all-purpose white flour

2 teaspoons baking powder

1/4 teaspoon salt

3/4 cup milk

Equipment

9×9×2-inch baking pan, 2 medium bowls, chef's knife, paring knife, chopping board, measuring cup, measuring spoons, wooden stirring spoon

Methods

Chopping, peeling, slicing, baking (see Chapter 3)

Quantity

6 servings

Preparation

1. Preheat the oven to 350°F.
2. Peel the peaches, slice, and place them in a medium bowl.
3. Add the pecans, sugars, and vanilla, stirring well to combine.
4. Cut the butter into 5 or 6 pieces, and place in the baking pan. Place the baking pan in the oven for 5 or 6 minutes to melt.
5. Combine the flour, baking powder, salt, and milk in a medium bowl. Stir well to blend.

6. Remove the baking pan from oven. Carefully pour the flour mix into the baking pan, distributing evenly. Do not stir, but if necessary, use the back of a large spoon to move the batter out to the edges to create a fairly even layer.

7. Carefully distribute the peaches evenly over the batter. Do not stir. The peaches need to sit on top of the batter layer.

Cooking Directions

8. Place the baking pan in the oven and bake for 1 hour. The batter will rise to the top forming a tasty crust over the peaches.

Variations

- Substitute blueberries, blackberries, plums, apricots, or nectarines for the peaches.
- At step 3 add 2 tablespoons of a fruit liqueur, amaretto, or Cointreau.

Pantry/Refrigerator Check

White sugar

Brown sugar

Vanilla extract

1 stick unsalted butter

All-purpose white flour

Baking powder

Salt

Milk

Shopping list

4 oz. pecans

2 medium peaches

Country-Style Strawberry Shortcake

Take advantage of ripe, in-season summer fruits. They are less expensive, likely to be on sale, and definitely have the best flavor. Check out a weekly farmers' market in your area for the best quality and deals.

Ingredients

4 *Sweet Biscuits* (page 80)

3 cups strawberries

1/4 cup white sugar

2 cups *Whipped Cream* (page 367)

> **tip**
>
> Fast Track by using purchased pound cake or sweet biscuits from your local bakery. In a pinch, use purchased whipped cream, but it is so easy to make your own and the results are far superior.

Equipment

Medium bowl, measuring cup, chef's knife, cutting board, wooden stirring spoon, 4 small plates or bowls

Methods

Slicing (see Chapter 3)

Quantity

4 servings

Preparation

1. Prepare Sweet Biscuits according to the recipe.
2. Wash the strawberries and slice. Place the berries in the bowl, add sugar, and gently stir to combine and coat.
3. Cover the bowl and let stand at room temperature for 1 hour. Stir occasionally for best flavor.

Assembly Directions

4. Halve the biscuits horizontally, and place the bottom half on individual plates.
5. Spoon 3/4-cup strawberries and some of the juice onto each biscuit half.
6. Top each serving with a 1/2-cup dollop of whipped cream.
7. Place the remaining biscuit halves on top of the cream and serve immediately.

Variations

■ Use blackberries, raspberries, sliced peaches, or any ripe summer fruit.

Pantry/Refrigerator Check

White sugar

Shopping List

1 1/2 pints fresh whole strawberries

note

Be sure to include ingredients needed for Sweet Biscuits and Whipped Cream.

Carrot Cake

Moist, rich, nutty and sweet, carrot cake is perfectly paired with a slightly sweet-tart *Quick Cream Cheese Frosting* (page 369). If you prefer a layered cake, use two 9×1 1/2-inch or 8×1 1/2-inch round cake pans. After baking, cool the cake and remove from the pans. Spread the frosting on the top of one cake and stack the other cake on top of it. Frost the cake, and garnish with 1/4-cup chopped walnuts. Store the cake in the refrigerator for up to 3 days.

Ingredients

3 cups lightly packed grated carrots

1 cup chopped walnuts

2 cups white sugar

1 cup canola oil

4 eggs

1 teaspoon vanilla extract

2 cups all-purpose flour

2 teaspoons baking powder

1 1/2 teaspoons baking soda

2 teaspoons cinnamon

1 teaspoon nutmeg

Equipment

9×13-inch baking pan, medium bowl, grater, wooden stirring spoon, fork, rubber spatula, measuring cup, measuring spoons, toothpick, wire rack

Methods

Grease and dust, peeling, grating, stirring, beating, baking, testing for doneness (see Chapter 3)

Quantity

12 servings

Preparation

1. Preheat the oven to 350°F.
2. Grease and flour-dust the baking pan.
3. Peel the carrots and grate using the large hole on the grater.
4. Coarsely chop the walnuts.

5. Stir together the sugar and oil in a medium bowl.

6. Add the eggs, beating with a fork to slightly scramble. Add the vanilla and stir well to combine.

7. Mix in the flour, baking powder, baking soda, cinnamon, and nutmeg. Stir to blend.

8.. Add the carrots and nuts. Stir to blend.

9. Pour the batter into the prepared pan, using a rubber spatula to scrap the batter from the sides and bottom of the bowl.

Cooking Directions

10. Place the pan in the preheated oven and bake for 45 minutes, or until a wooden toothpick inserted near the center comes out clean and the edges of the cake begin to pull away from sides of the pan.

11. Remove the pan from the oven and place on a wire rack. Let the cake cool completely in the pan before cutting or frosting.

12. Cover and refrigerate. Frost with *Quick Cream Cheese Frosting* (page 369) if desired. Serve chilled or at room temperature.

Variations

■ At step 3 substitute 1 cup crushed, well-drained pineapple for 1 cup grated carrot.

Pantry/Refrigerator Check

White sugar

Canola oil

Eggs

Vanilla extract

All-purpose flour

Baking powder

Baking soda

Cinnamon

Nutmeg

Shopping List

3 large carrots

4 oz. walnuts

Pound Cake

The versatile pound cake is a fabulous dessert, topped with butterscotch and a dollop of whipped cream or a warm breakfast bread, served with butter and fruit jam. It is also delicious used in fruit shortcake or tiramisu. This is another recipe for a baked good that is easily purchased at the grocery store, but with all the ingredients as close as your pantry, why bother?

Ingredients

3/4 cup unsalted butter

1 cup powdered sugar

3 eggs

1/2 teaspoon vanilla extract

1 1/4 cups + 2 tablespoons all-purpose flour

Equipment

9×5×3-inch loaf pan, large bowl, wooden stirring spoon, electric mixer, rubber spatula, wire rack

Methods

Grease and dusting, creaming, beating, baking, testing for doneness (see Chapter 3)

Quantity

10 servings

Preparation

1. Preheat the oven to 325°F.
2. Grease and flour-dust the loaf pan.
3. Use the back of a wooden stirring spoon to cream the butter and sugar until light and fluffy. This could take 10 minutes or more, so if you have an electric mixer then this is definitely the time to use it.
4. Add the eggs, one at a time, beating well after each addition. Add the vanilla along with the last egg.
5. Gradually beat in the flour, stirring constantly, until all of the flour has been added and is well blended. If using an electric mixer, use the lowest setting and scrape the sides of the bowl often.
6. Pour the cake batter into the prepared loaf pan, using a rubber spatula to scrap the batter from the sides and bottom of bowl.

Cooking Directions

7. Place the pan in the oven and bake for 60 to 75 minutes, or until a wooden toothpick inserted near the center comes out clean.

8. Remove from the oven and place the pan on a rack for 10 minutes.

9. Remove the cake from the pan by gently inserting a knife between the cake and the edge of the pan to loosen any area that may be sticking.

10. Place the rack on top of the cake and turn the pan, while hold the pan and rack, upside-down, allowing the cake to gently ease out of the pan and onto the rack. Turn the cake right-side up on the rack, and cool completely before cutting.

Variations

■ At step 5 alternate adding the flour with 1/2 cup chocolate chips and 1/2 cup sour cream.

Pantry/Refrigerator Check

Unsalted butter

Powdered sugar

Eggs

Vanilla extract

All-purpose white flour

New York Style Cheesecake

Cheesecake is always a favorite and festive dessert. Because it is an elegant dessert, it seems difficult to make, but it is actually simple. Due to the crumbly crust, the hardest part is getting the cheesecake out of the pan. Use a springform pan, which has a clamp that allows the sides of the pan to be removed from the bottom. Springform pans are inexpensive and available at most cookware stores. An electric mixer really helps with mixing the ingredients. Serve the cheesecake plain, with *Ginger-Pear Topping* (page 371), or with *Raspberry Sauce* (page 373).

Ingredients

1/2 cup + 1 tablespoon unsalted butter

3 8 oz. packages cream cheese

1 1/2 cup graham cracker crumbs

1 1/3 cups white sugar, divided

1 teaspoon vanilla extract

4 eggs

2 cups sour cream

Equipment

9-inch springform pan, small bowl or saucepan, medium bowl, large bowl, fork, wooden stirring spoon or electric hand mixer, rubber spatula, wire rack

Methods

Melting, whipping, beating, baking (see Chapter 3)

Quantity

14 to 16 servings

Preparation

1. Preheat the oven to 375°F.
2. Remove the butter and cream cheese from the refrigerator and set aside to soften.
3. Melt 1/2-cup butter in a small bowl in the microwave, or in a small saucepan over low heat.
4. In a medium bowl, combine the graham cracker crumbs and 1/3 cup sugar. Add the melted butter and mix with a fork until well blended.
5. Grease the bottom and sides of a 9-inch springform pan with 1 tablespoon softened butter.

6. With clean fingertips, press the crumb mixture into the bottom and part way up the sides of the pan. Set aside.

7. In a large bowl, use the electric mixer or wooden stirring spoon to whip together the cream cheese, remaining 1 cup sugar, and vanilla until soft and creamy.

8. Add the eggs one at a time, beating to blend after each addition.

9. Beat in the sour cream, stirring until well blended.

10. Pour the filling into the crumb-lined pan, using a rubber spatula to scrape the batter from the bottom and sides of the bowl.

Cooking Directions

11. Bake in the preheated oven for 50 minutes. Cheesecake is done when the center area jiggles slightly when shaken, but the 2-inch outer edge appears to be set without jiggling.

12. Remove from the oven and place the pan on a wire rack to cool to room temperature.

13. Cover and refrigerate for at least 3 hours before serving.

14. Remove the sides of the pan leaving the cheesecake on the bottom round of the pan.

Variations

■ At step 9 add any or all of the following:

- 1 cup chocolate chips
- 2 teaspoons instant espresso powder
- 1 tablespoon Cointreau or Kahlúa

Pantry/Refrigerator Check

2 sticks unsalted butter

White sugar

Vanilla extract

Eggs

Shopping List

1 13.5 oz. box graham crackers crumbs

3 8 oz. packages cream cheese

1 pint carton sour cream

Shortbread

It's a mystery why shortbread is fairly expensive. Using only three basic inexpensive ingredients, and taking no time to make, it must be the postage from Scotland that drives up the price. Homemade shortbread inside a tartan tin makes a thoughtful gift. Bake a double batch, and use half to make *Lemon Bars* (page 361). Serve plain with strawberry preserves, or orange marmalade, along with a spot of tea.

Ingredients

1 cup + 1 tablespoon unsalted butter

1/2 cup powdered sugar

2 cups all-purpose white flour

Equipment

9×9×2-inch baking pan, medium bowl, wooden stirring spoon, wire rack

Methods

Greasing, creaming, baking (see Chapter 3)

Quantity

25 squares

Preparation

1. Remove the butter from the refrigerator and let sit about 30 minutes to soften.

2. Preheat the oven to 325°F.

3. Lightly grease the 9×9×2-inch baking pan with 1 tablespoon softened butter and set it aside.

4. In a medium bowl, use the back of a wooden stirring spoon to cream the butter and sugar until light and fluffy.

5. Add the flour and combine with the butter and sugar. Using your clean hands, mix and crumble ingredients together until they begin to hold together and resemble coarse crumbs.

6. Gather the dough into a ball.

7. Set the dough in the baking pan. Gently press down and out to evenly spread the dough over the bottom of the pan.

Cooking Directions

8. Place the pan in the oven and bake for 40 to 50 minutes, or until very pale golden brown.

9. Transfer the pan to a wire rack. While still hot, cut the shortbread into 5 rows each way, creating 25 small squares.

10. Let the shortbread cool completely in the pan.

Variations

Pecan Shortbread

At step 4 substitute brown sugar for white sugar, and add 3 tablespoons finely chopped pecans.

Pantry/Refrigerator Check

3 sticks unsalted butter

Powdered sugar

All-purpose white flour

tip

Line the pan with a sheet of aluminum foil allowing it to lap over the ends. Spray the foil with nonstick cooking spray, and press the dough evenly over the bottom. This will make it easier to lift the cooked shortbread out of the pan for cutting.

Lemon Bars

The perfect balance of sweet and tart, lemon bars make a lovely dessert when cake or pie is too much of a commitment, and cookies just aren't enough. If making *Shortbread* (page 359), double the recipe and use half to make a batch of lemon bars.

Ingredients

Shortbread (page 359)

1 teaspoon lemon zest (optional)

4 eggs

1 1/2 cups white sugar

3/4 cup lemon juice from 4 to 6 lemons

1/4 cup all-purpose white flour

1 teaspoon baking powder

1/4 cup half-and-half

1/4 cup powdered sugar

tip

This recipe can be Fast Tracked by using purchased shortbread.

Equipment

13×9×2-inch pan, zester, strainer, fork, wooden stirring spoon, wire rack

Methods

Zesting, wire straining, beating, stirring, baking (see Chapter 3)

Quantity

24 2-inch squares

Preparation

1. Preheat the oven to 350°F.

2. Follow the instructions for short bread through step 7, pressing the dough into a 13×9×2-inch pan and reducing the shortbread baking time to 20 minutes.

3. While the shortbread is baking, zest the lemon and squeeze the lemon over the wire strainer to catch any seeds.

4. Beat the eggs until slightly scrambled in a medium bowl.

5. Blend in the sugar, lemon zest, lemon juice, flour, baking powder, and half-and-half, stirring vigorously to combine.

6. Remove the shortbread from the oven when done baking.

7. Carefully pour the lemon batter over the hot, baked shortbread and return the pan to the oven.

Cooking Directions

8. Bake for 15 to 20 minutes, or until pale gold and the center is set, and does not jiggle when gently shaken.

9. Remove from the oven, place the pan on a wire rack and let cool.

10. Sprinkle evenly with 1/4 cup powdered sugar. This is easily done by placing the sugar in a wire strainer and hitting the edge of the strainer against the side of your other hand while moving over the lemon bars.

11. Cut into 2-inch squares, cover, and store in the refrigerator.

Pantry/Refrigerator Check

Eggs

White sugar

All-purpose white flour

Baking powder

Powdered sugar

Shopping List

4 to 6 lemons

1/2 pint half-and-half

note

Be sure to include quantities needed for *Shortbread* (page 359) when making your shopping list.

Chocolate Chip Oatmeal Cookies

For a classic chocolate chip cookie, the basic recipe is the one found on the back of Nestlé Toll House chocolate chip packages. These types of cookies are called drop cookies because they are not rolled and cut, but rather dropped onto the baking sheet. They are less work, less clean-up, and less precise in size. We will be adding a twist to this recipe by including oatmeal.

Ingredients

1 cup unsalted butter

1 1/2 cups firmly packed brown sugar

2 eggs

1 teaspoon vanilla extract

1 1/2 cups all-purpose white flour

2 1/4 cups regular or quick-cooking rolled oats (not instant)

2 teaspoons baking soda

1 teaspoon salt

1 12 oz. package semisweet chocolate chips

1 cup chopped walnuts

Equipment

Nonstick baking sheet, large bowl, chef's knife, cutting board, measuring cups, measuring spoons, wooden stirring spoon, spatula, wire rack

Methods

Chopping, creaming, beating, stirring, baking (see Chapter 3)

Quantity

3 dozen cookies

Preparation

1. Preheat the oven to 350°F.
2. Cream the sugar into the butter in a large bowl using the back of a wooden stirring spoon, until light and fluffy.
3. Beat in the eggs and vanilla, stirring well to combine.
4. Add the flour, oats, baking soda, and salt, stirring well to combine.
5. Mix in the chocolate chips and nuts, and stir to combine.

6. Scoop out 1 tablespoon of cookie dough and hold it over the baking sheet. Use a second tablespoon to push the dough off of the spoon and drop it onto the baking sheet. Repeat this process, spacing the cookies about 1 1/2-inches apart from each other.

Cooking Directions

7. Place the baking sheet in the oven and bake for 10 to 12 minutes, or until the edges of the cookies are lightly browned.

8. Use a spatula to transfer the cookies to a wire rack, and cool completely.

Variations

■ At step 5 substitute chocolate-mint, butterscotch, or peanut butter chips for the chocolate chips.

■ At step 4 add 1 teaspoon cinnamon and 1/2 teaspoon of nutmeg to the flour. At step 5 omit the chips and add 1 1/2 cups dried cranberries or raisins.

■ At step 5 substitute pecans for the walnuts.

Pantry/Refrigerator Check

2 sticks unsalted butter

Brown sugar

Eggs

Vanilla extract

All-purpose white flour

Baking soda

Salt

Shopping List

1 18 oz. container regular or quick-cooking rolled oats, (not instant)

1 12 oz. package semisweet chocolate chips

4 oz. walnuts

Fudge Walnut Brownies

Unlike cake brownies, the centers of these chocolaty treats are moist, chewy, and rich. These brownies freeze well, so make a double batch. Cut the brownies into 2-inch squares, and then cut each in half diagonally for 48 little heavenly triangles.

Ingredients

3/4 cup walnuts

4 oz. unsweetened chocolate (4 squares)

1/2 cup + 2 tablespoons unsalted butter

2 cups white sugar

1/2 teaspoon salt

2 teaspoons vanilla extract

4 eggs

1 cup all-purpose white flour

1/4 teaspoon baking soda

Equipment:

13×9×2-inch baking pan, medium saucepan, small bowl, chef's knife, chopping board, measuring cup, measuring spoons, wooden stirring spoon, rubber spatula, toothpicks, wire rack

Methods

Chopping, grease and dusting, baking, toothpick doneness test (see Chapter 3)

Quantity

24 2-inch square brownies

Preparation

1. Coarsely chop the walnuts.
2. Coarsely chop the chocolate squares.
3. Preheat the oven to 350°F.
4. Grease and dust the baking pan.

Cooking Directions

5. In a medium saucepan, melt the butter and chocolate over low heat, stirring constantly until well-blended.

6. Remove the saucepan from the heat. Stir in the sugar, salt, and vanilla.

7. Add the eggs, one at a time, beating well after each addition.

8. Stir together the flour, baking soda, and nuts in a small bowl. Add to the saucepan, stirring well to blend.

9. Pour the batter into the prepared baking pan, using a rubber spatula to scrape the batter from the sides and bottom of the saucepan. Spread the batter evenly over the bottom of the baking pan, using the spatula to ease the batter out to the edges, if necessary.

10. Place the baking pan in the oven and bake for 20 to 25 minutes, or until a wooden toothpick inserted in the center comes out clean and the top of the brownies spring back when lightly touched.

11. Transfer the pan to a wire rack, and let the brownies cool completely before cutting.

Variations

- At step 1 substitute pecans or macadamia nuts for the walnuts.
- Frost with *Quick Chocolate Cream Cheese Frosting* (page 370).

Pantry/Refrigerator Check

2 sticks unsalted butter

Eggs

White sugar

Vanilla extract

All-purpose white flour

Baking soda

Shopping List

4 oz. unsweetened chocolate (4 squares)

6 oz. walnuts

Whipped Cream

Whip up some homemade whipped cream for superior flavor and quality. Less expensive than purchased, it takes only a few minutes to make and is more than worth the effort. For best results, chill the bowl and the beaters, or whisk. Add more or less sugar according to your taste.

Ingredients

1 cup heavy cream or whipping cream

2 tablespoons white sugar

1/2 teaspoon vanilla extract

Equipment

Electric mixer (or wire whisk), medium bowl, measuring cup, measuring spoons

Methods

Whipping (see Chapter 3)

Quantity

2 cups

Assembly Directions

1. Using an electric mixer on medium speed, whip the cream in a medium bowl until soft peaks form. If using a wire whisk, beat vigorously in circular motions.

2. The cream will double in volume during beating.

tip

Do not over-beat because the cream will become lumpy. Extremely over-beaten cream will eventually make butter.

Variations

■ At step 1 add 1 tablespoon flavored liqueur, amaretto, Cointreau, or Kahlúa.

■ At step 1 substitute 1/2 teaspoon of flavored extract such as almond, hazelnut, walnut, or maple for the vanilla extract.

Pantry/Refrigerator Check

White sugar

Vanilla extract

Shopping List

1/2 pint heavy cream or whipping cream

Quick Cream Cheese Frosting

The sweet-tart flavor of this frosting is a perfect foil for most baked goods. It is quick to make with ingredients most likely to be on hand. Dress up a purchased spice or poppy seed cake, shortbread, or brownies with this frosting and garnish with chopped nuts. To add chocolate chips or flavor the frosting with orange or lemon juice, see the variations below.

Ingredients

6 tablespoons unsalted butter

3/4 cup cream cheese

4 1/2 cups powdered sugar (approximate)

1 1/2 teaspoons vanilla extract

Equipment

Wire strainer or sifter, medium bowl, wooden stirring spoon, electric mixer (optional), rubber spatula

Methods

Sifting, creaming, blending (see Chapter 3)

Quantity

2 cups (enough to frost a 13×9-inch cake)

Preparation

1. Remove the butter and cream cheese from the refrigerator and let sit 30 minutes to soften.

2. Sift the powdered sugar with a sifter, or through a wire-mesh strainer, into a medium bowl.

Assembly Directions

3. In a medium bowl, cream together the butter, cream cheese, and vanilla until smooth. This can be done by hand or with an electric mixer.

4. Add 2 cups powdered sugar, and stir vigorously to blend. If you are using a mixer, set the speed to low.

5. Gradually add the remaining powdered sugar until the frosting is the desired consistency. It should be smooth and spreadable. If it's too thick, add a dash of milk; if too thin, add more powdered sugar.

Variations

Quick Chocolate Cream Cheese Frosting

At step 4 add 1/4 cup unsweetened cocoa powder to the butter and cream cheese with the first addition of powdered sugar.

Quick Lemon or Orange Cream Cheese Frosting

At step 3 substitute 1 1/2 teaspoon of lemon or orange juice for the vanilla extract, and add 1 teaspoon of lemon or orange zest.

Pantry/Refrigerator Check

1 stick unsalted butter

Vanilla extract

Powdered sugar

Shopping List

2 3 oz. packages cream cheese

Ginger-Pear Topping

This is a slightly spicy, chunky sauce that is not too sweet. It works great as a topping for desserts, waffles, yogurt, or ice cream. Make a double batch and store any unused portion in the refrigerator, tightly covered, for up to 1 week. Serve cold or warm up a tablespoon or two in the microwave before using.

Ingredients

1 cup sliced pears

1 teaspoon grated fresh ginger

2 tablespoons unsalted butter

1 tablespoon cornstarch

1 tablespoon cold water

3 tablespoons white sugar

3/4 cup pear nectar

Equipment

Medium saucepan, paring knife, chef's knife, cutting board, grater, small bowl, measuring cups, measuring spoons

Methods

Grating, slicing, mixing, boiling, simmering (see Chapter 3)

Quantity

1 cup

Preparation

1. Peel the pears, core, and slice.
2. Peel and grate the ginger.

Cooking Directions

3. Melt the butter in a medium saucepan over medium-low heat.
4. Add the pears and ginger, and sauté until the fruit softens.
5. Combine the cornstarch, water, sugar, and pear nectar in a small bowl.
6. Add to the saucepan, and bring to a boil.
7. Reduce the heat to medium-low and simmer, stir constantly until slightly thickened.

Variations

- At step 1 substitute 1 cup seasonal berries and berry juice for the pears.

Pantry/Refrigerator Check

1 stick unsalted butter

Cornstarch

White sugar

Shopping List

2 medium pears

1 small piece of fresh ginger

6 oz. pear nectar

Raspberry Sauce

Use your favorite fresh berries when in season. Add a tablespoon of flavored liqueur or a dash of nutmeg for a change. Serve warm or cold on cheesecake, pound cake, ice cream, breakfast loaves, or pancakes. Store any unused portion in the refrigerator, tightly covered, for up to 1 week.

Ingredients

2 cups fresh or frozen raspberries

1/4 cup white sugar

1 tablespoon cornstarch

1/3 cup water

Equipment

Medium saucepan, measuring cup, measuring spoons, wooden stirring spoon

Methods

Stirring, simmering (see Chapter 3)

Quantity

2 cups

Preparation

1. Wash the berries. Thaw if frozen.

Cooking Directions

2. In a medium saucepan, combine the sugar and cornstarch, stir well to combine.
3. Add 1/3 cup of water, and stir until the cornstarch is completely dissolved.
4. Set the pan on medium-low heat, and gently stir in the berries.
5. Simmer, gently stirring, until the sauce thickens.
6. Remove from the heat and use immediately.

Variations

■ Substitute blueberries, blackberries, or sliced strawberries for raspberries.

Pantry/Refrigerator Check

White sugar

Cornstarch

Shopping List

2 cups of fresh or frozen raspberries

Index